Alexander The Great In Afghanistan

A Reconstruction Of Cleitarchus

by

Andrew Michael Chugg

2011

First Edition

© 2011 by Andrew Michael Chugg. All rights reserved.
ISBN 978-0-9556790-3-2

The world's an older place today
Than it ever used to be.
One time I heard a minstrel say:
It hurts to peddle melody,
For fatal tunes we people play
Echo still most violently:
Notes that kill and songs that slay,
Tones for turning flesh to clay
Make many men to melt away!
My music murders silently.

Alexander the Great in Afghanistan
Contents

1. Introduction — 1
2. The Reconstruction Of Books Seven To Nine — 5

   Introduction; Alexander's Emulation of Cyrus and the Persianising; Geographical Errors; The Visit of the Queen of the Amazons; Prophthasia; The Culpability of Philotas and Parmenion; The Condemnation of the Branchidae; The Killing of Cleitus; The Culpability and Fates of Callisthenes and the Pages; The Marriage to Roxane; Fragments of Cleitarchus from Books Seven to Nine

3. Book 7: July 330BC – June 329BC — 39

   The Advance to Hecatompylus; Description of Hyrcania and the Caspian Sea; Surrender of Artabazus & the Greek Mercenaries; Theft of Bucephalus; Surrender of Nabarzanes; Visit of the Amazon Queen; Adoption of Persian Dress; Revolt of Satibarzanes; The Philotas Affair; Assassination of Parmenion; The Euergetae; First Crossing of the Paropamisus Range

4. Book 8: July 329BC – Autumn 328BC — 87

   Alexander's Advance to the River Oxus; Bessus Betrayed to Alexander; The Fate of the Branchidae; Alexander Wounded near Maracanda; The Revolt of Spitamenes; Alexander's Advance to the River Tanais; Annihilation of a Macedonian Column by Spitamenes and Alexander's Counterattacks; Capture of the Rock of Ariamazes

5. Book 9: Autumn 328BC – May 327BC — 117

   The Hunt in Basista; The Killing of Cleitus; The Treaty with Sisimithres; The Decapitation of Spitamenes; The Proskynesis Experiment; The Conspiracy of the Pages; The Army Caught in a Blizzard; The Marriage to Roxane

6. Alexander's Route Through Afghanistan — 144
7. Organisation And Sources — 149
8. An Update On The Organisation And Structure Of Cleitarchus And The Date Of Accession Of Alexander the Great — 157
9. Bibliography — 186
10. Acknowledgements — 193
    Index — 194

1. Introduction

This volume presents the third stage of an ongoing project to reconstruct the most influential of all the ancient accounts of the career of Alexander the Great: the history of his reign compiled by Cleitarchus of Alexandria, which has been lost since antiquity. I began this reconstruction with the three Indian books of Cleitarchus (books ten to twelve), which have been published together as *Alexander the Great in India*. Thereafter I reconstructed the final book of Cleitarchus' work (book thirteen), which treated events from the end of *Alexander the Great in India* through to the king's death and its aftermath. This has been published under the title of *The Death of Alexander the Great*. The work presented in the present volume constitutes a reconstruction of all the Cleitarchan material between the death of Darius and the opening of *Alexander the Great in India*, which constitutes a further three books of Cleitarchus' work covering the three year period between July 330BC and May 327BC. The successive highlights of the events recounted in this volume are therefore: the advance to Hecatompylus; the description of Hyrcania and the Caspian Sea; the surrender of Artabazus and the Greek Mercenaries; the theft of Bucephalus; the surrender of Nabarzanes; the visit of the Amazon Queen; Alexander's adoption of Persian dress; the revolt of Satibarzanes; the Philotas Affair; the assassination of Parmenion; the Euergetae; the first crossing of the Paropamisus Range; Alexander's advance to the River Oxus; Bessus betrayed to Alexander; the fate of the Branchidae; Alexander wounded near Maracanda; the revolt of Spitamenes; Alexander's advance to the River Tanais; the annihilation of a Macedonian column by Spitamenes and Alexander's counterattacks; the capture of the Rock of Ariamazes; the hunt in Basista; the killing of Cleitus; the treaty with Sisimithres; the decapitation of Spitamenes; the *proskynesis* experiment; the Conspiracy of the Pages; Alexander's army caught in a blizzard; the marriage to Roxane.

It is my intention eventually to produce as complete a reconstruction of Cleitarchus as may prove feasible and so supporting material already published in *Alexander the Great in India* has the scope of the entire work. However, the next section of this volume particularly provides a more detailed analysis of some key issues pertaining to the reconstruction of books seven to nine. The reconstruction itself comprises sections three to five. Then section six presents a review of the geographical issues pertaining to Alexander's route in the vicinity of Afghanistan, which was at its most tortuous and least intelligible during this period. Afterwards, section seven provides a tabulation of the source references against each episode. Finally, section eight offers an update and revision of the structure that may be inferred for Cleitarchus' work, which was originally published in *Alexander the Great in India*. This incorporates the special bonus of an argument for the precise date of accession of Alexander, which emerges directly from the new insights into Cleitarchus' book structure. Previously, speculation has ranged between summer and late autumn in 336BC, but it now appears highly likely that the festival at which Philip II was assassinated was held on the autumnal equinox in that year.

The reconstructed text is not merely a simple translation of passages from the surviving secondary sources, although virtually every sentence is founded upon evidence from those texts. Instead it has been necessary to meld overlapping and intersecting accounts together and continually to assess which source should have pre-eminence in the case of (usually slight) disparities. Furthermore, I have thought it fitting to attempt to echo the evidently flowery literary style of Cleitarchus to some extent, especially in the case of speeches and descriptive passages. To this end I have sometimes employed poetical devices including rhythmic or metrical passages, incidental rhyming or simple assonance and alliteration. However, it would also be true to say that some of this embroidery is already reflected in the surviving Latin and Greek texts of Curtius, Diodorus and even Justin and Plutarch. In this sense my own text is not merely a reconstruction, but also an evocation of the original.

Different passages may be attributed to Cleitarchus with widely varying degrees of confidence. Therefore, I have indicated the approximate confidence level using a textual hierarchy running from lowest to highest (the latter being defined as attributed fragments of Cleitarchus from surviving ancient texts). This is implemented as follows: *italic*; plain text; ***italicized bold***; **simple bold**; **underlined simple bold**. Although grey text has been reserved for connecting passages, where the Cleitarchan version is unfathomable, it has not been necessary to resort to its use for books seven to thirteen. Subject to a few minor exceptions, it is possible to read the reconstruction at a variety of confidence levels by ignoring all text below the desired level of fidelity.

This reconstruction is particularly founded on the premise that Curtius and Diodorus (Book 17 & Book 18.1-4) are largely abridgements of the History of Alexander by Cleitarchus, whereas Justin (Books 11 to 13.4) and Plutarch's *Life of Alexander* are believed to contain substantial Cleitarchan elements (this has been argued in detail in *Alexander the Great in India* – the interrelationship between various of the lost and extant ancient sources is summarized in Figure 2.2). Although I cannot be absolutely sure that Curtius did not employ another major source, the process of performing the reconstruction to date has had the incidental consequence of accumulating many minor points of evidence so as to formulate a cumulatively strong case that Curtius is in fact substantially (though not entirely) a Latin translation of an abridged version of Cleitarchus' Greek text. In particular, it has thus far transpired that this hypothesis resolves virtually all difficulties without generating significant inconsistencies.

However, reconstructed text solely based on material from only one of Curtius or Diodorus 18.1-4 or Justin 12-13.4 is indicated at a relatively lower level of confidence. Higher confidence is assigned to material exclusively derived from Diodorus 17. Still higher confidence is vested in cases where there are detailed

Introduction

matches between these sources and the highest confidence rests with the attributed fragments of Cleitarchus, although they are sadly sparse in general and almost non-existent in books eight and nine.

If the premise of a common source for the surviving texts were correct, then it would be expected that a relatively smooth and cogent version of the prototype could be reconstructed by merging them. However, if any of the extant sources had employed a significant secondary source, then it would be anticipated that the attempt to define a prototype that explained all the material in each of them should encounter numerous contradictions. It is a conclusion of the present research that it has been possible to reconstruct all seven years of Alexander's reign after the death of Darius without encountering significant contradictions when integrating all the appertaining material in Curtius, Diodorus and the *Metz Epitome* (with the obvious exception of a few passages in Curtius where that author is clearly offering his own comments and one instance, where he attacks Cleitarchus by name with reference to Ptolemy's version in a matter that concerned Ptolemy.) This is an important result, because it tends to reinforce the premise that Curtius, Diodorus and the *Metz Epitome* at least are essentially abridgements of Cleitarchus. Such an inference is not at all obvious in reading those sources individually.

In the case of Justin, we know from his manuscripts that he epitomised Trogus, although the latter probably used Cleitarchus (or else Timagenes who in turn used Cleitarchus). More difficulties tend to arise in reconciling his words with the tradition from the other Vulgate texts, as might reasonably be expected for such indirect transmission. A straightforward example is that Justin is more negative about Alexander's treatment of Philotas and Parmenion than either Curtius or Diodorus. Yet in fact this is easily explained as either an incidental consequence of successive stages of epitomisation via Trogus or else just another of the misunderstandings and over-simplifications, which are plainly attributable to Justin's rather careless epitomisation of Trogus. The process of reconstruction has also indicated significant amounts of Cleitarchan material in Plutarch, by virtue of some striking parallels between my text (reconstructed from Curtius and Diodorus) and some of Plutarch's anecdotes. But it is equally obvious that Plutarch used many early sources (as too did Cleitarchus himself), so I have used his material sparingly and at low confidence.

Neither do I intend that this should be the final and immutable version of the reconstruction, but rather hope that it may evolve and be revised in the light of new evidence or arguments as they emerge.

Finally, I would also commend the account of Cleitarchus to those readers who have little interest in the technical niceties of source research for Alexander studies. Cleitarchus' account rested on its literary merits for centuries in winning its place as the most popular version of Alexander's campaigns among the Hellenistic Greeks and the Romans. I believe that it retains good measures of readability, atmosphere, coherence and accuracy even in the present metamorphosed and imperfect form, sufficient anyway that it may be read in isolation as an authentic breath of the distant past by readers who are relatively unfamiliar with the particulars of the history of the most glamorous king who ever reigned.

2. The Reconstruction Of Books Seven To Nine

In spite of the objections of Tarn, I regard it as certain that whatever source Diodorus used, it was the same as that employed by Curtius. Schwartz assembled a formidable list of parallels between the two writers, without exhausting the subject. It is adequate to prove the point. To reconstruct this source would be a useful task.

C. Bradford Welles[1]

Introduction

The title of this volume refers to Alexander's activities in modern Afghanistan, although it actually starts with the 7th book of Cleitarchus' History Concerning Alexander, which opens after the death of Darius in July 330BC and ends with the close of Cleitarchus' 9th book 3 years later in the Summer of 327BC, when Alexander marched into India. For the first few months of this period Alexander was in fact operating in ancient Hyrcania and Parthia, which largely fall within the territory of modern Iran and there was probably a short excursion into Turkmenistan in the Autumn of 330BC. Furthermore, the campaigning appears to have strayed into parts of Tajikistan, Uzbekistan, Kyrgyzstan and even Kazakhstan in the course of 329-328BC. Tajikistan roughly corresponds to the northern and eastern districts of ancient Bactria, whereas Kyrgyzstan contains much of ancient Sogdiana, although Maracanda (Samarkand) lies in Uzbekistan.

Alexander's years in these territories were full of challenges, but in particular this was the period when the traditionalists among the Macedonians and Greeks accused the king of Persianising or going native, if you prefer. He evidently adopted some of the paraphernalia of the previous Persian monarchs, such as aspects of their dress. What really rankled, however, was the promotion of Persians into positions of influence within his regime. Darius's brother Oxathres was appointed to Alexander's inner group of "Friends". Artabazus was made governor of Bactria. But perhaps the conservatives were most offended when Alexander adopted Darius's eunuch Bagoas as his confidante and lover. A narrow section of traditionalist opinion regarded these things as a betrayal and launched bungled plots against their king's life.

The first seems to have occurred at Prophthasia (probably modern Farah) in the west of Afghanistan. A conspiracy by top Macedonians was revealed to Philotas, the commander of the Companion Cavalry. He failed to tell Alexander, but when the king was eventually told, one of the plotters called Dimnus committed suicide when Alexander tried to arrest him. Philotas was

---

[1] C. Bradford Welles, *Loeb edition of Diodorus Siculus*, Vol. 8 (Harvard, 1963), Introduction, 12.

accused of complicity in the plot and was executed after being tortured. His father, Parmenion, had been left behind to guard Alexander's supply lines, so the king had to send men on fast camels to execute him too.

Then there was another, equally painful plot, a couple of years later. Alexander had one of his teenage Pages called Hermolaus flogged for killing the king's prey in a royal hunt. This youth and a few of his friends hatched a plot to murder the king in his bed when they were supposed to be guarding his tent. The plot failed because Alexander stayed up drinking on the appointed night and the guilty Pages were tortured to death by their fellow Pages. At their trial, Hermolaus also referred to the Persianising as one of their main grievances.

But what was the outcome of the campaigning? Did even Alexander fail to subdue Afghanistan? Well it is true that Alexander could not rely simply on force of arms, but also needed to forge alliances with the natives in order to secure the territory. He himself married Roxane. This dual strategy was highly successful. We know that there were dynasties of Greek kings controlling Afghanistan for the next several centuries especially from the spectacular coins that they minted, which are sought after by numismatists.

How can the Afghan years be summed up? Basically, they were a blood-soaked slog, but through carrot and stick tactics Alexander eventually triumphed more completely that anyone else ever has in that land.

Alexander's Emulation of Cyrus and the Persianising

There are very strong reasons to believe that Alexander had read the *Cyropaidia* (Education of Cyrus) by Xenophon the follower of Socrates:

1) There are numerous anecdotal instances where Alexander appears to emulate Xenophon's Cyrus (visits to the wounded, *Cyropaidia* 5.4.18 & *Anabasis Alexandrou* 2.12.1; gifts of food and drink to those he wished to honour, *Cyropaidia* 8.2.4 & Plutarch, *Alexander* 23.5…).

2) Alexander's fond pilgrimage to the tomb of Cyrus at Parsagada and his furious reaction to its desecration upon his return from India are most readily explained by his having read the *Cyropaidia*. Strabo, *Geography* 11.11.4 actually describes Alexander as "a lover of Cyrus".

3) Diogenes Laertius 6.84 describes a parallel between Onesicritus, Alexander's chief pilot, who wrote perhaps the earliest complete account of Alexander's reign and entitled it How Alexander Was Led, and Xenophon the author of The Education of Cyrus. The parallel had probably been consciously and deliberately devised by Onesicritus himself, which suggests that Xenophon's *Cyropaidia* was a familiar point of reference among Alexander's circle of Friends.

4) Arrian actually has Alexander refer to episodes from Xenophon's *Anabasis* in his own *Anabasis Alexandrou* 2.7.8.

5) Alexander is known to have been widely read and it is obvious that he would have had a particular interest in books dealing with Persia, so it would be surprising, if he had ignored Xenophon's *Cyropaidia* and *Anabasis*, which were recent works about Persia by a writer of great repute, who had actually fought for Cyrus the Younger within the Persian Empire.

Xenophon's account actually bears only a passing resemblance to the true history of that Cyrus who had founded the Persian Empire. It seems instead to have been Xenophon's purpose, rather than penning an historically accurate work, to create an idealized model of kingship through the medium of a fictionalized version of the most influential recent king in his own time. It is the same species of motivation as stirred Plato to write the Republic. That is, a burning desire by an aristocratic Athenian, who had witnessed and suffered the excesses of Athens' democratic regime including the execution of his mentor, to develop a nobler alternative to democracy. In Alexander he found a willing and fervent disciple.

The relevance of Xenophon's influence upon Alexander in the matter of the Reconstruction of Book 7 of Cleitarchus lies in further connections with the *Cyropaidia* that may be discerned in the way that Alexander fell into the practice of so-called Persianising. For example, in Curtius 6.2.6-8 and Sections 7.3-4 of the Reconstruction, Alexander seeks to re-unite the captive granddaughter of Ochus, a former Great King (Artaxerxes III), with Hystaspes, her husband, who was a kinsman of Darius. This event, though superficially trivial, has the significance of inaugurating the Persianising phase of Alexander's career. However, it happens that we can use our knowledge of Alexander's enthusiasm for Xenophon's writings to gain special insight into Alexander's thinking on this matter, even beyond what would have been apparent to most of his contemporaries. Essentially, it appears that the king was emulating the chivalric model of kingship presented by Xenophon in the *Cyropaidia*, specifically the episode at *Cyropaidia* 6.1.45-48 wherein Cyrus reunites Pantheia with her husband Abradatas and thereby wins the latter's allegiance. There are some indications that Alexander originally planned to reunite Darius with his wife according to this model. He actually says so in his letter to Darius cited in Arrian, *Anabasis* 2.14.8: "If you are afraid you may suffer any harsh treatment from me when you come to me, send some of your friends to receive pledges of safety from me. Come to me then, and ask for your mother, wife, and children, and anything else you wish. For whatever you ask for you will receive; and nothing shall be denied you." But being thwarted in the ambition of perpetrating those reunions by the deaths of both Darius and his wife, he evidently found a convenient substitute in the wife of Hystaspes.

A further instance where Xenophon's influence seems to have been instrumental is Alexander's adoption of Persian dress. Cleitarchus recorded this with some disdain (Sections 7.35-36). To set this in context it is necessary to appreciate that Cleitarchus was one of the Cynics, a sect that considered abstemiousness to be next to godliness. They were an early manifestation of the asceticism that later launched Christianity and Islam. By contrast, Plutarch in his essays On The Fortune Or Virtue of Alexander (*Moralia* 329F-330A) actually praised the king for his rapprochement with the Persians by adopting elements of their dress. But even more interestingly Xenophon made a special virtue of the adoption of Median dress by the Persian Cyrus, when he had won control of that kingdom in *Cyropaidia* 8.1.40. This also explains why Alexander gave his companions Persian accoutrements, for Xenophon had Cyrus persuade his comrades to wear Median dress too.

The Cleitarchan sources show that Cleitarchus himself had given a particularly detailed account of exactly what it was that Alexander wore. However, it is a difficult matter to explain the appearance of clothing with a purely verbal description, so some clarification is appropriate. In fact, a good example of what the ancient Greek writers understood as Persian or Oriental dress is the attire of the ancient statue of Paris in the British Museum, which I have sketched in Figure 2.1. However, Cleitarchus noted that Alexander did not actually wear the trouser-leggings or the long-sleeves. What we are left with is a heavily pleated chiton or tunic, which in Alexander's case was dyed purple with a broad white stripe down the front (a similar tunic is worn by Darius in the Alexander Mosaic from the House of the Faun in Pompeii.) The tunic was tied just beneath the breast with a sort of cummerbund or belt called a *zona* and an ankle-length cloak (probably purple like those given to Alexander's companions) completed the clothing proper. Paris wears a type of cap, but Alexander had a diadem of purple interlaced with white bound about his head. This was simply a sort of elaborate ribbon tied in a bow at the back. Alexander is depicted wearing it in the silver tetradrachm coins minted by his Bodyguard Lysimachus after the king's death (the author's Lysimachus tetradrachm is depicted on page iii).

Of course the irony is that to modern eyes the dress of Paris looks quintessentially Greek and even more so if the long-sleeves and leggings are deleted. Even Alexander's own men must have recognized that his heavily edited compromise version of Persian dress was little more than a tweak to his previous range of raiment. But it seems that even the tiniest of Persian elements were deemed objectionable on principle. It was the symbolism of appeasing the Persians that mattered more than the reality.

Xenophon also gives a description of the Persian king's Royal Eunuchs in the Cyropaidia 7.5.60-65:

[Cyrus] knew that men with children or wives or favourites in whom they delight must needs love them most: while eunuchs, who are deprived of all such dear ones, would surely make most account of him who could enrich them or help them if they were injured or crown them with honour. And in conferring such benefits he was disposed to think he could outbid the world. Moreover the eunuch, being degraded in the eyes of other men, is driven to seek the assistance of some lord and master. Without such protection there is not a man in the world who would not

The Reconstruction Of Books Seven To Nine

Figure 2.1. Ancient statue of Paris in the British Museum wearing Oriental/Persian dress (sketch by the author)

think he had the right to over-reach a eunuch: while there was every reason to suppose that the eunuch would be the most faithful of all servants. As for the customary notion that a eunuch must be weak and cowardly, Cyrus was not disposed to accept it…. No men have shown more faithfulness than eunuchs when ruin has fallen on their lords. In bodily strength, perhaps, the eunuch seems to be lacking, but steel is a great leveller and makes the weak man equal to the strong in war. Holding this in mind, Cyrus resolved that his personal attendants, from his doorkeeper onwards, should be eunuchs one and all.

It is in this light that Alexander's appointment of Persian rod-bearers (ushers?) to his court (Diodorus 17.77.4 and Section 7.36 of the Reconstruction) should be viewed and most particularly so his eager acceptance of Bagoas the Eunuch, formerly the lover of Darius, into his retinue, perhaps among the rod-bearers, and soon into his bed too. Bagoas himself must surely have been influential in promoting the subsequent progress of the Persianising. This is probably why he is accused of being one of Alexander's most influential flatterers by Plutarch, *Moralia* 65D. Ultimately, however, the Persianisation project ran aground, when Callisthenes refused to perform *proskynesis*.

Geographical Errors

There are several geographical errors and ambiguities arising in the seventh to ninth books of Cleitarchus, which are potentially confusing to an unbriefed reader. However, a basic understanding of these issues will engender an appreciation that the Cleitarchan account is actually relatively accurate and self-consistent on matters concerning Alexander's route and itinerary. There are even some indications of the date and sources of Cleitarchus to be gleaned from his geography. It is therefore the purpose of this sub-section to furnish a suitable grounding in Cleitarchan conceptions of Asian geography.

    1) Uncertainty whether the Caspian Sea was a gulf of the Ocean.

This doubt of "some" concerning the nature of the Caspian is expressed at Curtius 6.4.19 as part of a geographical discussion of the region that includes fragments of Cleitarchus and parts of which are also echoed at Diodorus 17.75.3. Hence there is a strong implication that this material was sourced from Cleitarchus. Strabo 11.7.2 references Patrocles, who explored the Caspian for Antiochus I around 284-3BC and concluded that it was nearly as big as the Pontic Sea (Black Sea). The same view appears in Pliny, *Natural History* 6.36-38, who attributes it to Cleitarchus. Hence there may be some connection between Cleitarchus' writings on this topic and Patrocles' account of his explorations. It is difficult to believe that Cleitarchus considered it possible that the Caspian might be a gulf of the Ocean, because it would eliminate the possibility that the Jaxartes was the Tanais (which Cleitarchus evidently did believe – see below.) More

The Reconstruction Of Books Seven To Nine

probably, Cleitarchus was aware of Patrocles' explorations and was disparaging or at least questioning his view that the Caspian was a gulf.[2]

2) Flow of water between the Caspian and the Sea of Azov

Strabo 11.1.5 states that Cleitarchus allowed that water of either the Pontic Sea (a.k.a. Euxine, the modern Black Sea) or the Caspian might flood across the isthmus of land between them, which would appear to match the very similar comments at Curtius 6.4.18 regarding the supply of water from the Maeotic Marsh (vicinity of the Sea of Azov) into the Caspian. The land is indeed very low lying between the Sea of Azov and the northern Caspian, but actual transfer of water would seem unlikely even in antiquity. Nevertheless, the fact that Cleitarchus was able to discuss geographical issues pertaining to the northern Caspian region is suggestive of an awareness of the explorations of Patrocles (as in the preceding point).

3) The Bosphorus in Cleitarchus is usually the Cimmerian Bosphorus

Curtius 6.2.13, 7.6.12 & 8.1.7 is probably following Cleitarchus in referring to the "Bosphorus". To avoid confusion, it is important to realize that he means the Cimmerian Bosphorus, the modern Strait of Kerch at the entrance to the Sea of Azov, and not the more famous Bosphorus at the SW corner of the Black Sea by Istanbul.

4) The Caucasus mountain range extended eastwards to the Hindu Kush

Curtius 7.3.19-21 is probably following Cleitarchus in describing the Caucasus range as extending from the region of Armenia in NE Turkey eastwards across the whole of Asia to the Hindu Kush, when Alexander was about to cross the latter in the spring of 329BC. This is corroborated by the fact that Diodorus 17.83.1 also deems these mountains a part of the Caucasus, but notes that the Hindu Kush section was known as the Paropamisus Range. This slightly inaccurate view that the mountains stretch in an unbroken chain from west to east right across the center of Asia from Turkey to the Himalayas was common to a number of ancient geographers, being echoed somewhat in the maps of Claudius Ptolemy, for example.

5) The Syr-Darya was the upper reaches of the River Don

This is the most serious geographical distortion in Cleitarchus, because it engenders the view that Soviet Central Asia (now the various "Stans") was part of Europe and lay vaguely just to the NE of the Black Sea. Plutarch, *Alexander* 45.4 states that Alexander himself supposed the River Orexartes (elsewhere called the Jaxartes in ancient sources and now known as the Syr-Darya) to be the Tanais, which is the modern River Don. This has the effect of shifting the entire landscape some 2000km to the west of where it

---

[2] On the connection between Patrocles and Cleitarchus, see W. W. Tarn, Alexander the Great, Vol II, Sources & Studies, pp. 12-19.

actually lies on the globe. The expedition believed that the Scythian tribes that they encountered to the north of the Syr-Darya were identical to the Scythians with whom the Greeks had long been in contact to the north of the Black Sea (anciently the Pontic Sea or Euxine). It is quite probable that there were indeed pronounced similarities of language and culture, but this would have reflected the wide geographical range of the Scythian tribes rather than a contraction of the landscape. The implication that Bactria lay just to the east of the Pontic Sea at Curtius 7.4.27 is likely to be a further consequence of the same Cleitarchan misunderstanding of the geography, since Alexander was actually more than 1000km east of even the Caspian Sea when he was in Bactria. There is a strong connection to be drawn between the misidentification of the Syr-Darya as the Tanais, the spurious Cleitarchan link between the Caspian and the Sea of Azov and Fragment 7 of the work of the Alexander historian Polycleitus of Larissa (in Strabo 11.7.4), which also asserts these concepts. A strong possibility is that Polycleitus was among Cleitarchus' sources for this material (see Figure 2.2). Strabo himself knew these things to be in error, quite probably based on the geographical researches of Eratosthenes, whom he mentions in refuting the misconceptions. This tends to corroborate the view that Cleitarchus antedates Eratosthenes, who was active in the second half of the 3rd century BC.

6) India began in South Afghanistan in the vicinity of the Helmand River

According to Cleitarchan geography, India began in southern Afghanistan in the region of the Helmand River, which Alexander traversed towards the end of 330BC. This is most explicitly stated at Curtius 8.9.10, where the River Ethymantus, which appears to be the Helmand, is mentioned as being a part of India. There are many confirmatory instances of the same geographical concept. Polyaenus 4.3.10 and Plutarch, *Alexander* 57.1-2 corroborate the detailed account of baggage burning at Curtius 6.6.14-17 shortly prior to the entry of the army into Southern Afghanistan. Although the former pair place the burning just prior to the entry into India proper, the confusion might well have resulted from Cleitarchus counting Southern Afghanistan as part of India, for it was true that Alexander was about to cross the mountains moving southwards into Afghanistan in pursuit of Satibarzanes at this point. The reason that Southern Afghanistan had to be incorporated within India may have been that the territory of Arachosia extended from the vicinity of the Helmand as far as the west bank of the Indus. The manuscripts of Curtius 7.3.4 read that Arachosia extended to the *ponticum mare* meaning the Black Sea, which is complete nonsense. It is clear from Strabo 11.10.1 that ancient geographers actually asserted that Arachosia extended to the River Indus (cf. Curtius 8.13.3, 9.7.14 & 9.10.7). The inference must be that the Greek word for a river (*potamos*) has somehow been corrupted to give Pontic in the Latin.

The Reconstruction Of Books Seven To Nine

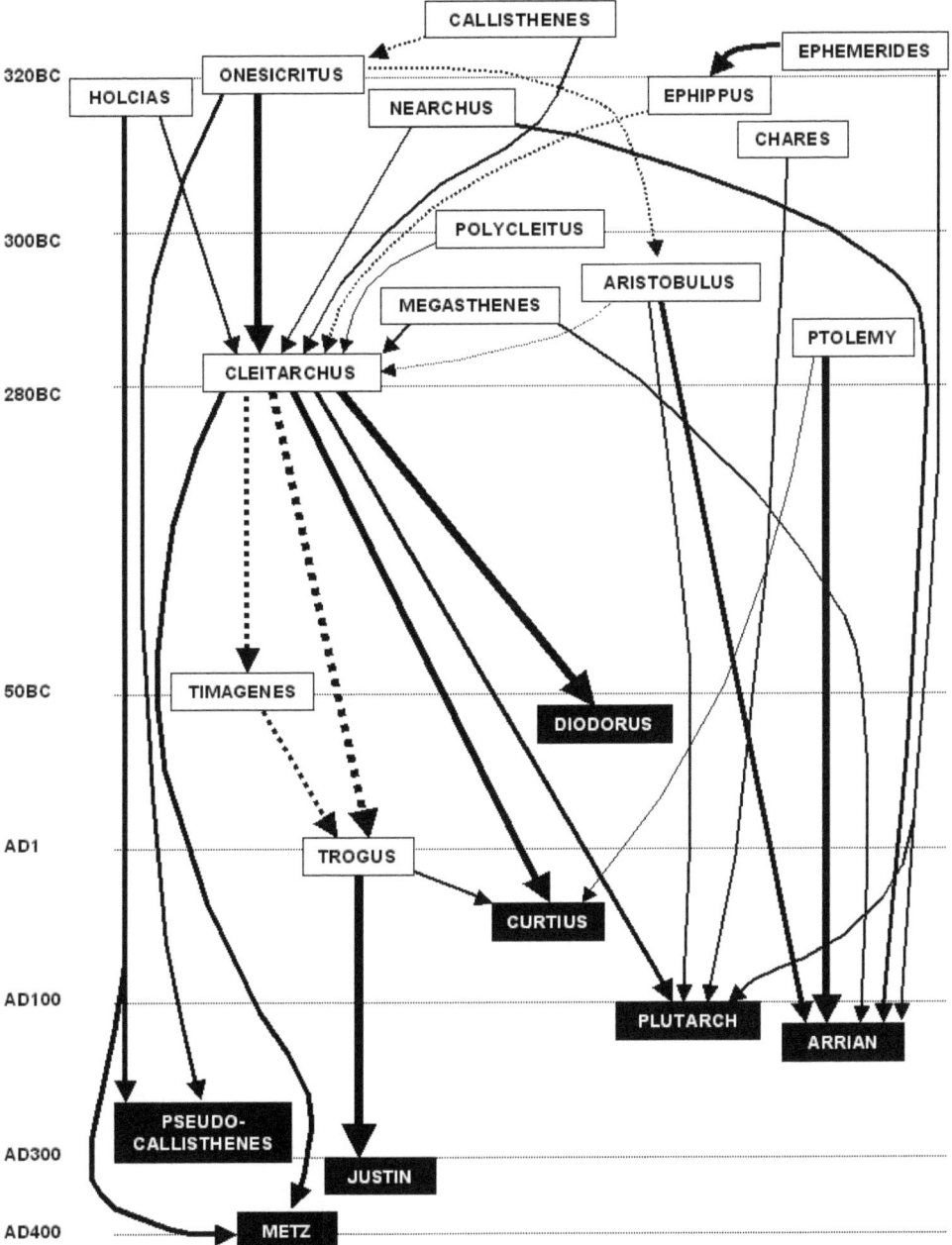

Figure 2.2. Relationships between ancient authors on Alexander's campaigns especially pertaining to Cleitarchus (white in black box = extant; and vice versa).

The Visit of the Queen of the Amazons

In the ancient world (as also today), Alexander's putative encounter with the Queen of the Amazons was one of the more controversial episodes in his career. The issue is neatly addressed by Plutarch in chapter 46 of his Life of Alexander:

Here [beyond the River Jaxartes] *the Queen of the Amazons came to see Alexander, as most writers say, among whom are Cleitarchus, Polycleitus, Onesicritus, Antigenes and Ister; but Aristobulus, Chares the royal usher, Ptolemy, Anticleides, Philo the Theban, and Philip of Theangela, besides Hecataeus of Eretria, Philip the Chalcidian, and Duris of Samos, say that this is a fiction. And it would seem that Alexander's testimony is in favour of their statement. For in a letter to Antipater, which gives all the details minutely, he says that the Scythian king offered him his daughter in marriage, but he makes no mention of the Amazon. And the story is told that many years afterwards Onesicritus was reading aloud to Lysimachus, who was now king, the fourth book of his history, in which was the tale of the Amazon, at which Lysimachus smiled gently and said: "And where was I at the time?" However, our belief or disbelief of this story will neither increase nor diminish our admiration for Alexander.*

It is certainly true that the daughter of the king of the Scythians dwelling beyond the Cimmerian Bosphorus was offered to Alexander in marriage, since this is also recorded by Arrian, *Anabasis* 4.15.2 and Curtius 8.1.9. Notionally, these were the Scythians dwelling in the vicinity of the Ukraine, but this may well be entangled with the geographical misconception that the Syr-Darya or Tanais or Jaxartes River was the border of Europe. If so, then the offer, which was received whilst Alexander was at Maracanda, may have come from a Scythian king perhaps based north of the Jaxartes. Some have supposed that Alexander's encounter with the Amazon queen was derived through embroidery of this incident, which is certainly a possibility. There is archaeological evidence for warrior women on the Russian Steppes in Alexander's era in the form of female ice-mummies preserved with their weapons in elaborate tombs dug into the Siberian permafrost. Hence the suggestion that Alexander encountered high status warrior women in this general vicinity may have some validity.

Curtius 6.4.17 appears to be following Cleitarchus in locating an Amazon homeland to Alexander's right as he approached the Caspian from the southeast. This would suggest that Cleitarchus placed it on the steppe to the east of the Caspian Sea. His source on this is likely to have been Onesicritus, who seems to be the earliest of the sources listed by Plutarch for Alexander having hosted a visit from the Amazon Queen. Subsequently, in giving the specific story of the visit of Thalestris, Cleitarchus suggested that she had travelled from the traditional Amazon homeland near the River Thermodon on the southern shores of the Black Sea (i.e. west of Hyrcania and very far to the west of the Caspian Sea.) It is likely that Cleitarchus or his source (Onesicritus?) has attempted to reconcile traditional legends of the Amazon nation with a visit to Alexander's camp of a high status warrior woman from east of the Caspian

Sea. This was perhaps facilitated by the haziness of Cleitarchus' grasp of the geography of the area.

Figure 2.3. Alexander with Thalestris (author's sketch of a fresco in Pompeii)

Whatever the degree of its authenticity, the story of the meeting between Alexander and Thalestris seems to have gripped the imagination of his readership in antiquity. A fresco found in Pompeii depicting Alexander with a queen (Figure 2.3) must surely have been intended to illustrate his meeting with Thalestris. She is a queen in her own right, since she bears a scepter and the helmet at her feet appears more likely to be her own than Alexander's.

Prophthasia

Prophthasia is the Greek for "Anticipation" (in the sense of forestalling something) and it is the name given to a town in the land of the Drangians by Alexander. It therefore seems to commemorate his having outrun fate in the form of the Dimnus conspiracy and hence it is considered to have been the site of the Philotas Affair, which is otherwise merely said to have transpired at the palace of the Drangians (Arrian, *Anabasis* 3.25.8).

Prophthasia is very likely to have been at or close to the modern city of Farah (Phraa) in the west of Afghanistan. Strabo 11.8.9, Claudius Ptolemy, *Geography* 6.19.4-5 and Pliny, *Natural History* 6.61 give the name Prophthasia to a town approximately 270km from Alexandria-in-Aria. If the latter is assumed to have been at or close to the modern city of Herat, which is likely, then 270km is about the correct distance for modern Farah. The specific distances cited by Strabo and Pliny give the route lengths abstracted from the records of the *bematists* (i.e. "pacers") of Alexander's expedition, the so-called Stages or *Stathmoi* in Greek. "Prophthasia" is listed among towns of Drangiana by Ptolemy[3] and Strabo 15.2.8 speaks of "Prophthasia in Drangiana", so it is clear that it lay south of Alexander-in-Aria. Stephanus Byzantinus in his entry for "Phrada" states that Alexander called this place Prophthasia and that it was a town among the Drangians (a.k.a. Zarangians) and there is also a mention by Isidorus of Charax, F2, 16 = Jacoby III C781. Hence it is beyond reasonable doubt that Prophthasia lay at or quite near Farah, despite that Tarn has gone against the grain by placing it considerably further south on Lake Seistan.

It is however a distinct possibility that Alexander's fort of Prophthasia was separate from the Farah that is the Phrada of Stephanus Byzantinus. Modern Farah lies down in the valley beside the river, but it is overlooked by crags of the nearby mountains, some of which are the sites of ancient fortresses. An adjacent refoundation could simultaneously explain the name change and the enduring association.

The old town of Farah, now in ruins, stood on the western bank of the river at a strategic point commanding the northern entrance into the province of Seistan. It used to be a major stage and tollhouse mid-way on the caravan road from Kandahar to Herat. A modern town, built on the opposite (eastern) bank, is now the center of all activities and accommodates the population.

---

[3] Ptolemy assigns Prophthasia coordinates of 110 pseudo-degrees of longitude and 32.33 degrees of latitude, whereas he places Alexander-in-Aria at 110 pseudo-degrees of longitude and 36 degrees of latitude. Ptolemy's longitude for Bactra (modern Balkh) was at 116 pseudo-degrees of longitude, which means that his longitude for Alexandria-in-Aria and Prophthasia is roughly consistent with Herat and Farah. The actual latitudes of Herat and Farah are 34.37N and 32.38N respectively and Farah is due south of Herat, so Ptolemy's separation is in the correct direction, but its magnitude is too large, although he has the latitude (which can be precisely derived from solar observations) almost exactly correct for Farah.

Farah was for centuries an important stronghold on the eastern frontier of the Sassanian Empire, possibly rebuilt by Peroz (AD457-84), since the province thereabouts was once named Fraxkar-Peroz. This might have been the occasion of its refoundation on a fresh site. The ancient citadel within Farah is seemingly Sassanian and there is scant evidence that much material of greater antiquity has been discovered in its immediate vicinity.

The Culpability of Philotas and Parmenion

The Philotas Affair, as it is commonly known, constitutes a real-life tragedy in three Acts, namely: The Dimnus Conspiracy, The Trial & Execution of Philotas and The Assassination of Parmenion. The account in Curtius is particularly full and vivid. Speculatively, Curtius found this quasi-judicial purgation especially interesting, since it bore comparison with the downfalls of some of the great political figures of his own time, such as Sejanus. Parallels with Diodorus, especially in the matter of how the plot of Dimnus and his fellow conspirators came to light, suggest that Curtius' version is highly likely to be derived from Cleitarchus, hence it probably constitutes a near verbatim and barely abridged Latin translation of a large section of Cleitarchus' text.

Alexander is often specially deprecated for his treatment of Philotas and Parmenion by both ancient and modern authorities and these critics often base their opinions on the Cleitarchan version of the affair, but it appears to me on the basis of the same account that Philotas was guilty of treason beyond reasonable doubt and that Alexander had no better option than to act as he did. However, the matter seems plagued with misunderstandings, which require explication.

There is no real doubt that Philotas concealed the existence of the Dimnus Conspiracy from the king, firstly, because he was stated to have confessed this much to Alexander by Cleitarchus and secondly, because Arrian, *Anabasis* 3.26.1-2 (citing Ptolemy and Aristobulus) reaches the same conclusion in his brief account of the matter:

Here also [at the palace of the Drangians] Alexander discovered the conspiracy of Philotas, son of Parmenio. Ptolemy and Aristobulus say that it had already been reported to him before in Egypt, but that it did not appear to him credible, both on account of the long-existing friendship between them, the honour, which he publicly conferred upon his father Parmenio, and the confidence he reposed in Philotas himself. Ptolemy, son of Lagus, says that Philotas was brought before the Macedonians; that Alexander vehemently accused him, and that he defended himself from the charges. He says also that the divulgers of the plot came forward and convicted him and his accomplices both by other clear proofs and especially because Philotas himself confessed that he had heard of some sort of conspiracy, which was being formed against Alexander. He was convicted of having said nothing to the king about this plot, though he visited the royal tent twice a day.

Alexander the Great in Afghanistan by Andrew Chugg

Neither is there any doubt that the Dimnus Conspiracy was a very real threat to Alexander's life, for Dimnus himself made dubiety impossible by committing suicide, when men were sent to arrest him. Legally speaking, the fact of having concealed the existence of a genuine assassination plot against the sovereign constitutes treason. However, there might be some moral mitigation, if Philotas' defence that he had not taken the plot seriously could be considered to have any credibility. However, this is not really a viable defence at all, because Philotas was at liberty to divulge the plot to Alexander, thus covering himself against accusations of concealment, whilst still expressing his personal skepticism about the matter, so there was actually no innocent motive for concealment. Conversely, Plutarch, *Alexander* 48.1-49.2 backs the comments of Arrian to the effect that Philotas' loyalty was already seriously suspected long before the Dimnus Conspiracy:

Now, Philotas, the son of Parmenion, had a high position among the Macedonians; for he was held to be valiant and able to endure hardship, and, after Alexander himself, no one was so fond of giving and so fond of his comrades. At any rate, we are told that when one of his intimates asked him for some money, he ordered his steward to give it him, and when the steward said he had none to give, "What meanest thou?" cried Philotas, "hast thou not even plate or clothing?" However, he displayed a pride of spirit, an abundance of wealth, and a care of the person and mode of life which were too offensive for a private man, and at this time particularly his imitation of majesty and loftiness was not successful at all, but clumsy, spurious, and devoid of grace, so that he incurred suspicion and envy, and even Parmenion once said to him: "My son, pray be less of a personage." Moreover, for a very long time accusations against him had been brought to Alexander himself. For when Darius had been defeated in Cilicia and the wealth of Damascus had been taken, among the many prisoners brought into the camp there was found a young woman, born in Pydna, and comely to look upon; her name was Antigone. This woman Philotas got; and as a young man will often talk freely in vaunting and martial strain to his mistress and in his cups, he used to tell her that the greatest achievements were performed by himself and his father, and would call Alexander a stripling who through their efforts enjoyed the title of ruler. These words the woman would report to one of her acquaintances, and he, as was natural, to somebody else, until the story came round to Craterus, who took the girl and brought her secretly to Alexander. He, on hearing the story, ordered her to continue her meetings with Philotas and to come and report to him whatever she learnt from her lover. Now, Philotas was ignorant of the plot thus laid against him, and in his frequent interviews with Antigone would utter many angry and boastful speeches and many improper words against the king. But Alexander, although strong testimony against Philotas came to his ears, endured in silence and restrained himself, either because he had confidence in Parmenion's good will towards him, or because he feared the reputation and power of father and son.

The glaring motivation for Philotas' concealment of the plot that remains was that he quietly hoped the conspiracy would succeed in eliminating Alexander, in which case his father was in an excellent position to seize power. Everything that we know about the circumstances drives towards the conclusion that this thought was exactly what kept Philotas' lips sealed. If so, then morally he was at

The Reconstruction Of Books Seven To Nine

least as culpable as the conspirators themselves and deserving of his fate. Note, however, that I very much distinguish between Philotas and the conspirators, for it is very unlikely that he was part of the plot. As he pointed out himself during his defence speech, if he had been the leader of the conspiracy or even just a member, he should both have set about having Cebalinus silenced and he should have advanced the timing of the perpetration of the plot, whereas he actually simply sat on his hands and did nothing. He seems to have believed that he could thereby exculpate himself, if the plot were discovered. He was almost correct, for Curtius suggests that Alexander's first instinct was to accept his excuses and forgive him. However, the king's Friends, notably Craterus, cogently made clear that Alexander simply could not afford to do so in the ensuing private council session. The recriminations had already gone too far, such that Philotas and Parmenion would now be driven to rebel by the perilousness of the cloud of suspicion that hung over them, even if they had not already contemplated insurrection.

The next matter that is disputed is the fairness of the ensuing trial. It is indisputable that such a trial took place before the Macedonian Assembly and that both Philotas and Parmenion (*in absentia*) were convicted, because, as we have seen, Arrian endorses the Cleitarchan version from Curtius using largely independent sources. Regarding its equity, Curtius 6.9.30-31 makes a point of having Alexander defend the right of Philotas to put his defence to the Assembly:

Then Coenus, despite that he had wed the sister of Philotas, fulminated against him more fiercely than anyone else, bellowing that he was a traitor to his king, to his country and to the army itself. And scooping up a stone that happened to lie by his feet he prepared to hurl it at him – many surmised out of a desire to spare him from torture. But the king stayed his hand, declaring that the defendant ought first to be afforded an opportunity to deliver his defence and that he would not allow the trial to proceed otherwise.

Hence Alexander himself apparently showed such meticulous attention to fairness as to insist that a man who had failed (by his own admission) to report a genuine assassination plot against the king's life should nevertheless be given a hearing before the entire army. However, the king's critics assert that he subsequently had Philotas tortured to elicit a confession, but this is mistaken. The torture did indeed take place, but according to Curtius (who gives by far the most detailed account) its purpose was not to secure a confession. Philotas gave a confession before the torturers began work in the hope of forestalling them. But in fact, it appears firstly that torture was a normal part of the punishment for those convicted of treason, since, for example, the Royal Pages were tortured to death after their conviction (Curtius 8.8.20), and secondly that it was designed to try to extract any further information about the plot that might not yet have been uncovered. In this particular case, it is clear that Alexander needed further evidence against Parmenion. He could not execute Philotas, Parmenion's last surviving son, without incurring the enmity of the general, so he was compelled to act against him. According to Curtius, Philotas did indeed provide evidence of Parmenion's treasonous intentions by describing an earlier pact with Hegelochus to kill Alexander after the death of Darius. Curtius also notes (and I agree with him) that such evidence given under torture was of doubtful validity. But that misses the point. Alexander had to move against Parmenion anyway, so it was better to do so on the basis of questionable evidence than on none at all.

Furthermore, Philotas had already made his defence and been condemned by the Assembly when the torture was applied to him. The torture occurs at Curtius 6.11.13-34, whereas Philotas was condemned with the Assembly having been roused against him at Curtius 6.11.8. That is the way the Assembly delivered its verdicts - by acclamation rather than an explicit vote. At this point all the evidence against Philotas had been heard and he had completed his defence, so the verdict was due. In the ensuing trial of Amyntas, Simmias and Polemon (who were acquitted), Curtius 7.2.7 actually states this by speaking of "the acclamations by which crowds express their favour". This is why the Bodyguards are starting to propose a sentence for Philotas (tearing him to pieces with their bare hands). It is true that the trials of the other suspects and Parmenion were conducted the following day. That was why Alexander only adjourned the Assembly. The next day, Philotas was merely a witness in the trial of his father, since the main evidence then available against Parmenion came from his testimony about Hegelochus under torture the previous evening.

Unfortunately, additional confusion has been sown by a slight mistranslation of Curtius 6.11.9 in the Penguin version of his text, which states that Curtius was about to experience *"further* torture in prison". There is in fact no word in the Latin of Curtius that translates as "further" in this passage, which is:

rex in contionem reversus, sive ut in custodia quoque torqueret, sive ut diligentius cuncta cognosceret, concilium in posterum diem distulit...

The word at issue is *quoque*, which means "also" or "as well". It is only necessary to look at the immediate context (the preceding sentences) to see what this torture/torment was as well as. A correct translation would be:

Then indeed the entire assembly was incensed and the Bodyguards made a beginning by bellowing that they should dismember the traitor with their bare hands. In fact, Philotas was scarcely scared on hearing this, since he feared far fouler suffering. But the king came back into the meeting and adjourned the proceedings until the following day, either in order to torment Philotas in prison as well or else to investigate the whole matter more thoroughly.

So in fact it is perfectly clear that the torture/torment in the prison is in addition to the proposal by the Bodyguards that they should dismember Philotas with their bare hands. The meaning of *torqueo* in Latin is actually literally to wrench or twist, so the dismembering would very much have been recognised by a Latin reader as another instance of it. There is also a strong reason in the structure of the Latin phrase, which means that it must really be a

The Reconstruction Of Books Seven To Nine

reference back to the proposed tearing to pieces. This is because *quoque* has a meaning very similar to the English "too" and just like "too" it almost always emphasises the word preceding it: in this case "in prison", so the meaning is "***in prison*** too". Hence Curtius is explicitly implying some kind of earlier mention of torment in a context outside of prison. The only thing this could possibly have been is the tearing to pieces, which would have formed part of a public execution. Thus there is no basis for the translation "further" in the Penguin Curtius, which infers something for which there is no evidence in the Latin.

It may also be noted that there has been no mention of Philotas having been tortured before, merely a proposal that he eventually should be. Hence, the translation "further" would make Curtius refer back to an event that he had not actually stated to have happened. So the Penguin translator (by the artifice of mistranslating a Latin word) would have us swallow that Curtius referred back to an episode of torture that he had forgotten that he had not already mentioned a few a pages earlier, which is preposterous.

Using "further" instead of "as well" was an artifice to give a particular slant to the Latin. But I do not at all suggest that the translator was committing a deliberate distortion. He probably put this slant on the Latin, simply because it was the only interpretation that he saw at the time. He simply did not notice on the spur of the moment that *quoque* should refer back to the tearing to bits by hand. However, the effect of this accident is unfortunate in seeming to provide evidence for pre-conviction torture where there is none.

It should be remembered that shortly after the trial of Philotas, Amyntas and Polemon were acquitted by the Assembly, so it is clear that trials before this body were not a foregone conclusion. But Philotas had the special problem that he had freely admitted to having concealed a genuine assassination plot against his sovereign, which would be sufficient to convict him of treason in most jurisdictions today.

There remains the question of the guilt of Parmenion. Many commentators, both ancient and modern, have assumed that he was innocent, since it is fairly unlikely that either he or Philotas were actually members of the Dimnus conspiracy. Two things, however, weigh significantly against him. Firstly, it is likely to be true that Philotas alleged under torture that Parmenion had consented to espouse Hegelochus' proposal that an opportunity should be sought to depose Alexander, once Darius had been dealt with. Although the truth of this accusation is in doubt, since it was made under torture, its falseness is equally in doubt, since it was credible to those present at the time and is relatively consistent with other information that has come down to us about the general context. For example, Hegelochus' reported accusation that Alexander had pardoned his father's assassins should probably be connected with the report at Justin 9.7 that Olympias had arranged getaway steeds for the assassin, Pausanias. It cannot refer to the pardoning of Alexander Lyncestes, because

Alexander had long since imprisoned him on suspicion of treason at the time when Hegelochus spoke.

Secondly, Alexander seems to have made an additional effort to secure evidence of Parmenion's disloyalty. Curtius 7.2.27 makes a point of the fact that Cleander and Polydamas waited until Parmenion was reading the letter purportedly penned by Philotas before slaying him. It was precisely at the point that he exhibited pleasure with the contents of this correspondence that the execution was perpetrated. Assuredly, the explanation must be that Alexander had included some treasonous material in this letter and had instructed his officers to await Parmenion's reaction before imposing the death sentence. Hence Parmenion's pleasure in learning of this treason from his son, as he supposed, provided Alexander and furnishes us too with some valid corroboration of the general's disloyalty.

The Condemnation of the Branchidae

It will be helpful to begin with a review of the more significant elements of the copious ancient source material on Alexander's destruction of the Branchidae.

Firstly, Strabo 14.1.5:

Next after the Poseidium of the Milesians, at the distance of 189 stadia from the seacoast, is the oracle of Apollo Didymeus among the Branchidæ. This, as well as the other temples, except that at Ephesus, was burnt by the order of Xerxes. The Branchidæ delivered up the treasures of the god to the Persian king, and accompanied him in his flight, in order to avoid the punishment of sacrilege and treachery.

Strabo 11.11.4:

And near these places [in Bactria and Sogdiana], they say, Alexander destroyed also the city of the Branchidae, whom Xerxes had settled there - people who voluntarily accompanied him from their homeland - because of the fact that they had betrayed to him the riches and treasures of the god at Didyma. Alexander destroyed the city, they add, because he abominated the sacrilege and the betrayal.

Plutarch, *Moralia* 557B, *De sera numinis vindicta* (On delays of divine vengeance):

Again, not even the greatest admirers of Alexander, among whom I count myself, approve his wiping out the city of Branchidae and his general massacre of young and old because their great-grandfathers had betrayed the temple near Miletus.

Curtius 7.5.28-35 (which is essentially the version used in this Reconstruction):

Whilst Bessus was leading him a merry chase, Alexander came upon an inconsequential citadel. Its populace comprised the Branchidae, who had migrated from Miletus at the bidding of Xerxes, when he was on his way back from Greece. They had set themselves up it this seat, since they had profaned the sanctuary called the Didymeon to appease Xerxes. In the interim they had hardly lapsed from the habits of their homeland, though they were now bilingual, having little by little been lured from their own languange by the local lingo. Therefore they

The Reconstruction Of Books Seven To Nine

were greatly gratified to greet Alexander and to set their city and themselves at his service. Then the king commanded that the Milesians who were serving in his forces should assemble. They nursed the ancient enmity against the Branchidaean folk. Hence he allowed those whom they had betrayed freely to judge whether they wished to recollect the kinship or the crime of the Branchidae. Then, having received various views from them, he himself undertook to weigh up what had best be done. The next day, when the Branchidae came before him, he called upon them to accompany him and, when they had come to the city, he himself got through its gate with a designated detachment. The phalanx he instructed to ring the ramparts of the fortress and to tear down the town at a given signal, since it was an asylum for quislings and these should be mown down to a man. Being defenceless they were massacred everywhere and neither their shared speech nor the beseeching of the suppliants with olive branches and prayer could curb the cruelty. Ultimately they undermined the foundations of the walls so that they could be cast down in order that no vestige of the town should stand. And in order to leave naught but wiped out waste and lifeless land with even its roots eradicated, they not only felled the copses and sacred groves, but also extirpated the stumps. Had this been contrived against the traitors themselves, then it would have been vindicated as valid vengeance rather than rated as ruthlessness. As it was the descendants suffered for the sins of their ancestors, though they had not even seen Miletus and hence never had the ability to betray it to Xerxes.

Diodorus, Contents of Book 17 (his main account is lost in a lacuna):

How the Branchidae, who of old had been settled by the Persians on the borders of their kingdom, were slain by Alexander as traitors to the Greeks.

Suda (Aelian fragment 54) s.v. *Branchidae* (Adler number: Beta 514):

Those living in Milesian Didyma, who, in seeking favor with Xerxes, betrayed the temple of the indigenous Apollo to the barbarians: the temple offerings, of which there were a great number, were plundered. The traitors, fearing vengeance from both the laws and the inhabitants of the city, asked Xerxes to pay them for this wretched betrayal and settle them in some Asian land. He agreed, and in exchange for what was evil and unholy, allowed them to live where they would never again set foot upon Greece and both they and future generations would be removed from the fear besetting them. Then, having obtained the land with birds of ill-omen, they established a city and gave it the name Branchidas, thinking they had not only escaped the Milesians, but also justice itself. But the watchfulness of the god was not asleep. For Alexander, when he obtained mastery of the Persian empire upon conquering Darius, heard of their daring and conceived a hatred for them and their successive generations; so he killed them all, judging that the offspring of evil is evil. He overthrew their pseudonymous city and razed it to the ground.

Given this wealth of source evidence, those that deny that this event ever happened are bound to expose their reputations to the taint of disingenuousness.[4] It is no excuse that Arrian omitted mention of the matter, for he omitted mention of many things that he considered distasteful.

---

[4] For the denial of the historicity of the event see W. W. Tarn, *Alexander the Great*, Vol II, Sources & Studies, "The Alleged Massacre of the Branchidae", pp. 272-275; Frank Holt, *Alexander the*

By modern standards the destruction of the Branchidae was an atrocity. By the standards of Alexander's era, the issue is far more complex. It appears that contemporaneous religious law, which then enjoyed genuine respect, dictated that the descendants of serious religious criminals inherited the guilt. Plutarch's dialogue On Delays in Divine Vengeance in his *Moralia* attacks the application of this religious law through various examples, including the case of the Branchidae, but it nevertheless treats it as axiomatic that such a law was applied and even cites an attack upon the same principle by Euripides at *Moralia* 556E. It was a sacred duty of Alexander to uphold religious law, but he would probably have been conscious that this particular tenet was controversial and that the passage of 150 years could be seen as a major mitigation. It was probably his sense of a dilemma that led him to seek a sentence from his Milesians. Curtius is usually translated to the effect that these Milesians could not decide, so Alexander took the decision instead, but actually he need not mean more than that Alexander imposed a punishment in accordance with the preponderance of the varied views of the Milesians. Translations that make Alexander override his own policy of consultation are unnecessarily implying irrationality and vindictiveness on the part of the king, which is not substantiated by the actual words of Curtius. Among the ancient sources Aelian and Strabo seem to endorse or accept the justice of Alexander's treatment of the Branchidae, whereas Curtius and Plutarch express doubts.

The Killing of Cleitus

The killing of Cleitus was arguably the worst thing Alexander ever did. Certainly, he seems to have thought so himself, even reportedly attempting suicide, as he realized the full horror of what he had done. Cleitus had ranked among the most senior of his Friends, and, what was worse, was the brother of Alexander's nurse. Worst of all, the man had saved Alexander's life at the Battle of the Granicus. The killing was utterly dishonorable and the king found his shame hard to bear.

Nevertheless, the behaviour of Cleitus himself in the matter was also foolish and disgraceful. Just how biting some of the taunts with which he provoked Alexander were likely to have proven requires some explanation.

Cleitus began by quoting Euripides, *Andromache* 693-698:

Alas, what perverse customs prevail in Greece! Whenever the army sets up a trophy over the foe, men no more consider this the work of those who really toiled, but the general gets the credit

---

Great and Bactria, p. 74, refutes Tarn's case, which is essentially that the temple and oracle had already been burnt and plundered by Darius I in 494BC (according to Herodotus 6.19), so there was nothing left for Xerxes to deal with 15 years later. However, there is reason to believe that the temple was re-constructed in the interim. Alternatively, there may be some undetected confusion between Darius and Xerxes among the Alexander historians.

The Reconstruction Of Books Seven To Nine

for it. He brandished his spear as one man among a myriad others and did no more than a single warrior, yet he gets more praise than they.

The particular passage may be firmly identified by the snatch quoted by Plutarch, *Alexander* 51.5. It argues that generals were too eager to claim too much of the credit for victories won by the exertions of their troops. It is plain enough how this might needle Alexander in itself, but Cleitus may additionally have been parodying a habit of Alexander, who is himself frequently cited as having quoted passages from Euripides to make pointed observations. Plutarch, *Alexander* 10.4 reveals that Alexander quoted an equivocal line from the *Medeia* to Pausanias, before the latter assassinated his father, whilst Nicobule (Athenaeus 12.537D) has the king recite an entire scene of *Andromeda* during the banquet at which his fatal illness began. Plutarch, *Alexander* 53.2-3 also records Alexander quoting from the *Bacchae* and another, unidentified play of Euripides in criticism of Callisthenes. Arrian, *Anabasis* 7.16.6 cites Alexander reciting Euripides to express cynicism to the Chaldean priests, who were warning him against entering Babylon.

As the tension rose, Cleitus suggested that Alexander of Epirus, the brother of Olympias, who had been killed on campaign in Italy in the winter of 331-330BC, had had to contend with much stiffer opposition than the Persians, who were women by comparison. Cleitus' quote is also referenced by Livy 9.19.10-11 and Aulus Gellius 17.21.33. It was an outright assault on Alexander's self-esteem. To add insult to injury, Cleitus combined this dig with praise for Parmenion, who was officially a convicted traitor. But perhaps the most stinging insult of all was his last, when he ridiculed the Oracle of Ammon and Alexander's official status in Egypt as Ammon's son. This was an attack on Alexander's religious sensibilities and was just as incendiary then as such things are apt to prove nowadays.

The sources are united in attributing the uninhibited and unrestrained foolishness to mutual inebriation, which rings very true. However, Plutarch and Arrian do differ markedly from Curtius in the precise circumstances of the killing itself. The version found in Curtius gives a more cold-blooded account of the killing by making Alexander wait for Cleitus outside the hall, where they had been banqueting. Also Alexander's taunting of the corpse regarding Cleitus' praise for Philip is only reported by Curtius 8.1.52 and Justin 12.6.4, which is a strong indication that Curtius is following the Cleitarchan version. Arrian, *Anabasis* 4.8.9 and Plutarch, *Alexander* 51 recount a variant version where Cleitus is successfully dragged from the hall, but bursts back in reciting Euripides' *Andromache* 693 and is speared in the doorway by Alexander on the spur of the moment.

Arrian, *Anabasis* 4.8.4-9:

It was well known that Cleitus had long been vexed at Alexander for the change in his style of living in excessive imitation of foreign customs, and at those who flattered him with their speech. At that time also, being heated with wine, he would not permit them either to insult the deity or, by depreciating the deeds of the ancient heroes, to confer upon Alexander this gratification which deserved no thanks. He affirmed Alexander's deeds were neither in fact at all so great or marvellous as they represented in their laudation; nor had he achieved them by himself, but for the most part they were the deeds of the Macedonians. The delivery of this speech annoyed Alexander; and I do not commend it, for I think, in such a drunken bout, it would have been sufficient if, so far as he was personally concerned, he had kept silence, and not committed the error of indulging in the same flattery as the others. But when some even mentioned Philip's actions without exercising a just judgment, declaring that he had performed nothing great or marvellous, they herein gratified Alexander; but Cleitus being then no longer able to contain himself, began to put Philip's achievements in the first rank, and to depreciate Alexander and his performances. Cleitus, being now quite intoxicated, made other depreciatory remarks and even vehemently reviled him, because indeed he had saved his life, when the cavalry battle had been fought with the Persians at the Granicus. Then indeed, arrogantly stretching out his right hand, he said: "This hand, O Alexander, preserved thee on that occasion." Alexander could now no longer endure the drunken insolence of Cleitus; but jumped up against him in a great rage. He was however restrained by his drinking companions. As Cleitus did not desist from his insulting remarks, Alexander shouted out a summons for his shield-bearing guards to attend him; but when no one obeyed him, he said that he was reduced to the same position as Darius, when he was led about under arrest by Bessus and his adherents, and that he now possessed the mere name of king. Then his companions were no longer able to restrain him; for according to some he leaped up and snatched a javelin from one of his Bodyguards; according to others, a long pike from one of his ordinary guards, with which he struck Cleitus and killed him. Aristobulus does not say whence the drunken quarrel originated, but asserts that the fault was entirely on the side of Cleitus, who, when Alexander had got so enraged with him as to jump up against him with the intention of making an end of him; was led away by Ptolemy, son of Lagus, the Bodyguard, through the gateway, beyond the wall and ditch of the citadel where the quarrel occurred. He adds that Cleitus could not control himself, but went back again, and falling in with Alexander who was calling out for Cleitus, he exclaimed: "Alexander, here am I, Cleitus!" Thereupon he was struck with a long pike and killed.

Arrian states that he found this account of the killing in Aristobulus: it is circumstantially more credible than Curtius, who makes Alexander stalk Cleitus in the courtyard in a more pre-meditated mode of action.

Plutarch, *Alexander* 50-51:

Not long after [the Philotas Affair] came the affair of Cleitus, which those who simply learn the immediate circumstances will think more savage than that of Philotas; if we take into consideration, however, alike the cause and the time, we find that it did not happen of set purpose, but through some misfortune of the king, whose anger and intoxication furnished occasion for the evil genius of Cleitus. It happened on this wise. Some people came bringing Greek fruit to the king from the seaboard. He admired its perfection and beauty and called Cleitus, wishing to show it to him and share it with him. It chanced that Cleitus was sacrificing, but he gave up the sacrifice and came; and three of the sheep on which libations had already been poured came following after him. When the king learnt of this circumstance, he imparted it to his soothsayers, Aristander and Cleomantis the Lacedaemonian. Then, on their telling him that the omen was bad, he ordered them to sacrifice in all haste for the safety of Cleitus. For he himself, two days before this, had seen a strange vision in his sleep; he thought he saw Cleitus sitting with the sons of Parmenion in black robes, and all were dead. However, Cleitus did not finish his sacrifice, but came at once to the supper of the king, who had sacrificed to the Dioscuri. After boisterous drinking was underway, verses were sung which had been composed by a certain Pranichus, or, as some say, Pierio, to shame and ridicule the generals who had lately been defeated by the Barbarians. The older guests were annoyed at this and railed at both the poet and the singer, but Alexander and those about him listened with delight and bade the singer go on. Then Cleitus, who was already drunk and naturally of a harsh temper and wilful, was more than ever vexed, and insisted that it was not well done, when among Barbarians and enemies, to insult Macedonians who were far better men than those who laughed at them, even though they had met with misfortune. And when Alexander declared that Cleitus was pleading his own cause when he gave cowardice the name of misfortune, Cleitus sprang to his feet and said: "It was this cowardice of mine, however, that saved thy life, god-born as thou art, when thou wast already turning thy back upon the spear of Spithridates; and it is by the blood of Macedonians, and by these wounds, that thou art become so great as to disown Philip and make thyself son to Ammon." Thoroughly incensed, then, Alexander said: "Base fellow, dost thou think to speak thus of me at all times, and to raise faction among Macedonians, with impunity?" "Nay," said Cleitus, "not even now do we enjoy impunity, since such are the rewards we get for our toils; and we pronounce those happy who are already dead, and did not live to see us Macedonians thrashed with Median rods, or begging Persians in order to get audience with our king." So spake Cleitus in all boldness, and those about Alexander sprang up to confront him and reviled him, while the elder men tried to quell the tumult. Then Alexander, turning to Xenodochus of Cardia and Artemus of Colophon, said: "Do not the Greeks appear to you to walk about among Macedonians like demi-gods among wild beasts?" Cleitus, however, would not yield, but called on Alexander to speak out freely what he wished to say, or else not to invite to supper men who were free and spoke their minds, but to live with Barbarians and slaves, who would do obeisance to his white tunic and Persian girdle. Then Alexander, no longer able to restrain his anger, threw one of the apples that lay on the table at Cleitus and hit him, and began looking about for his sword. But one of his Bodyguards, Aristonous, conveyed it away before he could lay his hands on it, and the rest surrounded him and begged him to desist, whereupon he sprang to his feet and called out in Macedonian speech a summons to his corps of guards (and this was a sign of great disturbance), and ordered the trumpeter to sound, and smote him with his fist because he hesitated and was unwilling to do so. This man, then, was afterwards held in high esteem on the ground that it was due to him more than to any one else that the camp was not thrown into commotion. But Cleitus would not give in, and with much ado his friends pushed him out of the banquet-hall. He tried to come in again, however, by another door, very boldly and contemptuously reciting these iambics from the Andromache of Euripides: "Alas! in Hellas what ill government!" And so, at last, Alexander seized a spear from one of his guards, met Cleitus as he was drawing aside the curtain before the door, and ran him through. No sooner had Cleitus fallen with a roar and a groan than the king's anger departed from him. And when he was come to himself and beheld his friends standing speechless, he drew the spear from the dead body and would have dashed it into his own throat, had not his bodyguards prevented this by seizing his hands and carrying him by force to his chamber.

Alexander's distress initially proved intractable, despite the fact that an Assembly of the Macedonians retrospectively exculpated his actions by declaring the killing to have been lawful. They had missed the point. It was not the legality of the killing that troubled the king so much as the consequential dishonour. Perhaps, therefore, it was the arguments of the courtiers and philosophers that were more successful in eventually persuading Alexander to abandon an attempt to starve himself. They seem to have argued that the expedition could not afford to be deprived of his leadership. His loss in such perilous territory would endanger all of them, so it was the more honourable course that he should rise above his shame.

The Culpability and Fates of Callisthenes and the Pages

Some commentators have sometimes sought to argue or imply that the fact that there were two assassination plots launched against Alexander during his reign shows that he was an unpopular monarch. However, history actually teaches us that there is no clear correlation between the popularity of a ruler and the number of attempts on his or her life. Many popular rulers have suffered assassination (e.g. Abraham Lincoln or John Kennedy) or attempted assassination (e.g. President Reagan or Pope John Paul II). James Garfield was shot by a man (Charles Guiteau) who had supported his presidency and who mistakenly believed that his support had earned him a political appointment. Conversely, unpopular rulers have often been removed by legitimate means instead. Nero, having made himself unpopular through excessive taxation, was removed by a vote of the Senate, whereas Gaius Caligula, who remained popular with the Roman masses, could only be removed by assassination when he upset certain narrow sections of the Roman elite. It is a false syllogism to argue that assassins dislike their victims and Alexander was a victim of assassination attempts, therefore Alexander was generally disliked.

Regarding the second assassination attemp against Alexander's life, commonly known as the Conspiracy of the Pages, the instigators seem to have been inspired by special personal motives in the first instance. It is clearly reported by our sources that it came about simply because Alexander had Hermolaus flogged for having slain the king's prey (a boar) in the hunt, which was in itself a perfectly proper punishment by Macedonian standards for a significant offence against royal etiquette.

According to Macedonian custom Hermolaus needed to kill a boar to achieve the right to recline at supper, but was short of opportunities. Instead of talking the matter through with Alexander, he simply slew the first boar that came his way, despite the embarrassment caused to the king. This is classic misbehaviour by teenagers. Alexander had no choice but to treat it as insubordination. It could be argued that in an ideal world he should have been more sensitive to the issue beforehand, but that would be to apply 20:20 hindsight.

Subsequently, the complaints and moans of the Macedonian traditionalists concerning Alexander's Policy of Fusion were raised by Hermolaus during his trial in an attempt retrospectively to justify his unjustifiable behaviour. But are even these motives to be condoned? The basic premise of the traditionalists was that Persians were barbarians and should be treated as second-class citizens in their own country. Their central complaint against Alexander was that he treated the Persians too well and even admired aspects of their culture.

Others argue that the pages were partly motivated by the recent refusal of their tutor Callisthenes to perform *proskynesis* before Alexander. Although Callisthenes does not appear to have actually been in the plot, he does seem slyly to have encouraged Hermolaus in his rebellious tendencies – possibly due to his disillusion over the *proskynesis* issue.

The coterie of six or eight conspirators among the Pages (more accurately the "Royal Youths", who served as squires to the king) seems to have been selected either because they were boyfriends or ex-boyfriends of existing conspirators or because they also harboured known grudges against the king. Of course the plot was rationalised in terms of the widespread dissent over the Policy of Fusion. Of course there was a large traditionalist faction (probably even a majority) among the Macedonians that opposed Fusion. But the latter were not fundamentally disloyal and would not have supported killing Alexander (indeed the associated crisis would have been acutely dangerous for everyone). They would on the other hand have been unscrupulous in exploiting Alexander's premature death to seek the enslavement of the Persians.

It would be overly to rationalise the circumstances even to assume that this group of conspirators believed that they could necessarily avoid death, if successful. They felt personally outraged – Sostratus, the lover of Hermolaus, was said to be even more outraged than Hermolaus himself. It seems that Alexander was normally rather mild in his treatment of the Pages (the king says so himself at Curtius 8.8.4), so the flogging and horse-deprivation imposed upon Hermolaus rankled all the more bitterly. Teenagers are not normally perfectly rational in their behaviour and these teenagers do not seem to have thought much beyond their immediate objective: simple revenge. It is unlikely that the conspiracy would ever have happened without the flogging. That was what transformed mild resentment into murderous intent. The significance of the flogging was that it was the essential catalyst for a variety of less burning resentments to be formulated into tangible treason.

The greater area of controversy in the context of the Conspiracy of the Pages is the implication of Callisthenes in the plot and his ensuing arrest and maltreatment. Hephaistion claimed that he had agreed to perform *proskynesis* (a form of obeisance practiced by the Persians) before Alexander at a specially convened formal dinner held perhaps just weeks beforehand (Plutarch,

Alexander 55.1). However, he had made a point of refusing *proskynesis* at the actual event and instead had delivered an oration defending his stance. This had probably damaged his standing with the king. He was Alexander's officially appointed historian of the expedition, but as a leading scholar had also been assigned responsibility for the education of the Pages. Callisthenes was said to have heard Hermolaus' complaints against Alexander and his whipping with sympathy. He had reportedly made ambiguous remarks to the Page that he should remember that he was a man and that he might become the most illustrious of men by killing the most illustrious (Curtius 8.6.25 & Plutarch, *Alexander* 55.2). Although none had named him as a participant, Callisthenes was arrested and imprisoned following the betrayal of the plot on the basis that he had used his position to influence the conspirators against the king.

Hermolaus called for Callisthenes to be brought before the Macedonian Assembly at his trial in order to employ his oratory in their mutual defence. However, Alexander refused, explaining his decision with the Latin phrase: *nunc Olynthio non idem iuris est*. It is unfortunate that this has been given a pejorative spin in the Penguin translation: "He is an Olynthian and does not enjoy the same rights". The word "enjoy" supposes that Callisthenes rights were inferior, which is not implied by the Latin, which literally has the meaning that "being Olynthian he does not come under the same jurisdiction." It was in fact a neutral statement of the legal position that the Macedonian Assembly was not the correct body to try Callisthenes, since he was not Macedonian. It specifically does not mean that he had no right to a trial: that is the whole point of *idem*, which would be unnecessary, if Alexander were trying to say that Callisthenes had no rights. The Penguin translation would almost be correct, if it were read as: "He does not enjoy **the same** rights." But, of course, everyone reads it incorrectly as: "He does not enjoy the same **rights**."

Immediately thereafter Curtius 8.8.20-21 reports:

With that Alexander closed the meeting and had the condemned men [the Pages] transferred to members of their own unit. The latter tortured them to death so that they would gain the king's approval by their cruelty. Callisthenes also died under torture. He was innocent of any plot to kill the king, but the sycophantic character of court life ill-suited his nature.

But again it is worth referring back to the Latin in Curtius for Callisthenes' fate: *Callisthenes quoque tortus interiit*. This does not have to mean more than that "Callisthenes also died in torment". It is not inconsistent with the most credible of the various extant ancient accounts of Callisthenes' end, which is attributed to Chares, Alexander's chamberlain. Plutarch thought him reliable on this matter and I concur, because Chares was uniquely in a position to know the truth. Plutarch, *Alexander* 55.5 wrote:

Chares says that after his arrest Callisthenes was kept in fetters seven months, that he might be tried before a full council when Aristotle was present, but that about the time when Alexander was wounded in India, he died from obesity and the disease of lice.

The Reconstruction Of Books Seven To Nine

Thus Alexander evidently intended a trial should take place. Chares seems to have been the manager of Alexander's court. This and the fact that we find him making authoritative and detailed statements on Callisthenes' disagreement with Alexander and his ultimate fate would suggest that he was probably responsible for royal prisoners, in which case he would have had privileged knowledge on the matter. However, there is one notably dissonant version in Arrian, *Anabasis* 4.14.1-3:

As for Callisthenes, Aristobulus says he was bound with fetters and carried round with the army, but at length died of sickness, Ptolemy son of Lagus that he was racked and put to death by hanging. Thus not even those whose narratives are entirely trustworthy and who actually accompanied Alexander at the time agree in their accounts of events which were public and in their own knowledge. There are many other varying accounts of the same events in different histories, but I must be content with what I have recorded.

My view is that Ptolemy's history bore the hallmarks of having been sanitised prior to publication, especially because it exhibited significant blandness and surprising omissions of scandalous anecdotes etc. Where possible it seems to have suppressed embarrassing details. In some cases the event was too prominent to gloss over and then we see signs of whitewash. The suspicion should be that Ptolemy or his editor (Philadelphus?) has substituted a clean death for Callisthenes, because the truth was embarrassing.

The fact that disparate contemporaneous accounts of Callisthenes' death exist means that it must have happened in private. If he had been publicly executed, then there could not be room for doubt. But hanging is only likely to have been used as a public means of execution in Alexander's era. Private killings are dominated by stabbings (e.g. Eumenes), but also include poisonings (Alexander IV and Roxane) and strangulations in familiar cases (e.g. Heracles the son of Alexander and Barsine). It is difficult to prove a negative, but secret hangings do not seem to have been common in Alexander's world and it would seem unnecessarily elaborate. If you believe that secret hanging is unlikely, then it is similarly improbable that Ptolemy's account gave the truth on this matter.

The Marriage to Roxane

The marriage to Roxane formed the finale of Book 9 of Cleitarchus. It comes as a rather abrupt surprise, stimulating intense discussion of Alexander's motives anciently as well as today. Why wed this girl, when he could simply have taken her as his mistress? However, Alexander could simply be regarded as seeking to emulate his father, Philip, who took on new wives as an extension of his war policy, the idea being to build a victory by the formulation of pacts with suitable allies as much as by the defeat of irreconcilable enemies in battle. This is explained by Athenaeus 557B:

And Philip the Macedonian did not take any women with him to his wars, as Darius did, whose power was subverted by Alexander. For he used to take about with him three hundred and fifty concubines in all his wars; as Dicaearchus relates in the third book of his Life in Greece. "But Philip," says he, "was always marrying new wives in war time. For, in the twenty-two years, which he reigned, as Satyrus relates in his History of his Life, having married Audata the Illyrian, he had by her a daughter named Cynna; and he also married Phila, a sister of Derdas and Machatas. And wishing to conciliate the nation of the Thessalians, he had children by two Thessalian women; one of whom was Nicesipolis of Pherae, who brought him a daughter named Thessalonice; and the other was Philinna of Larissa, by whom he had Arrhidaeus. He also acquired the kingdom of the Molossians, when he married Olympias, by whom he had Alexander and Cleopatra. And when he subdued Thrace, there came to him Cothelas, the king of the Thracians, bringing with him Meda his daughter, and many presents: and having married her, he added her to Olympias. And after all these, being violently in love, he married Cleopatra, the sister of Hippostratus and niece of Attalus. And bringing her also home to Olympias, he made all his life unquiet and troubled. For, as soon as this marriage took place, Attalus said, 'Now, indeed, legitimate kings shall be born, and not bastards.' And Alexander having heard this, smote Attalus with a goblet, which he had in his hand; and Attalus in return struck him with his cup. And after that Olympias fled to the Molossians; and Alexander fled to the Illyrians. And Cleopatra bore to Philip a daughter who was named Europa."

Another factor was Alexander's pressing need to beget a legitimate heir, for which purpose marriage was a prerequisite. The successive threats to his life were perhaps making the matter seem more imperative. The king seems to have fathered Heracles on his mistress Barsine at about this time, but she was politically unsuitable for marriage, especially because she had children by her previous husbands.

Before considering the Cleitarchan version of the marriage, it will be illuminating to review the accounts in Plutarch and Arrian. It was a final reason for his marriage (though perhaps not the most important) that Alexander had genuinely fallen for Roxane as Plutarch, *Alexander* 47.4 affirms:

His marriage to Roxana, whom he saw in her youthful beauty taking part in a dance at a banquet, was a love affair, and yet it was thought to harmonize well with the matters, which he had in hand. For the Barbarians were encouraged by the partnership into which the marriage brought them, and they were beyond measure fond of Alexander, because, most temperate of all men that he was in these matters, he would not consent to approach even the only woman who ever mastered his affections, without the sanction of law.

Arrian, *Anabasis* 4.19.5-6 & 4.20.4:

The wives and children of many important men were there [at the Sogdian Rock] captured, including those of Oxyartes. This chief had a daughter, a maiden of marriageable age, named Roxana, who was asserted by the men who served in Alexander's army to have been the most beautiful of all the Asiatic women whom they had seen, with the single exception of the wife of Darius. They also say that no sooner did Alexander see her than he fell in love with her; but though he was in love with her, he refused to offer violence to her as a captive, and did not think it derogatory to his dignity to marry her. This conduct of Alexander I think worthy rather of praise than blame... Oxyartes, hearing that his children were in the power of

Alexander, and that he was treating his daughter Roxana with respect, took courage and came to him. He was held in honour at the king's court, as was natural after such a piece of good fortune.

Arrian is clear that Oxyartes was not present when Alexander met Roxane, but the reader will discover in most modern texts of Curtius 8.4.21 that it was he who introduced them. However, this is a horrible mistake, dating back to Renaissance attempts to disambiguate Curtius' text in a section where there are indeed some significant manuscript problems. In fact the name rendered as "Oxyartes" in modern versions of Curtius read "Cohortandus" in the manuscripts. Aldus spuriously altered it to Oxyartes. This was done to reconcile Curtius' ensuing statement that Roxane was the daughter of this Cohortandus. But in fact it was this latter statement that was the true error. The reason this was not clear to Renaissance editors like Aldus is that they were unaware of the parallel text (also from Cleitarchus) in Sections 28-29 of the *Metz Epitome*, which states that Roxane danced among Corianus' daughters, but was herself the daughter of one of his friends:

Corianus welcomed Alexander to be entertained at his place and brought in his own virgin daughters and those of his friends as dancers. Among these was the daughter of Oxiatris, Rhoxane, the loveliest of them all.

This Cohortandus/Corianus appears to be the chieftain called Chorienes by Arrian. It seems probable on balance that Arrian himself is in error in placing the meeting with Roxane at the Sogdian Rock rather than at the Rock of Chorienes.

My reconstruction of Cleitarchus' version of the marriage is therefore a synthesis of Curtius with the *Metz Epitome*, using the latter to correct and elaborate upon the former. The most important Cleitarchan detail that was omitted by Curtius was the fact that Alexander arranged parallel marriages between the daughters of the local dignitaries and his Friends. The mention of this by the *Metz Epitome* is validated as originating with Cleitarchus by the Contents List of Diodorus 17th Book (although his detailed account is lost in a lacuna):

How Alexander, enamoured of Roxane, daughter of Oxyartes, married her and persuaded numbers of his friends to marry the daughters of the prominent Barbarians.

This obviously presages the Susa marriages between the senior Macedonians and eligible Persian ladies. It is fascinating to learn that Alexander had already conceived and begun to implement this politically crucial policy years beforehand.

Fragments of Cleitarchus from Books Seven to Nine

The named fragments of Cleitarchus are sparse across these three books and those that can be assigned are concentrated into the first third of Book 7 (see

Table 2.1). They particularly concern the geography, the fauna and the Amazons. They are listed with brief explanatory descriptions below:

1. Jacoby Fragment 12 of Cleitarchus, in which Pliny, *Natural History* 6.36-38 describes the various names of the Caspian (e.g. Hyrcanian Sea) as deriving from the peoples living upon its shores (cf. Curtius 6.4.18 & Diodorus 17.75.3), then attributes comparable sizes to the Euxine (Pontic or Black Sea) and the Caspian on the authority of Cleitarchus. This size comparison is fairly accurate and also appears in Strabo 11.7.2, where it is attributed to Patrocles, who explored the Caspian in about 284-283BC.

2. Jacoby Fragment 13 of Cleitarchus, wherein Strabo 11.1.5 says that Cleitarchus allowed that water of either the Euxine (Pontic or Black Sea) or the Caspian might flood across the isthmus of land between them, which would appear to match up with comments from Curtius 6.4.18 regarding the supply of water from the Maeotic Marsh (vicinity of the Sea of Azov) into the Caspian. The land is indeed very low lying between the Sea of Azov and the northern Caspian, but actual transfer of water would seem unlikely even in antiquity.

3. Jacoby Fragment 14 of Cleitarchus is from Demetrius, *De Eloc.* 304, who criticizes a passage, wherein Cleitarchus gave a colourful description of a wasp, as repellent due to its overblown character. (There is similar phraseology at Diodorus 19.2.9, which appears to be sourced from Timaeus, co-author of a couple of the other fragments with Cleitarchus.)

4. Jacoby Fragments 15 (Plutarch, *Alexander* 46) and 16 (Strabo, *Geography* 11.5.4) confirm that Cleitarchus was one of the writers to record the visit of Thalestris, Queen of the Amazons, to Alexander for the purpose of conceiving offspring by him, although both writers express skepticism about the trustworthiness of his account.

5. Jacoby Fragment 32 of Cleitarchus comes from a scrap of papyrus (Pap. Oxyrh. II 218 col. II). It is uncertain whether it belongs with the account of Alexander's encounter with the Amazon Queen, although some of the historical review of Amazons in Justin 2.3-4 might have been sourced from Cleitarchus, making it more credible that he gave lost background information about them. A secondary possibility is that it is the corollary of suttee for men who murder their wives (cf. Cleitarchus Reconstruction 11.13). The papyrus co-attributes the report to "Zopyrus", probably Zopyrus of Magnesia, who seems to have written a history on *The Foundation of Miletus* perhaps around 300BC, which might have said something about Amazons.

6. At Section 9.15 of the Reconstruction, I place Fragment 49 = Antonii Melissa I 13 p. 805 D, considered doubtful by Jacoby, but apposite

The Reconstruction Of Books Seven To Nine

here. It reads, "If you defend your misdeeds, you will double your disgrace." With exactly this sentiment Arrian, *Anabasis* 4.9.6, concludes a passage giving the Cleitarchan stories of the attempted suicide of Alexander, the king's guilt regarding his nurse and a neglected sacrifice to Dionysus. He may well have been inspired in this too by Cleitarchus.

Apart from these explicitly attributed Fragments found in the surviving literature, there are many detailed matches between Curtius and Diodorus or Curtius and the *Metz Epitome* or even between Diodorus and the *Metz Epitome* in these books of Cleitarchus. Some of them are identified in Table 2.2.

TABLE 2.1: The Books and Fragments of Cleitarchus (7-9)

BK	START	END	FRAGMENTS
7	JULY 330BC Advance to Hecatompylus	JUNE 329BC First crossing of the "Caucasus" (actually Paropamisus– modern Hindu Kush) "These were the concerns of Alexander" Diodorus 17.83.3	F12 – Caspian Sea equal to the Euxine F13 – Flooding of isthmus between Euxine and Caspian F14 – a wasp in Hyrcania F15 & F16 - Visit of Thalestria, Queen of the Amazons F32 – Castration of man (spouse of an Amazon?) for adultery
8	JULY 329BC Digression on quarrel of Bessus & Bagodaras at a banquet	AUTUMN 328BC Capture of the Sogdian Rock	
9	AUTUMN 328BC Scythian king offers Alexander his daughter in marriage	MAY 327BC Marriage to Roxane	F49 – "If you defend your misdeeds, you will double your disgrace" on Alexander's shame after killing Cleitus

TABLE 2.2: The *Einquellenprinzip*: close matches between Curtius and Diodorus 17

C=Curtius, D=Diodorus, J=Justin, S=Schwartz, H=Hamilton in Cleitarchus & Diodorus 17, cf.=vergleiche in Schwartz

C3.2.1=D17.30.7 S
C3.11.7-11=D17.34.2-6 S
C3.11.20,23-6=D17.35.2,36.5,2,4 cf.J11.9.11-12 S
C3.11.27=D17.36.6 H
C3.12.15-17=D17.37.5-6 H
C3.12.26=D17.38.2 H
C4.1.15-26=D17.47.1-6 H
C4.1.27-33=D17.48.2-4 S
C4.1.39-40=D17.48.1-2 S
C4.2.7=D17.40.4 S
C4.2.12=D17.41.3-4 S
C4.2.18=D17.40.5 S
C4.2.20=D17.41.1 S
C4.3.6,9,11-12=D17.42.5-6,43.3 S
C4.3.20=D17.41.2 cf.J11.10.14 S
C4.3.22=D17.41.8 H
C4.3.25-26=D17.44.1-3 S
C4.4.1-2=D17.45.7 S
C4.4.3-5=D17.41.5-6 H
C4.4.10-12,17=D17.46.2-4 S
C4.5.11=D17.48.6 S
C4.6.30=D17.49.1 S
C4.7.1,5,9=D17.49.2-4 S
C4.7.12-14=D17.49.4-5 S
C4.7.16-17,20-28=D17.50.3-51.3 S
C4.9.4-5=D17.53.1-2 H
C4.13.26-29=D17.57.1-4 S
C4.15.9-11=D17.59.6-7 S
C4.15.16-17=D17.58.4-5 S
C4.15.28-29,32=D17.60.2-4 S
C4.16.31-32=D17.61.3 S
C5.1.10-11=D17.64.3 S
C5.1.40-42=D17.65.1 S
C5.1.43-45=D17.64.5-6 S
C5.1.25-26=D2.7.3-4 (Jacoby F10) S
C5.1.34-35=D2.10.4,1 S
C5.2.1-7=D17.65.2-4 cf.D17.27.1-2 S
C5.2.8, 12-15=D17.65.5,66.2-7 S
C5.3.1.2,4-5,10=D17.67.1-2,4-5 S
C5.3.17-18,23&C5.4.2-4,10,12,18=D17.68.1-6 S
C5.5.2-4=D17.69.1-2 S

C5.5.5-9,12,23-24=D17.69.2-8 cf.J11.14.11-12 S
C5.6.1-5,8,9=D17.70.1-71.2 S
C6.2.15=D17.75.1 S
C6.4.3-6=D17.75.2 S
C6.4.18,22=D17.75.3,6 S
C6.5.11-12,18-21=D17.76.3-8 S
C6.5.24-26,30-32=D17.77.1-3 cf. J12.3.5-7 & Strabo11.5.4 S
C7.1.5-9=D17.80.2 S
C7.2.18=D17.80.3 S
C7.2.35-37=D17.80.4 cf. J12.5.4-8 S
C7.3.1,3=D17.81.1-2 S
C7.3.5-18=D17.82 S
C7.3.22-23=D17.83.1-2 S
C7.4.33,38=D17.83.4-6 S
C7.5.28-35 cf. Dκ S
C7.10.4-9 cf. Dκβ S
C7.10.15-16 cf. Dκδ S
C8.1.11-19 cf. Dκς S
C8.5.4 cf. Dλα, J12.7.5 S
C8.10.5-6 cf. Dλβ S
C8.11.2=D17.85.1-2, J12.7.12 S
C8.11.3-4=D17.85.4-5 S
C8.11.7-8,25=D17.85.3,8-9&D17.86.1 S
C8.12.1-3=D17.86.2 S
C8.12.4-10,14=D17.86.3-7 S
C8.14.3=D17.87.5 S
C9.1.1,3-4,6=D17.89.3-6&D17.90.1 S
C9.1.8-12=D17.90.4-7 S
C9.1.24-33=D17.91.4-D17.92.3 S
C9.3.10-11=D17.94.2 S
C9.3.19=D17.95.1-2, J12.8.16 S
C9.3.20,23=D17.95.3,5 S
C9.4.1-2,5=D17.96.1-3 S
C9.4.8-14=D17.97.1-3 S
C9.7.16-26=D17.100.2-D17.101.6 S
C9.8.4-8=D17.102.1-4 S
C9.8.13-15(Jacoby F25)=D17.102.6 S
C9.8.17-28=D17.103, J12.10.2-3 cf. Cic. de divin. 2.135 S
C9.10.5-11,17-18,27=D17.104.4-D17.106.1 S
C10.2.4,8-12,30=D17.109.1-2 S
C10.5.21-25=D17.118.3, J13.1.5-6 S
C10.10.14,18-19=D17.117.5&D17.118.2 cf. J12.13.10 S

3. Book 7: July 330BC – June 329BC

The Advance to Hecatompylus; Description of Hyrcania and the Caspian Sea; Surrender of Artabazus & the Greek Mercenaries; Theft of Bucephalus; Surrender of Nabarzanes; Visit of the Amazon Queen; Adoption of Persian Dress; Revolt of Satibarzanes; The Philotas Affair; Assassination of Parmenion; The Euergetae; First Crossing of the Paropamisus Range

KEY
<u>**Underlined bold text for attributed Fragments of Cleitarchus**</u>
Bold text where there is overwhelming evidence
Bold italic text where there exists direct-firm evidence
Normal text where direct-weak evidence applies
Italic text where the evidence is conjectural
Grey text for connecting passages, if Cleitarchus' version is indeterminate

7.1 *At the beginning of the seventh year of Alexander's reign, Darius being dead, Bessus accompanied by Nabarzanes, Barzaentes and many of their fellows eluded the king's grasp and bore towards Bactria. Bessus had been set up as satrap of this dominion under Darius and, being familiar to its folk in respect of his rule, he roused them to defend their freedom. He noted that the nature of their terrain would greatly aid them, since it was awkward of access and was settled with sufficient manpower to assert its independence. He proclaimed that he would personally prosecute the war and with the approval of the people he declared himself king. Then he engaged upon recruiting troops, forging abundant arms and keenly configuring to confront the encroaching crisis.*

7.2 Yet as soon as a mind that was more amenable to military matters than to peace and quiet was disburdened of bothers, Alexander succumbed to sensual pursuits and he who had not been worsted by the weapons of the Persians was vanquished by their vices. There were perpetual parties, the demented delight of drinking till dawn, sundry entertainments and herds of whores. Everyone lapsed into outlandish mores. By copying such customs, as though they were preferable to his own, he so offended the feelings of his folk and equally their gaze that many of his former friends found in him a foe. For his countrymen kept to their own schooled fashions and were inured to nourishing their natural longings with sparing and readily reaped rations, but he pressed upon them the depravity of foreign and defeated nations. Hence the hatching of conspiracies against his person occurred more often as also insurrections of his soldiers and more resort to resentment amidst mutual recriminations. Hence too he was for his own part at some points vexated and at others distrustful due to groundless fears and suchlike sores as shall later be related.

7.3 Therefore when he was devouring days and nights alike in prolonged banquets, he used to introduce diversions at the consummation of the courses. Yet he was not satisfied by the swarm of artists that he had gathered from Greece, since captive women were bidden to sing songs in the vernacular fashion that were dissonant and repellent to the ears of their visitors. Among them the king himself caught sight of one who seemed sadder than the rest in ashamedly resisting those who looked to lead her forward. She cut a fine figure that was accentuated by her bashfulness. Her eyes were downcast and her visage veiled inasmuch as was allowed, causing the king to sense that she was of too refined a pedigree to be exhibited amongst the entertainments in the revelry. Therefore she was asked about her ancestry and she said that she was the granddaughter of Ochus, sometime sovereign of Persia. His son had fathered her and Hystaspes had been her husband, who was a kinsman of Darius and had himself led a large army.

7.4 The king still retained in his mind some modicum of his former morality. Thus out of respect for the lady's royal roots and so celebrated an ancestor as Ochus, he not only released her from captivity, but also bade that her fortune be refunded and even that her husband should be sought, so that the king might hand his wife to him when he was brought.[1] Furthermore, the following day he instructed Hephaistion to order that every captive be convened at his headquarters. There one by one he looked into their lineages, segregating those of eminent descent from the commoners. He found a thousand of the former, including the brother of Darius, Oxathres, who was no less a luminary for his intellectual talents than for his family.

---

[1] This event, though superficially trivial, has the significance of inaugurating the so-called "Persianising" phase of Alexander's career, but it happens that we are in the privileged position of being able to gain special insight into Alexander's thinking on this matter, even beyond what would have been apparent to most of his contemporaries. Essentially, it appears that the king was emulating the chivalric model of kingship presented by Xenophon in his *Cyropaidia*, specifically the episode at *Cyropaidia* 6.1.45-48 wherein Cyrus reunites Pantheia with her husband Abradatas and thereby wins the latter's allegiance. There are some hints that Alexander originally planned to reunite Darius with his wife according to this model, but being thwarted in that ambition, he evidently found a convenient substitute in the wife of Hystaspes.

Book 7: July 330BC – June 329BC

7.5 Alexander *performed the funeral rites for his fatalies in the flight of Darius with extra extravagance for he* **had garnered a great booty** *in the pursuit, including eight thousand talents taken from the* Persian *royal treasurers.* **What was dispersed as gifts among the** *surviving* **soldiers** *comprising such stuff as clothing and cups* **came to** *nearly* **thirteen thousand talents, whereas what fraudsters pilfered or purloined as plunder was perceived to match or even exceed this sum.** *Most of the mounts had also been lost or lamed due to the intense heat. However,* **Alexander's main monies, which amounted to between a hundred & eighty and a hundred & ninety thousand talents, were deposited at Ecbatana in the custody of Parmenion.**[2] A Persian nobleman named Oxydates, who was found in fetters due to having been condemned to death by Darius, Alexander set at liberty and made satrap of Media. The king also appointed a bevy of bodyguards and **Oxathres the brother of Darius was welcomed into the fraternity of his Friends** *with all the dignity due to his distinguished dynasty.*

7.6 Alexander now reached Parthia, whereof the Scythians had seized the fertiles fields. They have homesteads in both Europe and Asia. Those who dwell beyond the Bosphorus are attributed to Asia and those that are in Europe hold the land from the western strand of Thrace through to the Borysthenes and thence the stretches straight on to the Tanais.[3] This river runs down the boundary between Europe and Asia. There is no doubt that the Scythians that sired the Parthians penetrated into those parts rather by roaming from the region of Europe than from *beyond* the Bosphorus.

7.7 The king now headed for Hyrcania and halted near a city called Hecatompylus *on the third day. This wealthy town had been founded by Greeks and afforded a profusion of everything required for recreation and relaxation, so he rested his army there for several days, whilst supplies were gathered in from everywhere round about. Hence hearsay, the habitual sin of soldiers at leisure, was whispered without warrant that the king, being content with his accomplishments, stood ready to return right away to Macedonia. They ran off as if raving mad to their tents and prepared their packs for the trek. It might have been believed that the signal to bundle up the baggage of the entire camp had been given. The cacophony carried to the king's ears as here they hallooed their tent-mates and there they weighed down the wagons.*

7.8 Alexander perceived from his perspective that the Macedonians saw the death of Darius as the conclusion of the campaign and yearned to

---

[2] 180,000 talents according to Diodorus 17.80.3 and 190,000 in Justin 12.1.3 – perhaps respectively rounding down and up an intermediate figure in Cleitarchus.

[3] These things are: the Cimmerian Bosphorus, which is the Strait of Kerch at the eastern tip of the Crimea; the River Borysthenes, which is the Dnieper; the River Tanais, which is properly the Don, but which Cleitarchus confused with the ancient River Jaxartes or modern Syr-Darya.

return to their own land *and farms. In the mind's eye of each man he was already enfolding his wife and children in his arms.* The king had convened an assembly of the allied levies from the Greek cities, at which he had commended their conduct and released them from soldiering service. As well as their awaited wages, he had awarded a talent to each of their cavalrymen and ten minas to each of their footsoldiers plus supplementary sums fully to fund their journeys home.[4] *Although* he had tendered retainers of three talents to any that would remain enrolled in the royal regiments, *the disbandments had leant credence to the view of the rest of the army that the end of their own service would duly ensue.*

7.9 *Being no less than duly alarmed by this, seeing as he was seeking to set off for India and the uttermost Orient, the king convened the commanders of his contingents in his headquarters. On the verge of tears, he loudly lamented that he was being recalled with his conquests but half accomplished, so as to carry back to his country a name more famed for its failures than its victories. Nor was it the war-weariness of his warriors that was thwarting him, but rather the spite of the gods, who had inspired fellows of the finest fortitude with a sudden desire for their land of domicile, whither they would withdraw more worthily and with better repute in just a little while.*

7.10 *Then indeed each commander present proffered his efforts in Alexander's cause, ardently asking for the most awkward tasks and trumpeting the tractability of his troops, were the king willing to mollify the men's minds with a mellow and meet address. They had never withdrawn dispirited and dejected, so long as they had been able to elicit inspiration from Alexander's ardour and the valour of so sublime a spirit. Thus the king responded that he would inspire them: let them but ready the ears of the rank and file and he would speak fire in them. Hence when every appropriate preparation appeared to have been put in place,* the king commanded that his soldiers be summoned to an assembly, at which he delivered a stirring address.

7.11 "When you study our stupendous successes, soldiers, it is little wonder that you hanker after peace and feel fed up with glory. Let me leave aside the Illyrians, the Triballians, Boeotia, Thrace and Sparta and the Achaeans in the Peloponnese, some of which I have myself subjugated, whilst others have been subdued in the name of my power and authority.[5] Instead let me commence my account of our campaign at the Hellespont, from which point we have freed the

---

[4] A talent was a weight of 6000 drachms and a mina was one hundred drachms, where a drachm was approximately 4.3g (of silver) according to the Attic standard, which was popular at that time.

[5] Alexander means that he had personally led the campaigns against the Illyrians, the Triballians, Boeotia (Thebes) and Thrace in 336-335BC, whereas Antipater had defeated the rebellion of the Spartans and Achaeans in the Peloponnese in 331BC.

Book 7: July 330BC – June 329BC

Ionians and Aeolis from servitude to despotic foreigners and we have put in our power Caria, Lydia, Cappadocia, Phrygia, Paphlagonia, Pamphylia and the Pisidians, Cilicia, Syria, Phoenicia, Armenia, Persia, the Medes and Parthia. Rivals have seized fewer cities than the number of countries that I have occupied and I am unsure whether in enumerating such a number of them I have detracted from the sum of our triumphs. Therefore, if I considered that our control of the regions that we have so rapidly reduced were soundly secured, I myself, soldiers, would hurtle homewards to my mother, sisters and fellow citizens, though you strove to restrain me. For there especially I might bask in the praise and glory that we have together instigated, where the most magnificent rewards of victory may be anticipated: the joy of our parents, wives and offspring, the ease of peace and the tranquil enjoyment of everything gained through our daring."

7.12 "Yet our rule here is recent and in reality precarious, should we care to confess it, for the barbarians are still stiff-knecked in yielding to its yoke. It will take time, soldiers, till they cultivate more congenial characters and healthier habits sap their savagery. Similarly, crops reserve their ripening pending the appointed date, since even insensate things mellow at their own rate. Well then, can you believe that so many nations inured to another monarch's name and command and lacking any commonality of custom or communication or creed with us were tamed in the same combat in which they were overcome? Actually, it is your arms that restrain them rather than their own manners and those who are in dread of us while we are here, will emerge as enemies if we disappear. We are dealing with fierce beasts, which, being captured and confined, cannot calm their tempers save through a longer lapse of time."

7.13 "And up till now I have reflected, as if our arms have subjected all the domains that Darius directed. Yet Nabarzanes has seized Hyrcania and the murderer Bessus not only possesses Bactra, but also makes menaces against us. The Sogdiani, Dahae, Massagetae, Sacae and the Indians have fallen under their own jurisdiction. As soon as they see us turn tail, they will all of them be harrying our heels, since they are each of the same race, whilst we are outsiders bred in a foreign place. Everyone is more amenable to someone from his own society dominating, even when the outland lord can be more intimidating. It follows either that what we have seized must be forsaken, else we must also occupy what we have not yet taken."

7.14 "Just as a surgeon, soldiers, will leave nothing festering in the bodies of the ill, so let us cut away at whatever would withstand our will. There's many a time that a tiny, disrespected spark has kindled a colossal conflagration. And so there is no such foe as may safely be spurned, for him whom you despise is made that much mightier when a blind eye's turned. Nor did even Darius receive the rule of Persia through inheritance, but rather he was set upon the throne of Cyrus by the beneficence of Bagoas the eunuch. So let you not suppose that Bessus need greatly struggle to reap a realm that is rulerless. Certainly, we have sinned, soldiers, if we have defeated Darius simply to surrender his sovereignty to his servant, who has dared to commit the ultimate miscreancy. For when his sovereign was even in want of succour from foreigners, he set him in fetters like a common captive, though we the victors would assuredly have spared him.[6] And then in the end he slaughtered him in order that we should not be able to save him."

7.15 "So will you suffer such a wretch to reign? Personally, I am impatient to see him suffer crucifixion, since for the sake of every ruler and race and for his violation of loyalty he merits such a conviction. But, by Heracles, if you should shortly hear it heralded that he has annihilated the Greek settlements or even ravaged the Hellespont, what massive remorse will mortify you when the gains from your victories have been seized by such as Bessus? Then you will snatch up your arms. Then you will rush to recover the situation. But how much more majestic it would be to scupper him whilst he's scared and scarcely coping with his consternation."

7.16 "There remains a march of four days for us, who have trampled so many snowfields, traversed so many rivers and surmounted so many mountain ranges. Neither can a surging sea that roils across the route cause us delay nor can Cilician gulches and gulleys box us in today, but rather it is smoothly downhill all the way. We stand on the very verge of victory. Before us but a few fugitives and murderers of their master remain at liberty. A lovely labour, by Heracles, that shall be enumerated amongst the most remarkable of the feats that you bequeath to posterity and the halls of fame. They will say that having ended your enmity towards Darius upon his death, you even avenged your foe by killing his killer in order that no faithless fellow should elude your grasp. And this being done, how much more compliant do you suppose the Persians will be, when they perceive that you crusade against disloyalty and that it is the betrayal by Bessus that riles you rather than his whole society?"

7.17 These winning words were heard with wholehearted acclaim by the troops, who bade Alexander to lead them wheresoever he wished for what remained of the campaign. *Nor did the king impede their impetus, so they pushed on through Parthia and reached the rim of Hyrcania on the third day.* He had left Craterus behind with the forces that were under his command and the company led by Amyntas augmented by six hundred cavalry and just as many bowmen with the mission of safeguarding Parthia against barbarian invasion. He ordered Erigyius to lead the baggage train on a route through the plain, assigning him an adequate escort. **Alexander himself**

---

[6] I have previously argued in *Alexander's Lovers* p.28 that the mention of Alexander having uncharacteristically halted his pursuit of Darius for 5 days when he reached the Caspian Gates (Arrian, *Anabasis* 3.20.3) suggests that Darius had agreed to surrender. The Latin of Curtius 6.3.13 (on which my Reconstruction relies at this point) could be translated to mean that Darius was known to have been considering seeking help from foreigners at the time that Bessus deposed him: most probably Patron's Greek mercenaries (7.19 below), but possibly even the Macedonians.

Book 7: July 330BC – June 329BC

advanced one hundred and fifty stades *from Hecatompylus* **with the phalanx and the cavalry** and established a fortified base in the valley that leads into Hyrcania, *which is shaded by a lofty and dense forest of trees, where streams that flow out from beneath huge overhanging crags irrigate the fertile soil of the dale.* From a cavern at the very roots of the pinnacles the River Stiboeites[7] flushes forth on a torrential scale and gushes on in a single bed for *almost* three stades, until it swirls against the block of a breast-shaped rock and its confined current cascades into two channels, *as though perpetrating a parting of its waters.* Roaring on from there, it is stirred to seethe more fervently by rushing over rocks, before falling forcibly into a fissure and foaming up from the thunderous shocks. Through three hundred stades it coasts along a concealed course and then surges back to the surface, *as if conceived from a second source.*

7.18 *These waters then spread into a new bed far wider than before, for their breadth broadens to thirteen stades, then again fades when forced between narrower banks once more. They eventually drain into another river that is known as the Rhidagnus.* The locals related that whatsoever were washed down the fissure nearer the source would emerge from the further orifice perforce. Therefore Alexander bade that two *horses* be hurled in where the waters went underground and where the river resurges, by those he sent to see, their cast up carcasses were found.

7.19 Alexander had already rendered a rest of four days to his soldiers in this same vicinity, when he received a letter from Nabarzanes, who had been in league with Bessus in the detention of Darius. The gist of his epistle was that he had not been the enemy of Darius, but rather had contributed what he considered valuable advice, but for proffering this faithful counsel to his king, he had come close to being killed by him. Darius had discussed conveying the custody of his person into the hands of the foreign recruits in contravention of propriety and sanctity and vilifying the loyalty of his compatriots that they had maintained immaculately under consecutive kings for two hundred and thirty years. Nabarzanes had stood on a slippery slope, such that the pressures of his predicament had dictated his conduct. Darius too, when he had done away with Bagoas, had pacified the populace by explaining that he had been dispatched on account of his own treachery. Miserable mortals are more enamoured of nothing than the breath of life and it was love of life that had driven him towards deeds of despair. But he had simply collaborated in the affair rather than actively desired it. When catastrophe is everywhere, each man must look to his own welfare.

7.20 If Alexander should bid Nabarzanes to appear before him, then he would turn up without trepidation. He had no fear that so fine a king would violate his

---

[7] Perhaps the modern Chesmeh-i-Ali about 25km NW of Hecatompylus: cf. P. Pédech, "Deux campagnes d'Antiochus III chez Polybe," *Revue des Études Anciennes*, 60 (1958), 67-81.

sacred pledge of safe conduct. It would be extraordinary for the gods to be deceived by a fellow divinity. However, if Nabaranes were deemed undeserving of Alexander's good faith, many lands lay open to him as a refugee. Wherever a brave man's chosen base stands becomes his current home country. But Alexander did not hesitate to grant assurances in the form in which the Persians conventionally embraced them, such that, should he come before him, he would not be harmed.

7.21 Nevertheless **Alexander advanced into Hyrcania** in tight formation and square array, repeatedly sending out scouts ahead of him, who reconnoitred the region. The light-armed levies led the order of march and the phalanx followed after them with the baggage trailing after the infantry. Both the inaccessible nature of the territory and its hostile inhabitants caused the king to continue with caution. For in fact *there is a seamless valley that reaches as far as the Caspian Sea, where two tracts of land run out from it resembling arms, these being moderately flexed near their middles to make an arc most like the Moon when it has horns, whilst the face of its orb is far less than full. Leftwards lie the lands where the Cercatae, Mossyni and Chalybes reside, whilst the Leucosyri and the plains of the Amazons are on the opposite side, the former where the land is northwards depressed and the latter where it leans towards the west.*[8]

7.22 *Alexander took every town down to the Caspian, which is less salty than similar seas and* especially spawns sizable serpents in considerable numbers. Its fish too are truly distinguished from those elsewhere through their hue. <u>This body of water is known by numerous names nominated by the nations that inhabit its shores, the commonest being the Caspian or the Hyrcanian. In extent it is not inferior to the Euxine</u>[9] and indeed <u>there are those who hold that the Maeotic Marsh percolates into the Caspian.</u>[10] These base their case on the theory that it is fresher than many another sea due to dilution of its salinity by the inflow from its Maeotic tributary. *Further to the north stormy seas batter the shore*

---

[8] This location for the Amazon homeland (taken from Curtius 6.4.17) would suggest that Cleitarchus placed it on the steppe to the east of the Caspian Sea. His source on this is likely to have been Onesicritus, who seems to be the earliest of the sources listed by Plutarch (Life of Alexander 46.1) for Alexander having hosted a visit from the Amazon Queen.

[9] Jacoby Fragment 12 of Cleitarchus, in which Pliny, *Natural History* 6.36-38 describes the various names of the Caspian (e.g. Hyrcanian) as deriving from the peoples living upon its shores (cf. Curtius 6.4.18 & Diodorus 17.75.3), then attributes comparable sizes to the Euxine (Pontic Sea) and the Caspian on the authority of Cleitarchus.

[10] Jacoby Fragment 13 of Cleitarchus, wherein Strabo 11.1.5 says that Cleitarchus allowed that water of either the Euxine (Black Sea) or the Caspian might flood across the isthmus of land between them, which would appear to refer to these comments from Curtius 6.4.18 regarding the supply of water from the Maeotic Marsh (vicinity of the Sea of Azov) into the Caspian. The land is indeed very low lying between the Sea of Azov and the northern Caspian, but actual transfer of water would seem unlikely even in antiquity.

Book 7: July 330BC – June 329BC

shoving their waves far inland such that much of that strand is immersed beneath lagoons. But in other weather, these seas are expelled with the same seething with which they had swelled and the turf returns to its normal nature as the surf is dispelled. And some have deemed it credible that this might not be the Caspian Sea at all, but that the Ocean ranges round from India to enter upon Hyrcania, the Highlands of which dip down into an unbroken vale, as there has already been reason to retail.

7.23 *From this place for twenty stades* the king proceeded *via a practically impassable path, which was overgrown with woodland, and torrents and floods further protracted his progress. Yet since no foe opposed him, he pushed on through and eventually came* into *more* cultivated country. These were the fields of the Favoured Villages as they are dubbed and indeed duly so designated, for their farmland is far more fecund in fine fare than is found elsewhere. Since it is said that every vine furnishes a full metretes of wine, whilst some of their fig trees can provide ten medimni of figs, when dried.[11] *The grain that is missed during the reaping and tumbles down upon the earth germinates without a sowing and leads to a harvest of lavish worth.* Another source of lusciousness in the lives of local folk is a type of tree that is common there with the characteristics of an oak and from each of its leaves there drips a honeydew cloak, but unless the natives gather it ere the sun rises, hardly any heat ensures that it volatilizes. <u>A winged creature that infests the hill-country is called the anthredon, which, though smaller than a bee, is everywhere set eyes upon. It roves the ranges raiding nectar from all sorts of blooms and nests in lightning-struck trees and rock wombs. It fashions wax combs and secretes a syrup so sweet as our own honey can barely beat.</u>[12]

7.24 *Alexander had gone forward a further thirty stades, whereupon Phrataphernes came before him surrendering himself and those who had deserted due to the death of Darius. The king gave them a kindly reception* and then progressed to the town of Arvae, where he was met by Craterus and Erigyius. They had escorted Phradates, the governor of the Tapurian people. Alexander also accepted him into allegiance, **and this was a model for many in pursuing a pardon from the king, for he became famed for his fairness.** Thereafter he assigned the Satrapy of Hyrcania to

---

[11] Strabo 11.7.2 says sixty medimni; a metretes was about 40 litres, whereas a medimnus was around 55 litres, so each tree produced over half a cubic metre of dried figs (Diodorus 17.75.5).

[12] Jacoby Fragment 14 of Cleitarchus from Demetrius, *De Eloc.* 304, who criticizes the passage as repellent due to its overblown description of a mere wasp.

Manapis,[13] who had come to Philip as an exile during the reign of Ochus. He returned the Tapurian people to the rule of Phradates too.

7.25 Just when the king had come into the furthest reaches of Hyrcania, he was approached by *Artabazus in the company of his own offspring as well as the kindred of Darius and* a humble contingent of Greek troops. *His utmost loyalty to Darius has already been described. Upon his arrival Alexander proffered his right hand in friendship, for in the first place he had been a guest of Philip whilst in exile during the reign of Ochus, but more movingly he had kept faith with his king to the bitter end. Being therefore welcomed as a comrade, he said: "I pray to god, Sire, that you should prosper in perpetual happiness. I myself, though otherwise blessed, am tormented by this alone, that my impending dotage means I cannot long enjoy your kindness." He was soldiering through his ninety-fifth year and was escorted by nine youths, all of them his sons by the same mother. These he caused to clasp the king's right hand, praying that they should survive only so long as their lives were lived to the benefit of Alexander. The king generally went about on foot, but in this instance he commanded that mounts be brought for both Artabazus and himself in order to spare the old man the shame, if he rode whilst his sovereign strode.*

7.26 *Upon pitching camp,* Alexander bade that the Greeks, *who had been brought in by Artabazus,* be called to an assembly. *Yet they responded that they would have to consider their options, unless a pledge of safe-conduct were also extended to the men from Sparta and Sinope. These were the emissaries that had been sent by the Spartans to Darius. Following his defeat, they had joined forces with the Greek mercenaries serving on the Persian side. But the king commanded that they come before him and take their chances as to what he would offer without either promises or assurances. After protracted hesitation and vacillation they eventually consented to come. But Democrates the Athenian, always to the fore in fomenting opposition to Macedonian power, despaired of pardon and ran himself through with his sword. All the rest, as they had resolved,* put themselves in the power of Alexander. They numbered fifteen hundred seasoned soldiers *plus ninety men sent to Darius in delegations.* The troops were fully forgiven for their former enmity and were distributed as reinforcements across Alexander's army at the same pay rates as his own levies. *The others were sent home, except the Spartans, whom he commanded to be kept in custody.*[14]

---

[13] Arrian, *Anabasis* 3.22.1 calls him Amminapes; he had been involved in the surrender of Egypt to Alexander and had then joined his entourage.

[14] At this time Alexander may not have been sure that the Spartan rebellion of Agis had ended.

Book 7: July 330BC – June 329BC

7.27 Alexander marched westwards along the shoreline and reached the territory of the Mardians, who were a nation neighbouring upon Hyrcania. These people were scarcely civilized and had become habituated to banditry. They counted on their combat capability and deprecated the king's pre-eminence. Therefore they alone disdained to dispatch delegates to him or to show any sign that they would respect his rule. Rather they occupied their passes with eight thousand men and audaciously defied Alexander's dominion. *Hence the king was vexed that a single tribe should deny him the name of invincibility, so, having left the baggage guarded, he advanced with an invincible vanguard in his company. The march being made by night,* their foes were found *at first light* and it was rather a rout than a real fight with most of them slain and the rest put to flight. *Hurled from the hills that they had held,* the barbarians were rapidly repelled *and the nearby towns were taken that the natives had forsaken.*

7.28 *However, their heartlands were hardly accessible without the army enduring a great deal of trouble. For* they were ensconced by *unscalable cliffs, towering forests and* mountainous massifs *and, where the way was flat, the barbarians had barricaded that with a fresh form of fortification. For this purpose trees are designedly planted in thick array and whilst their stems are still pliable they are pleated by hand and thus twisted are bent back into the soil. Thence, seemingly out of another root, shoots spring forth more vigorously. But these are not left to mature naturally, for the twigs are intertwined like a lattice. When they are cloaked in profuse foliage, they completely cover the land and hence their boughs, concealed like snares, choke the route with an unbroken fence. The only recourse was to cut a corridor through this coppice cultivation, yet even this meant a major operation. For their numerous knots had made the trunks intractable and the interlaced limbs of the timber, dangling like rings* forming chains, *would cushion the chopping with their springy canes.*

7.29 *Moreover the natives were wont to burrow beneath the bushes in the manner of beasts. Thus they had then too infiltrated the thickets and whilst well hidden were harrying their opponents with missiles. Alexander in huntsman mode tracked and transfixed quite a few of them in their hidy-holes and in the end he ordered his troops to go around the woodland and to burst in through any opening that they found. But* being strangers in this district many stragglers went astray *whilst he was laying waste to the land with fire* and some were seized *by the foe*. The youths who escorted the monarch's mounts drifted a little apart from Alexander and were ambushed by the barbarians, who captured the king's most outstanding steed, which he esteemed above the rest of his herd. This beast was called Bucephalus. Alexander had acquired him as a gift from Demaratus of Corinth. He had carried the king into all of his combats in Asia. Whilst he was not caparisoned, he would only allow his groom to sit upon his back, but not even him when harnessed in the royal trappings. Then he stood still for Alexander alone and voluntarily bent his knees to aid the king's ascent, seeming to sense just whom he conveyed.

7.30 Such was the distinction of this steed that Alexander was aggravated into greater grief and aggression than was proper. He bade that his beast be tracked down and that proclamations be made by interpreters that none of the natives would survive were his horse not brought back alive. Cowed as he commenced to commit this threat, the Mardians returned the horse together with their most precious presents. Yet even this did not appease Alexander, but rather he directed that the forests be felled and he fetched earth from the fells to pile into the passes where they were choked with branches. The mounds had already been raised to a considerable height, when the barbarians abandoned hope of holding out in their haunts and put forward fifty of their fellows to surrender their nation and crave the king's pardon. Alexander held as hostages the most eminent of these *and made their people subject to Phradates.*

7.31 On the fifth day thereafter Alexander arrived back at his established basecamp. Thence he sent Artabazus back home after redoubling the distinctions that Darius had vested in him. At this time he came to that Hyrcanian city that housed the palace of Darius,[15] where, having accepted the king's pledge of safe-conduct, Nabarzanes came before him proffering prodigious presents. Amongst these was Bagoas, a eunuch of uniquely lovely looks and just then in the very flower of his youth, whom Darius had been wont to penetrate and with whom Alexander used later to mate. Mainly through this youth's pleas he was driven to agree that Nabarzanes be forgiven.

7.32 **There is**, as already mentioned, **an Amazon people bordering upon Hyrcania and dwelling in the fields of Themiscyra on the banks of the River Thermodon and in the mountains beyond.**[16] **Their queen at that time was Thalestris,** who ruled the entire region between the Caucasus Range and the River Phasis. She was distinguished by her combination of bodily strength with beauty and her Amazon army much admired her bravery. **Being fired with desire to visit Alexander, she set forth from Thermodon** and *for thirty-five days* she travelled *amidst the most truculent tribes* **via the Caspian Gates and came to the Hyrcanian frontier.** From here she sent emissaries ahead to make it known that she was keen to call upon and consort with him who held the throne. She was

---

[15] Perhaps Arvae as in 7.24, which is Zadracarta in Arrian, *Anabasis* 3.23.6 - possibly modern Sari.

[16] This was noted at the end of Section 7.21, but then placed to the east of the region. It is likely that Cleitarchus or his source (Onesicritus?) has attempted to reconcile traditional legends of an Amazon nation near the Thermodon on the southern shores of the Black Sea (i.e. west of Hyrcania) with the visit of a warrior queen from east of the Caspian Sea to Alexander's camp in this vicinity. This underlines the haziness of Cleitarchus' grasp of the geography of the area.

Book 7: July 330BC – June 329BC

Figure 7.1. The meeting of Alexander with the Amazon Queen, Thalestris (from a French translation of Curtius by de Vaugelas, 1696)

at once forwarded a welcome, whereupon she bade the bulk of her battalion to abide at the border and went on with an escort of three hundred women each armed as an Amazon. Sporting two spears in her right hand, she alighted from her steed as soon as Alexander was sighted.[17]

7.33 *The monarch and his men were amazed by the Amazons, for what they wore was wierd for women. Amazon dresses do not drape the entire torso, since the left side of the chest is bared to beneath the breast, although they do veil all the rest. However, the hem of the skirt, which is girt with a knot, does not descend beneath the knee. They leave their left nipples intact so as to suckle their female offspring,* the boys being forwarded to their fathers for mothering. *But the right ones they sear, the better to bend a bow or cast a spear.* When one of these warrior women dies, her male partner is allowed to stay alive, **so long as her corpse survives and he does not dally with other wives. But if this law be violated, he is summarily castrated and his genitals are incinerated at her tomb.**[18]

7.34 *Displaying a dauntless demeanour Thalestris scrutinized the king, her perception of his appearance failing to match up to the fame of his deeds, for all the barbarians vest their veneration in individuals of vast stature. They consider that none is capable of colossal accomplishments, save him that Nature has favoured with a fabulous physique. But Alexander was bedazzled by her dashing dismount and by the dignity of the dame. Therefore he enquired as to whether she wished to present a request and she unabashedly confessed that she came to conceive offspring by the king. She was the strongest and most stalwart of women and he had made it manifest that he was the most remarkable of men through his achievements. The children of such a pair should surpass the rest of mankind in excellence, so with her he might beget a worthy heir. Though she should retain any female child, any male would be forwarded to his father without fail. Then Alexander asked her whether she would like to set off soldiering with him? She excused herself on account of having left her realm lacking a guard, but pressed her appeal that he should not let her leave forlorn in her longing. With the queen's wish for copulation being keener than the king's,* she obliged him to tarry there through the thirteen days that were required to indulge her desires.

---

[17] The Jacoby Fragments are 15 (Plutarch, *Alexander* 46) and 16 (Strabo, *Geography* 11.5.4).

[18] This is Jacoby Fragment 32 of Cleitarchus from a scrap of papyrus (Pap. Oxyrh. II 218 col. II). It is uncertain whether it belongs with the account of Alexander's encounter with the Amazon Queen, although some of the historical review of Amazons in Justin 2.3-4 might have been sourced from Cleitarchus. A secondary possibility is that it is the corollary of *suttee* for men who murder their wives (cf. Cleitarchus Reconstruction 11.13). The papyrus co-attributes the report to "Zopyrus", probably Zopyrus of Magnesia, who seems to have written a history on *The Foundation of Miletus* perhaps around 300BC, which might have said something about Amazons.

Book 7: July 330BC – June 329BC

Finally, *when she believed that she had conceived,* Alexander allowed her to leave *laden with his lavish presents* and thence he pursued his own path to Parthia.

7.35 It was actually at this juncture that Alexander gave vent to his inclinations and turned away from temperance and continence, venerable virtues at the peak of prosperity, veering *instead* towards loftiness and licentiousness. **From this point onwards the king** *considered that he incontestably possessed the throne of Asia. Hence he regarded his own country's customs, the healthily restrained traditions of the Macedonian kings and their citizenlike dispositions, as too mean for the magnificence of his monarchy. Therefore, he* **assumed the imperial pomp of the Persians that was on a par with the power and prestige of the gods.** He anticipated that the conquerors of so many countries would prostrate themselves upon the ground in veneration of him and would gradually become used to servile obsequiousness. *In this* he welcomed their becoming equal to the conquered people.[19]

7.36 *First of all he installed Asiatic rod-bearers to orchestrate his court and he mandated that the most eminent of their men should serve as his sentries and among them was the brother of Darius, Oxathres. Then* **Alexander donned the diadem such as Darius had once worn, which is a purple fillet interlaced with white** *that no former Macedonian monarch's head had borne.* **He also attired himself in the tunic** *of purple* **with a central white stripe and the cummerbund** *and the scepter.* **In fact he adopted all of the Persian rulers' raiment, except for the trousers and the long-sleeved garment.** *Nor was he even nervous about the portent in exchanging the victor's insignia for the routed realm's regalia. Actually he used to say that he was displaying the spoils picked from the Persians, but he had seen fit to assume their customs as well as their costume and habitual hauteur came with the haute couture. Additionally, the letters that would be delivered to Europe he sealed with the device cut into the gem of his old ring, whereas he impressed those that he wrote to Asia with the ring of Darius, so as to suggest that a single charisma could not captivate both cultures.* **He also distributed both Persian apparel and harnesses for their horses to his companions and to the cavalry, since these were his senior soldiers. Despite that they despised the cloaks with their purple hems** *embroidered with gold,* **they did not dare not to wear what the king would behold.**

---

[19] To set Sections 7.35-37 in context the reader should appreciate that Cleitarchus was one of the Cynics, a sect that considered abstemiousness to be next to godliness. They were an early manifestation of the asceticism that later launched Christianity and Islam. Plutarch in his essays *On The Fortune Or Virtue of Alexander, Moralia* 329F-330A actually praised the king for his *rapprochement* with the Persians by adopting elements of their dress.

7.37 During the dominion of Darius there were kept at court three hundred and sixty-five women of such superlative loveliness as selection from all the lands of Asia could gather in. Nightly they processed around the king's bower, so he could choose which he wished to deflower. Alexander too retained in his retinue concubines as numerous as the days of the year *accompanied by herds of eunuchs, who, though not whole, were practised in performing the passive sexual role.* In fact Alexander rarely employed their services and generally stuck to his established practices, for fear of offending his fellow Macedonians. *Finally, so as not to seem to stint or starve the extravagance, he convened vast banquets that he embellished with entertainments in keeping with kingly magnificence. For he had forgotten that great resources are not customarily produced by such practices, but rather rapidly reduced.*

7.38 These activities, being tainted with ostentation and foreign tradition, were openly despised by the veteran troops of Philip, a faction who were unfamiliar with suchlike luxuries. And throughout the camp but a single sentiment and subject of conversation was rife: the thought that they had lost more in victory than they had gained during the strife. For now they were most completely overcome, in giving themselves up to every alien and outlandish custom. How could they face returning home when they were dressed as if they were conquered men? Actually, they were already ashamed, since their sovereign resembled one of the vanquished rather than a victor, being recast as a Satrap of Darius instead of a Macedonian commander. Indeed, the king perceived that both his principal friends and his forces were seriously aggrieved, so he sought to regain their goodwill through benefactions *and some reforms he had conceived.*

7.39 *So as not to seem isolated in succumbing to the corrupt customs of the conquered countries, he permitted his men to marry any of the captive women with whom they were sleeping. For he calculated that they would be less likely to hanker after heading homewards, if they had in the camp some semblance of a hearth and a household. He also held that the hardships of the campaign would make the blessings of marriage more amenable. Furthermore, to facilitate reinforcing his soldiery without stripping Macedon of manpower, he planned that the sons of his veterans should succeed their fathers in serving as recruits upon the palisades within which they had been born. He deemed that they would be the more steadfast for having spent not just their training but also their infancy within his own camp. Indeed, this policy even persists under Alexander's successors. Accordingly, as boys they received regular rations and as youths they were outfitted with arms and steeds and their sires were assigned premiums in proportion to the number of their sons. If the sire of any son were slain, the orphan still drew his father's entire pay, and they spent their boyhood engaged upon sundry military operations. Hence having been hardened by hardships and hazards from a tender age, they formed a force that was found invincible. They knew naught but the camp as their country and*

Book 7: July 330BC – June 329BC

they fought no fight but that it led to victory. These progeny were proclaimed to be the Epigoni.[20]

7.40 In order that the muttering not be magnified into mutiny, the king called for campaigning to curtail their leisures, because cause was conveniently mounting for measures. For **Bessus, *having arrayed himself in regal raiment, had commanded that he be called Artaxerxes,*[21] *and he was summoning up the Scythians and the rest of the races from the region of the Tanais. Satibarzanes, an accomplice of Bessus in the murder of Darius, announced this news.*[22] Alexander had accepted his fealty and reinstated him in the Arian Satrapy. But because the king's columns, being overladen with luxurious paraphernalia and plunder, were barely mobile, Alexander ordered that firstly his own and thereafter the entire army's baggage, excepting absolute essentials, be fetched into their midst. The weighed down wagons were wheeled whither there was a wide and level field. Whilst everyone was watching out for what he would next compel, the king bade that the draught animals be led away and touched a torch to his own baggage first, then required that the rest be fired as well. Kindled by their owners, there were combusted those riches that to rescue unwrecked from the cities of their foes they had often had to quench infernos. And though these rewards had been won with their blood, none dared voice laments, when the selfsame flames were consuming their king's own affluence. Soon after the sense of it assuaged their sorrow, since, set up for soldiering and ready for anything, they rejoiced that they had jettisoned their baggage instead of their fitness for fighting.*[23]

7.41 Therefore they were bound for the Bactrian territories, but then Nicanor, the son of Parmenion, was suddenly seized by death and a great grief for him enfolded everyone. More mournful than anyone, their monarch was minded to halt the march to attend his funeral, but a lack of provisions harried him into hurrying on. Hence he left Philotas with two thousand six hundred men to furnish a fitting send-off for his brother and **Alexander** himself **hastened to confront Bessus.** But letters were delivered to him from the surrounding satraps **whilst he was on his way**, from which **he learnt that his foe was in**

---

[20] Literally the "Afterborn" or alternatively the "Descendants": the Greek term is preserved in the Latin manuscripts of Justin 12.4.11. The original *Epigoni* were the sons of the *Seven Against Thebes*, who renewed the war of their fathers (e.g. the two plays with these titles by Aeschylus).

[21] The regnal name of several former Persian Great Kings.

[22] This occurred at Sousia (Arrian, *Anabasis* 3.25.1-3), which is probably the modern Tus.

[23] The detailed account of baggage burning in Curtius 6.6.14-17 is corroborated by Polyaenus 4.3.10 and Plutarch, *Alexander* 57.1-2; although the latter pair place the burning just prior to the entry into India, this is probably due to the fact that Cleitarchus counted southern Afghanistan as part of India and it was true that Alexander was about to cross the mountains moving southwards into Afghanistan in pursuit of Satibarzanes at this juncture.

fact faring forth to confront him in arms. Though bemused by the boldness of Bessus, Alexander *also* heard that Satibarzanes, whom he himself had placed in charge of the Satrapy of the Arians, had murdered his Macedonian minders and defected to Bessus. He was holed up in Artacana[24], a considerable citadel of that satrapy that was situated upon a naturally tenable site. Therefore, though keen to cow Bessus himself, he rather reckoned he should first turn his attention to tackling Satibarzanes, who was the nearer of his enemies. Hence he led his light infantry, comprising the Agrianians and the hypaspists, together with his contingents of cavalry via the mountains into Aria. Performing forced marches throughout the night, he came upon his opponents unawares. On realising that he had arrived and fearful of both the magnificence and the fame of his forces, Satibarzanes fled for Bactra with but two thousand mounted troops, because he could not muster more on the spur of the moment. He instructed the remainder of his men to hold out among the nearby mountains.

7.42 There is a towering rock in that range that is precipitous *on the side facing westwards but presents a slighter slope slipping down to the east and is thickly forested with a perennial spring, its circumference stretching to thirty-two stades. It has a grassy ground at its crest, upon which the Arians ordered all men unfit for war to rest. They themselves stacked up stones and tree trunks where the cliff edge was depressed. They numbered thirteen thousand men-at-arms, whom* Alexander *left Craterus to invest, whilst he himself pressed on in pursuit of Satibarzanes. But upon finding that his foe was far ahead in his flight, he turned back to overwhelm those who held the mountain height. Initially, he ordered his men to clear away the barricade wherever headway could be made, but then, when they encountered sheer cliffs and unscalable scree, it seemed that Nature's opposition made for pointless industry. Since to advance was arduous and to retreat was risky, Alexander, being ever of a mind to wrestle with adversity, pondered plan after plan, resorting to every expediency, as is wont to happen when we ditch our initial strategy.*

---

[24] Artacana in the manuscripts of Curtius 6.6.33 and Artacoana in Arrian, *Anabasis* 3.25.6, but Chortacana in Diodorus 17.78.1; its location remains uncertain: most have assumed that it lay at or in the vicinity of modern Herat, but Donald Engels has argued in *Alexander the Great and the Logistics of the Macedonian Army*, pp.87-91 that the "rock" in the nearby mountains was Kalat-i-Nadiri 60km north of Tus; a reconciliation of this with the order of events in the Cleitarchan tradition is not apparent, since, for example, Engels reverses the order of the attack on Artacana and the siege of the rebel stronghold in the mountains; it is easier to accept the traditional view, which would place Alexander on the borders of Bactria near Kushka immediately north of Herat when he heard of the defection of Satibarzanes; hence Artacana was near Herat, which is also the site of Alexandria in Aria (cf. *Geographies* of Strabo 11.10.1 & Ptolemy 6.17).

Book 7: July 330BC – June 329BC

7.43 *Whilst the king was in a quandary, Fortune put forward a scheme beyond the reach of rationality. There blew in a wild wind from the west and the troops had felled loads of lumber in looking to lay a causeway up the scree. This timber was now dessicated by the searing heat, so Alexander ordered other trees to be piled up to fuel a bonfire and it rapidly matched the mountain crest as the logs were raised higher. Then burning brands were cast in all around it, so that the whole heap was simultaneously lit. The gale flung the flames into the faces of their foes and the sky was veiled as if by clouds as voluminous fumes arose. The woods resounded with the roar of the conflagration and parts that the troops did not ignite caught alight, so that all about them suffered incineration. The barbarians sought to evade terminal torment, wherever the blaze had abated, but where the flames gave way, there their opponents waited. Therefore they were dispatched by a medley of deaths: some rushed into the midst of the infernos; from the crags others went a-leaping; some consigned themselves to the arms of their foes, whilst a few, half-fried, came into their keeping. Thus* **by aggressing without cessation, the king compelled their capitulation.**

7.44 From there Alexander rejoined Craterus, who was besieging Artacana. Having completed the preparations, he was waiting for the coming of the king, so as to tender him the title of taker of that town in accordance with etiquette. Hence Alexander ordered that the siege-towers be trundled forward and the sight itself so intimidated the natives that they stretched their arms beyond their ramparts palms skyward. Then they began to beseech the king to focus his ferocity upon Satibarzanes, the fomenter of their defection, whilst sparing such suppliants as put their own selves into subjection. Alexander did pardon them and he not only lifted his blockade but saw that restitution of all the inhabitants' property was made. ***Thus thirty days after the rock's reduction, every Arian city was brought into submission.***

7.45 As he was quitting this city, he was met by reinforcements in the form of fresh recruits: Zoilus had fetched five hundred cavalrymen from Greece; Antipater had dispatched three thousand men from Illyria; a hundred and thirty Thessalian horsemen had come with Philip; two thousand six hundred foreign troops had arrived from Lydia and three hundred cavalry of the same country accompanied them. With his augmented army, **Alexander advanced upon the Drangians,** *a warlike nation, whose satrap was* **Barzaentes.** *He* **had been the accomplice of Bessus in his treason against their king. Now he fled into India in dread of retribution,**[25] *of which he was deserving. Alexander marched to the capital of Drangianê, where he paused to rest his army.*[26]

---

[25] Barzaentes is called Ariobarzanes in *Metz Epitome* 3: "India" means Southern Afghanistan.

[26] This is very likely to have been at or close by the modern Farah (Phraa) in the west of Afghanistan. Strabo 11.8.9, Ptolemy 6.19.4-5 and Pliny 6.61 give the name Prophthasia to a site

7.46 *It was on the ninth day that* the king *had been encamped in this locality that he* was betrayed into perpetrating a dire deed, *which was alien to his characteristic probity. When he was not simply safe from foreign forces, but actually invincible, he was assailed by insider villainy. Dimnus was a man of modest influence and esteem with Alexander, a member of his monarch's circle of Friends, but on some account he became discontented with the king and incautiously conspired in a plot against his life.*[27] Dimnus was fervently infatuated with his catamite called Nicomachus, *fixated by the favours of a body that was surrendered solely to him.* Virtually frantic, as was transparent in his countenance, he drew the youth aside unseen into a temple, first confiding that he had a secret and unrepeatable matter to reveal. With the young man held in suspense, Dimnus entreated him to swear in the name of their mutual love and the vows they had exchanged that he would keep silent concerning what Dimnus was about to share. So Nicomachus swore such an oath by the gods of that shrine, not reckoning on being obliged to expose, even at the cost of being forsworn, the secret that Dimnus was now to disclose. For what Dimnus divulged was that he was a member of a conspiracy comprising courageous and illustrious men that had planned upon the third day thereafter to attempt the assassination of their sovereign. Upon hearing this, the youth resolutely refuted that he had vowed to participate in a treasonous murder and asserted that no sacred oath could bind him to conceal treachery either. Out of his mind with both infatuation and fear, in tears Dimnus grasped the right hand of his beloved and first of all implored that he pledge himself to the plot and its implementation, but then begged, if he could not bear actually to be involved, that he should at least agree not to betray his lover. For the devotion of Dimnus to Nicomachus beyond everything else particularly had this strongest proof: that he had entrusted his life to the trueness of the untried youth.

---

approx. 270km from Alexandria in Aria (Herat), which is about the correct distance for modern Farah (they give the route distances seemingly taken from the *bematists* of Alexander's expedition). Stephanus Byzantinus in his entry for "Phrada" states that Alexander called this place Prophthasia and that it was a town among the Drangians (a.k.a. Zarangians). Hence it is clear that Prophthasia was very probably at or near Farah, although Tarn has differed by placing it further south on Lake Seistan. The name Prophthasia ("Anticipation" in the sense of forestalling something) assigned by Alexander seems to refer to him having outrun fate here in the form of the Dimnus conspiracy, which ensues. The place is therefore believed to be the scene of the Philotas Affair.

[27] So began the Philotas Affair, a tragedy in three Acts, namely: *The Dimnus Conspiracy*, *The Trial & Execution of Philotas* and *The Assassination of Parmenion*. The account in Curtius is particularly full and vivid. Speculatively, Curtius found this quasi-judicial purgation especially interesting, since it bore comparison with the downfalls of some of the great political figures of his own time, such as Sejanus. Parallels with Diodorus suggest that Curtius's version is highly likely to be derived from Cleitarchus, hence it probably constitutes a near verbatim and barely abridged Latin translation of a large section of his text. However, I follow my standard practice of only using bold characters where relatively direct corroboration of a Cleitarchan source is available from Diodorus or elsewhere.

Book 7: July 330BC – June 329BC

7.47 However, in the end, when Nicomachus maintained his revulsion for the treason, Dimnus tried to terrify him with a threat of death, saying that the conspirators would inaugurate their most admirable enterprise with the murder of Nicomachus. Then, alternating between calling him an effeminate and womanish coward, the betrayer of his lover and promising lavish incentives even including a kingdom, Dimnus sought to warp a mind to which such a crime was utterly abhorrent. Thereupon he drew his sword and set it first to his beloved's throat, then to his own, combining begging with belligerence and thus at last **Dimnus extorted a promise from Nicomachus not just of silence but even of assistance.** Yet the youth possessed a staunchly steadfast spirit such as suits a person of conscience, so he had not veered from his previous view, but rather affected to feel such affection for Dimnus that he could deny him nothing. He then proceeded to gather intelligence as to the identities of Dimnus's associates in such a fateful undertaking. It mattered greatly, he said, what sort of men had agreed to put their hands to so distinguished a deed. Out of his mind with a mixture of amour and remorse, Dimnus simultaneously expressed his gratitude and his congratulations to Nicomachus for not having hesitated to ally himself with the bravest young men including Demetrius the Bodyguard,[28] Peucolaus and Nicanor. To these he added Aphobetus, Iolaus, Dioxenus, Archepolis and Amyntas.

7.48 When he was dismissed from this dialogue, *being as yet underage,* **Nicomachus related what he had learnt to his** *elder* **brother. This man was called Cebalinus** *and he was acutely concerned in case a conspirator should confess the plot to the king before they could.* It seemed best that Nicomachus should remain in the tent lest the conspirators realised that they were being betrayed, if he were uncustomarily conveyed into the royal quarters to see the king. Consequently, **Cebalinus himself went and stood at the entrance to the courtyard of the royal quarters,** *for he was not allowed any further forward. There he waited for anyone from the upper echelon of Alexander's Friends who would admit him to the king's presence. Of these by chance all had already gone save for* **Philotas the son of Parmenion,** *who had* **remained there** *for reasons known to none. Blithering and blatantly in a considerable state of consternation,* **Cebalinus blurted out to him what he had heard from his brother and called for the king to be informed without demur.** *Whereupon he was warmly praised by* **Philotas,** *who at once* **went in to Alexander and engaged him in lengthy conversation on a variety of topics, but made no mention of what he had learnt from Cebalinus.** *At twilight* **the youth intercepted Philotas as he emerged** *into the courtyard of the royal quarters and queried whether his mission had been accomplished?* **But Philotas, professing that he had found no opportunity to talk to the king,**

---

[28] Demetrius was a *Somatophylax*, i.e. a member of the elite seven-man bodyguard of the king and therefore one of the most senior officers in the Macedonian court.

said that on the following day he would see Alexander alone on the matter *and went on his way.*

7.49 *It may be that Philotas was in fact a party to the conspiracy or perhaps he just failed to treat the matter sufficiently seriously. At all events,* the next day *Cebalinus was already at hand when Philotas arrived at the royal quarters and as he entered he prompted him to recall the matter he had made known to him the day before.* Philotas *retorted that he was attending to it, yet* even then did not declare the affair to the king. Cebalinus grew suspicious and forsook his faith in Philotas. He deemed that there should be no further delay, lest another betray the plot and imperil *his brother and* him. Hence he pestered one of the Royal Pages, a noble youth named Metron, who had charge of the armoury, and he apprised him of the planned perfidy, beseeching him to report it immediately. Having concealed Cebalinus in the armoury, Metron went at once to the king, who happened to be bathing, and revealed what his informer had imparted, adding that he had him in hiding. Alexander reacted with alarm, sending his attendants to apprehend Dimnus *and entering the armoury, where Cebalinus was exultant, exclaiming: "Sire, you are saved, rescued from the blows of faithless fellows." Thereupon the king interrogated him as to his whole story and put together a complete picture. And then he returned to the question of how many days it had been since Nicomachus had brought him this information? And when Cebalinus conceded that it had happened the day before yesterday, Alexander considered him hardly trustworthy in waiting so long to report what he had heard and ordered that he be fettered. But Cebalinus began to bellow that he had dashed off to Philotas the instant he had heard, so it was Philotas who had covered up what he had discovered.*[29]

7.50 *Then Alexander likewise interrogated the youth as to whether he had gone to Philotas and whether Cebalinus had pressed for them to approach the king.* When Cebalinus resolutely reaffirmed his assertions, Alexander held his hands up to the Heavens and with his eyes flooding with tears he deplored that one who was formerly his fondest friend had rendered him such a reward. Meanwhile, Dimnus, *not at all innocent of why he was summoned by his sovereign and happening to have his sword strapped on,* dealt himself a mortal wound. *Then the men from the royal retinue rushed to restrain him and conveyed him to the king's quarters.* Glaring at him, Alexander asked: "What atrocity have I intended to commit against you that you should feel that Philotas is fitter than I myself to rule the Macedonians?" But Dimnus was already rendered speechless and so he simply sighed and, turning his face from

---

[29] Adopting Jeep's emendation of Curtius 6.7.27 to read *ab eo operiri comperta* instead of the manuscript reading of *ab eo percomperta.*

the king's gaze, he at once collapsed and died. Yet the king had already learnt everything from his suicide.³⁰

7.51 The king, *having* commanded that Philotas report to the royal quarters, *addressed him thus: "If for two days Cebalinus covered up a conspiracy primed to take my life, he has merited capital punishment. But he has shifted the blame for his felony onto Philotas through his claim that he immediately imparted the information to him. The closer your status of friendship ties you to me, the more villainous is your duplicity, although indeed I concede that this conduct better becomes a Cebalinus than a Philotas. You have a sympathetic judge, if you are at least able to absolve yourself, Philotas, of what should never have come to pass." To this Philotas responded without the least trepidation, if his emotions were to be measured by his expression, saying that Cebalinus had indeed retailed some talk from a tart to him, but that he himself had given scant credence to so fickle an informant. He had worried that he would not be able to tell of a tiff between a catamite and his lover without arousing derision from others. However, since Dimnus had done away with himself,* Philotas confessed that the information, *whatever its pedigree,* should not have been suppressed. *Then he embraced the king and commenced cajoling him to concentrate upon his career to date rather than this current misdemeanour, which was merely muteness rather than anything mutinous.* It is hard to say whether the king believed him or withheld his anger deep within himself. He proffered Philotas his right hand to seal their reconciliation and said that it seemed to him a case of spurning rather than hiding the information.

7.52 Yet the king convened a council of his Friends, to which however Philotas was not invited, and he bade that Nicomachus be brought before them, who set out the sequence of events just as they had been imparted to the king. Few were closer to Alexander than Craterus, who was consequently hostile towards Philotas as his rival for preferment. He was well aware that Philotas had often overburdened Alexander's ears by vaunting his valour and the value of his services excessively and hence was suspected of waywardness rather than criminality. Reckoning that there would be no better opportunity to disparage his enemy by obscuring his antipathy with a veneer of loyalty, he commented: "Would that you had discussed this affair with us from the start! If you had wished to forgive Philotas, we would have coaxed you to keep him in innocence of the degree of his debt to you, rather than have him meditate more often on his jeopardy, after having been put in fear of his life, than on your generosity. For Philotas will perpetually be in a position to conspire against you, yet you will not perpetually be in a position to pardon Philotas. There is no reason for

---

³⁰ Diodorus 17.79.5 says Alexander learnt everything on arresting Dimnus, but must mean from his behaviour rather than from speech, since he agrees with Curtius regarding Dimnus's suicide.

you to imagine that a man who has manifested such audacity can be reformed by forgiveness. He knows that those who have exhausted one's clemency cannot expect any more mercy. But even if, overcome either by repentance or by your indulgence, the man himself should wish to shun strife, I am confident that his father Parmenion will be discontent to be indebted to you for his son's life. He heads so huge an army and holds such long-standing influence with the troops that he occupies a position scarcely inferior in authority to your own. There are such kindnesses as cause us to recoil. Since the man is dishonoured who declares himself deserving of death, Philotas will foster the feeling that he has received injustice rather than been reprieved. Therefore be assured that you must make war on these fellows for your safety's sake. Sufficient foes remain amongst those whom we are about to pursue. Let you protect your flank against internal opponents too. If you but rid yourself of these, I fear no foreign enemies."

7.53 So spoke Craterus and neither did the rest doubt that Philotas would not have stifled the story of the plot unless he were either its instigator or a conspirator. Indeed, what loyal and well intentioned man - not necessarily a Friend *of the king*, but even the lowest of the low - on hearing the accusations made to Philotas would not have run off to his ruler right away? Yet the son of Parmenion, the commander of the cavalry and a consultant on all his sovereign's secrets, was not even inspired by the example set by Cebalinus, who had brought him everything from his brother's briefing. Philotas had even pretended that the king had not had a moment to talk to him, so that his informer should not seek an alternative intermediary. Nicomachus had hastened to disburden his conscience, despite being bound by an obligation to the gods. Yet Philotas had frittered away almost the entire day on mere horseplay, loth to introduce a few words pertaining his sovereign's preservation during such protracted and perchance inconsequential conversation. If indeed he had disbelieved such testimony out of the mouths of mere youths, why then would he have strung them along for two days as if he trusted in their allegations? Cebalinus should have been sent away at once, if Philotas had discounted his accusations. Chivalry should be shown in the face of one's own jeopardy, but, when there is concern for the sovereign's safety, there is a duty of credulity, such that even groundless allegations should be taken seriously.

7.54 They were therefore unanimous that Philotas should be put to the question in order to press him to name his accomplices in the treachery. Before dismissing them the king bound them to silence concerning the outcome of the council. Then he ordered that that a march be announced for the following day, so that no signal of the council's decisions should be betrayed to the traitors. Philotas was even invited to what was to be his last banquet and Alexander deigned not merely to dine but also to gossip with the man he had condemned. Then in the second watch of the night with the extinction of every light there congregated in the king's quarters Hephaistion, Craterus, Coenus and Erigyius from among the Friends plus Perdiccas and Leonnatus from the Bodyguards

Book 7: July 330BC – June 329BC

together with a few others. Orders were issued by these that those on watch at the headquarters should stand to in arms. Cavalry detachments had already been deployed to all the exits from the camp and they had also been ordered to seal the roads in order that nobody should covertly abscond to Parmenion, who at that time commanded Media and vast contingents of troops. Furthermore, Atarrhias entered the royal quarters with three hundred men-at-arms. Ten deputies were seconded to him, each escorted by ten guardsmen. These were detailed to apprehend the other plotters, whilst Atarrhias was dispatched to Philotas with the three hundred. With the support of fifty of his readiest recruits he set about forcing the barred entrance to his house, for he had commanded the rest completely to surround the premises, lest Philotas should slip away via some secret access. But either on account of a carefree conscience or else overcome by fatigue he had succumbed to slumber and he was still only half-awake when he was seized by Atarrhias. When at last he was fully alert and fetters were fastened upon him, he groaned: "O Sire, your goodness has been soured by the bitterness of my antagonists!" And without further oratory he was led into the king's quarters with a hood over his head.

7.55 On the following day **the king decreed a general assembly of the Macedonians in arms in order to try Philotas.** Around six thousand soldiers as well as a crowd of camp-followers and servants congregated and were crammed into the royal enclosure. Files of guardsmen screened Philotas in order that he should not be glimpsed by the masses until the king had addressed his troops. It was the ancient custom of the Macedonians that the army - or the populace in time of peace - should try capital cases and the king's influence counted for nothing unless they had been swayed by his evidence before their decision. Accordingly, the corpse of Dimnus was introduced at the outset, the majority being ignorant of what he had plotted or how he had died. Thereupon the king made his entry to the gathering, his sense of sorrow being revealed in his expression and the solemnity of his Friends as well inspired no small apprehension of what was about to transpire.

7.56 For a long while **the king** seemed stunned and stupefied as he stood staring at the ground, then, recovering his self-possession, he **began to speak**: "I have very nearly been wrenched from you by the villainy of certain individuals and it is through the providence and mercy of the gods that I am still alive. The awesome sight of you so congregated has compelled me to be the more vehement in seeking vengeance against the traitors, since it is the primary or rather the sole profit of my existence to be able to render due rewards to such men of the utmost valiance and most meriting of my beneficence." Gasps and sighs from the assembled soldiers necessitated the suspension of his speech, whilst tears welled up in the eyes of each. Then their sovereign resumed: "How much more marked are the emotions I shall stir in your senses, when I expose the instigators of such foul offences. These I still shrink from defaming and, as if they could still be redeemed, I refrain from naming. Yet I must overcome the recollection of my former affection, since a conspiracy of corrupt countrymen

Alexander the Great in Afghanistan by Andrew Chugg

Figure 7.2. The trial and execution of Philotas (from a 1696 edition of Curtius)

Book 7: July 330BC – June 329BC

requires revelation, for how can I keep quiet concerning such an abomination? Though behoven to me and to my father for so many favours, though the eldest of all our Friends and despite his age, **Parmenion proposed himself to lead this heinous outrage. His confederate, Philotas,** suborned Peucolaus, Demetrius and this very Dimnus whose body you behold before you together with the rest of the demented men who meant to murder me." All about him howls of indignant resentment broke out from the whole host, just as is wont to occur with a crowd, and especially an assemblage of soldiers, when it is aroused by partiality or fury. At that point Nicomachus and Metron and Cebalinus were led forward and each testified concerning his story. Yet none of the information from any of them fingered Philotas as a participant in the treachery. Therefore, following the first outburst of outrage, the evidence of the informants was absorbed in silence.

7.57 Thereafter the king continued: "What, then, does it seem to you is the mindset of a man, who, when the matter was disclosed to him, withheld the information, considering that the death of Dimnus demonstrates that the affair was not without foundation? Cebalinus was not intimidated by his liability to be tortured in reporting a deniable crime and Metron even burst into my bathroom, so as not to delay disburdening himself of the betrayal even for a short time. None but Philotas feared nothing and disbelieved everything. What a man of mettle! Yet should not such a man be stirred to action by his king's jeopardy? Should his expression not alter in anxiously hearing out the accuser of such a conspiracy? Assuredly it is perfidy that lies behind his silence and a keen craving for kingship sped his spirit headlong unto the ultimate treachery. His father is the master of Media and he himself covets more than he can properly command by dint of his overpowering influence with many commanders in my army. He would even have removed me whilst lacking heirs, insofar as I am without issue. Yet in this Philotas errs, for I do possess kindred, parents and progeny in all of you! Whilst you survive, I cannot be completely deprived of family." Then he read aloud a letter that Parmenion had written to his sons, Philotas and Nicanor, which had been intercepted, although it did not really reveal evidence that they had sinister plans in store. For this was the nub of it: "First of all concern yourselves with caring for your own advantage and then for the advantage of those close to you, since we shall thereby bring about what we envisage." And the king remarked that it was couched in such terms, so that, should it reach the sons, it could be understood by the conspirators, but, should it be intercepted, it would not be decoded by outsiders.

7.58 Alexander continued: "Yet it may be objected that Dimnus failed to finger Philotas, when he indicated the rest of his comrades in crime. This need not be evidence of his innocence, but rather of his influence, insofar as even those who could have disclosed his name were so much in dread of him that they still hid his identity, when they made known their own. But the history of his own behaviour in fact fingers Philotas. At that time back in Macedon that Amyntas,[31] who was my cousin, concocted a treasonous plot to murder me, Philotas was consorting with him as his ally and crony. And this is the man who gave his sister in matrimony to Attalus,[32] than whom I had no deadlier enemy. Then, when I wrote to him in the context of our close camaraderie and friendship regarding the response rendered to me by the Oracle of Zeus-Ammon, this is that very man who had the insolence to write back that, though he congratulated me on being recognized among the gods, he nevertheless pitied those that must live under one who transcends the bounds of humanity. These things indicate that his heart has long since been estranged from me and is jealous of my glory. These signs, soldiers, so long as was viable I suppressed in my mind. Indeed it seemed to me as though I wrenched out part of my own guts, if I were to vitiate men that I had made so great. But now it is not mere words that must be punished: rash rant has reached the point of swords. If you believe me, Philotas has honed these blades against me, else, if you believe him, he has allowed them to be."

7.59 "Where shall I turn, soldiers? To whom shall I entrust my life? I have placed him in sole command of the cavalry, the finest force in my army, the flower of our young noblemen. My safety, my aspirations and my conquests I have consigned to his good faith and guardianship. I have elevated his father to share the same pedestal upon which you have set me. I have made Media, than which no region is richer, subject to his mandate and authority, as well as so many thousands of our compatriots and confederates. Where I had sought support, a threat juts forth. How much happier to have fallen in the fighting, felled by a foe, rather than die by a countryman's blow! Now, preserved from the only perils that I feared, I am beset by threats that should never have appeared. Soldiers, you are accustomed repeatedly to plead with me to take fewer risks with my safety. Of this policy that you have urged upon me, you are now able to answer for the implementation. It is in your hands and through your arms that I seek my salvation. If you are unwilling to save me, I do not wish for safety, and you cannot intend my preservation, unless you act for my protection."

7.60 Then he bade that, with his hands tied behind his back and his head enfolded in a shabby cloak, Philotas be led in. It was plain to see that the men were moved by the wretched state of a man whom it had not been feasible to view without envy until that date. Just yesterday they had beheld him as

---

[31] This Amyntas was the son of Perdiccas III, the elder brother of Philip II, Alexander's father. Alexander had him executed some time between coming to the throne in the Autumn of 336BC and the Spring of 335BC (Justin 12.6.3 & Arrian, *Anabasis* 1.5.4) evidently for plotting the assassination of the king.

[32] Attalus had married his niece to Philip II, thereby threatening Alexander's succession in the case of male progeny. He managed to imply that Alexander was a bastard by loudly hoping for a *legitimate* heir at the wedding feast (Plutarch, *Alexander* 9.4 & Athenaeus 557B).

Book 7: July 330BC – June 329BC

commander of the cavalry, whom they knew to have attended the king's banquet. Now, suddenly, they surveyed him as a defendant in fact, but already doomed, indeed even in bonds. The fate of Parmenion too loomed in their minds. What a giant of a general! What a coruscating countryman! But lately bereaved of two of his boys, Hector and Nicanor, he must now stand trial in his absence along with the sole son spared to him by calamity. Therefore, since the assembly was inclining towards mercy, Amyntas, from among the king's commanders, revived their antagonism towards Philotas through his oratory: "In fact Philotas sought to betray us to the barbarians. None of us would ever have made it back to our wives and parents in our home country, but like a decapitated body turned zombie, without identity and astray in strange lands, we should have made fine sport for the enemy." But this speech by Amyntas was by no means so pleasing to the king as its speaker had expected, because by reminding the soldiers of their wives and their homeland he had made them the more reluctant to endure the rest of their term of service.

7.61 Then Coenus, despite that he had wed the sister of Philotas, fulminated against him more fiercely than anyone else, bellowing that he was a traitor to his king, to his country and to the army itself. And scooping up a stone that happened to lie by his feet he prepared to hurl it at him – many surmised out of a desire to spare him from torture. But the king stayed his hand, declaring that the defendant ought first to be afforded an opportunity to deliver his defence and that he would not allow the trial to proceed otherwise. Then, when bidden to speak, Philotas was fuddled and stunned, neither venting his mouth nor raising his gaze, either due to a sense of guilt or the awfulness of his predicament. Thereupon he burst into tears and fainted into the embrace of him that held him. But, his eyes being dried with his mantle, he gradually recovered his bearing and his voice and appeared to be on the point of speaking. Staring intently at him, Alexander thought to interject: "The Macedonians are ready to hear your case, so I would ask whether you will address them in their native dialect?" Philotas responded: "As well as the Macedonians there are many here, who will more readily appreciate what I have to say, if I use the same tongue as you yourself have been uttering today, for no other reason I believe than that your speech could be understood by more in the crowd." To this the king retorted: "Can anyone not see how Philotas loathes even the language of his patrimony, since he alone dislikes its study? But let him indeed speak in whatsoever way he deems wise, whilst keeping in mind that it is our ways as much as our speech that he seems to despise." And with that the king quit the assembly.

7.62 Then Philotas began: "It is easy for an innocent man to conceive of word after word, but for a wretched chap to choose them is awkward. Therefore, beleaguered between the clearest of consciences and the most perverse adversity, I do not know how to suit both my sentiments and the opportunity. In fact, the best judge of my case is no longer here, though, by Heracles, I cannot fathom why he should not wish to grant me his ear. When he is aware of both sides he may as legally condemn me as acquit me. But if he does not hear me, I cannot be set at liberty when he is absent, who condemned me whilst present. A defence by a fellow in fetters is not just in vain but also invidious, since he seems not to be enlightening but laying the blame upon his judge. Nevertheless, in whatever I am allowed to tell, I myself shall not falter nor foster the impression that I am guilty in my own opinion as well."

7.63 "In truth, I cannot see of what crime I am accused. None among the conspirators has named me. Nicomachus said of me not a word and Cebalinus could not know more than he had heard. Yet the king credits me with the leadership of the conspiracy. Could Dimnus have withheld mention of the man whom he abetted, especially since, being asked about his confederates, he ought to have named me, even if falsely, the more readily to recruit him whom he tempted? For when Dimnus laid bare their wickedness he did not omit my name in order to appear to have spared an accomplice. In confessing to Nicomachus, whom he thought would keep his own secret safe without doubt, all others being named, I alone was left out. Consider, comrades, if Cebalinus had not come to me, if he had wanted me to know nothing concerning those in the conspiracy, would I this day be delivering my defence, when none has named me in the offence? Definitely Dimnus so long as he lived forbore to name me, but how about the rest? Patently, those that currently incriminate themselves still maintain my anonymity! Adversity is vindictive, so a villain in torment will normally consent to the torture of another. So can so many plotters fail to confess facts even when stretched upon racks? Just as nobody gives quarter to a condemned man, it is true that a condemned man gives quarter to nobody in my view."

7.64 "I need return to the one true charge laid against me: 'Why did you keep silent concerning the matter that was reported to you? Why did you hear it with such serenity?' This, such as it is, being acknowledged by me was pardoned by you, Alexander, wherever you may be. I clasped your right hand to pledge our restored amity and even attended last night's revelry. If you believed me, then I was absolved. If you pardoned me, then the matter was resolved. Let you abide by your adjudication. What did I do last night after leaving your refection? What fresh villainy has been revealed to you to alter your conception? I lay deep in sleep oblivious of my troubles when my antagonists woke me as they set me in shackles. How did a traitor and betrayer come by such sound slumber? Miscreants cannot readily slip into sleep due to the nagging of their conscience. For the Furies harry them not merely after the perpetration of their treason but also in its anticipation. But my sense of security was founded firstly in my innocence and then bolstered by your right hand. I had no apprehension that you would allow others' inhumanity to outweigh your own inclination towards clemency."

7.65 "But let you not regret your belief in me, for the affair was unfolded to me through a mere boy who could produce neither proof nor any witness for his

Book 7: July 330BC – June 329BC

story and who could have caused comprehensive consternation, if people had begun to pay heed to his information. Unfortunately, it was my opinion that my ears had been taxed by a tiff between a lover and his minion and I doubted his good faith when he did not tell me to my face, but briefed his brother to act in his place. I feared that he would abjure what he had consigned to Cebalinus in that briefing and I would then be seen as a source of insecurity for sundry associates of the king. Even so, though I have denounced nobody, I have uncovered someone who would prefer to see me perish rather than secure safety. How much more resentment do you reckon I would have evoked, had I provoked the innocent? And yet, indeed, Dimnus slew himself. Do you honestly suppose that I should have been able to foresee that he would do so? Hardly! Hence the sole fact that has since confirmed the allegation could not convince me when Cebalinus cornered me with his information. But, by Heracles, had I really been in league with Dimnus in such treachery, I ought not to have kept it in the shade for those two days that we had been betrayed and Cebalinus himself could have been disposed of without difficulty. Furthermore, after the information, which I was to withhold, had been made known, I entered the king's bedchamber all alone and even girt with a blade. Why then would I have let the deed be delayed? Did I dare nothing without Dimnus? Then he was thus the leader of the escapade and Philotas, whilst manoeuvring to be monarch of Macedon, was sheltering in his shade. *Manoeuvring to be king!* Which among you have I bought with my presents? What captain, what commander did I cultivate at excessive expense?"

7.66 "There is even laid against me the accusation that I disdain to communicate in the language of my nation, that I recoil from the customs of the Macedonians, which would suggest that I covet the kingship of that which I detest. That native speech has long since faded out through our dealings with nations round about. Both the conquered and the conquerors must learn the language of foreigners. By Heracles, such charges made against me are no more scathing than that Amyntas the son of Perdiccas intrigued against the king. That I stood on friendly terms with him I shall not shy from defending, unless it was never our duty to adore a cousin of the king.[33] But if it was required that we even reverence such an exalted royal, am I indicted because I lacked foresight or is death also to be be dealt to the blameless friends of the disloyal? If that is just, why let me live so long? Else why am I now at last to die, if it is wrong?"

7.67 "It is indeed the truth that I wrote that I pitied those who had to live under one who believed himself to be Zeus's son. O faithful friendship with the perilous liberty to tender candid counsel, you have beguiled me! It was you that dispelled my reticence in revealing my sentiments. I confess that I wrote this thing for the king's own reading, though I wrote nothing of it to others about

---

[33] The Latin of Curtius 6.10.24 uses *frater* (brother), but the term extends to cousins, which was the actual relationship between Amyntas and Alexander.

the king. For I sought not to expose him to odium, but rather I feared for him. It seemed to me more seemly for Alexander to acquiesce to his descent from Zeus without communication, rather than to broadcast it by public proclamation. But since we are convinced of the verity of the oracle, let its god bear witness in my case. Keep me fastened in fetters, whilst Ammon is asked whether I instigated a furtive and sinister disgrace. He who has distinguished our king as his son will not suffer the concealment of anyone who has conspired against his race. Yet if you consider torture to be more reliable than prophecy, even from that version of validating the truth I do not beg for mercy."

7.68 "Those accused in capital cases are accustomed to call upon their kin to come before you. But I have recently been bereaved of my two brothers and I am unable to present my father to you. Nor will I venture to invoke his name, since he himself has been implicated in this awful shame. For it is not enough that he, who was lately the father of many a son and now seeks solace in a single one, losing him too should be left with none, unless also he himself be put upon my pyre. So, dearest father, you are due to die due to me and with me. It is I who cause your life to expire. It is I who terminate your antiquity. Why indeed did you sire unhappy me against divine mandate? Was it in order to gather this harvest from me, which is now your fate? I do not know whether my youth or your age is the more distressing. I am reaped in my prime, whilst in your case the executioner will cut short a life, which, had fate been willing to wait, nature was already soliciting."

7.69 "Mention of my father has reminded me how timorous and hesitant I was obliged to be in divulging what Cebalinus had told me. For Parmenion, when he heard that poison was being concocted for the king by Philip the Physician, wrote Alexander a note to deter him from drinking the potion with which the doctor had decided to dose him. You will recall that my father was disbelieved and that his message was paid no heed. How often I myself have confided what I have heard and been rebuffed with derision for my gullibility. If our information attracts odium and our silence inspires suspicion, what ought our recourse to be?" And when one among the encompassing crowd had retorted, "Not to plot against your benefactors!" Philotas responded, "You are correct, whoever you may be. Hence, if I am guilty of such conspiracy, I do not entreat you for exemption from due sentence and I make an end of eloquence, since it appears that my final words have offended your ears." Thereupon he was led away by those in whose hands he lay.

7.70 There was among the commanders a certain Bolon, a formidable fighter, but unskilled in the arts of peace and urbane manners, an old trooper in fact, who had risen through the ranks to reach his current captaincy. He, when the host was hushed, began with discourteous and defiant audacity to remind them how frequently they had been kicked out of quarters they had requisitioned in the cause of accommodating the filth among Philotas' servants in the places

Book 7: July 330BC – June 329BC

whence his comrades had been evicted. His carts crammed with gold and silver had been parked throughout entire precincts, but not a single man among his fellow fighters had been admitted even to the vicinity of his lodgings. Rather they had all been banished into the distance by those he had disposed as wardens of his repose, so that that sissy should not be disturbed by the hush rather than the hubbub of their murmurings. Those that came from the countryside, whom he had nicknamed Phrygians and Paphlagonians, were martyrs to the mockery of him, who, though Macedonian by birth, was not ashamed that he had to hear men whose native tongue he shared through an interpreter. Now he desired that Ammon be consulted, the very same man who accused Zeus of lying when he recognized Alexander as his offspring, supposedly suffering anxiety lest this gift from the gods should engender jealousy. He never referred the matter to Zeus, when he conspired against the life of his sovereign and friend. Only now he wished to send to the oracle, whilst his father suborned those he commanded in Media and disbursed the funds consigned to his regency to induce outlaws to ally with him in his treachery. The army would indeed send envoys to the oracle, not to quiz Zeus on what they already knew from the king, but instead to tender their thanks and redeem the promises in their prayers for the preservation of their sovereign.

7.71 Then indeed the entire assembly was incensed *against Philotas*[34] and the Bodyguards made a beginning by bellowing that they should dismember the traitor with their bare hands. In fact, Philotas was scarcely scared on hearing this, since he feared far fouler suffering. But the king came back into the meeting and adjourned the proceedings until the following day, either in order to torment Philotas in confinement as well[35] or else to investigate the whole matter more thoroughly. And despite that the day was dimming into dusk the king convened a council of his Friends. **The consensus** of the rest **was that Philotas should be put to death according to the custom of the Macedonians *by stoning*, but** Hephaistion, Craterus and Coenus declared **that the truth should be extracted from him by torture first** and those who had argued otherwise came round to their view. Therefore, the council being dissolved, Hephaistion with Craterus and Coenus arose as one to subject Philotas to inquisition.[36] The king called Craterus aside and had a quiet word with him, the substance of which has not been published, before withdrawing

---

[34] This constitutes the conviction verdict against Philotas: the verdicts of the Macedonian Assembly were by acclamation rather than a formal vote as is explained by Curtius 7.2.7.

[35] That is to say, as well as the preceding proposal by the Bodyguards that they should tear Philotas to pieces in public. The Penguin Curtius is wrong to give the translation "to subject Philotas to further torture in prison", since this infers earlier torture, which Curtius has not mentioned.

[36] The Latin of Curtius 6.11.11 grants primacy to Hephaistion among this group, because he was Commander of the Bodyguards (*Hegemon* of the *Somatophylakes*) according to Diodorus 17.61.3 and possibly already *Chiliarch*.

into the private part of the royal quarters. There, having dismissed all onlookers, he waited up deep into the night for the outcome of the tortures.

7.72 The torturers arrayed all the tools of their brutality before the gaze of Philotas and he volunteered: "Why tarry in exterminating the king's enemy, who confesses he sought to assassinate him? What need is there for interrogation? I conceived the thing and wanted to bring it about." But Craterus required that he reiterate his confession under torture. Then he was seized and, whilst he was being blindfolded and stripped of his clothing, he invoked the gods of his fatherland and human rights, but futilely in the face of deaf ears. He was mangled by the most excruciating torments, seeing as he was a condemned man being tortured by his bitter rivals for the favour of the king. Though assaulted successively with fire and the scourge, no longer for inquisition but to induce suffering, he initially curbed not only his screams but even his groans. But after his body had become swollen with weals, he could no longer bear the swipes of the scourges that cut to the bare bone, so he promised that he would tell them what they wished to know, if they would relent from tormenting him. But he wanted them to swear by Alexander's life that the interrogation would end and the torturers would withdraw. And when both things had been effectuated, Philotas said: "Tell me, Craterus, what you would have me say." However, when Craterus was indignant at such mockery and was calling the torturers back again, Philotas began to beg for time to recover his composure, whereupon he would divulge everything that he knew. Meanwhile, after they had got wind of the torturing of Philotas, the cavalry, including all those of the noblest birth and any with family ties to Parmenion in particular, were panic-stricken due to the Macedonian law that provided for the relatives of a traitor to share his death. Some did away with themselves whilst others fled into remote mountain ranges and desert wastes as abject terror stalked through the entire camp, until the king became conscious of the consternation and rescinded the law that allowed for the penalisation of the kindred of the convicted by a proclamation.

7.73 It is ambiguous whether **Philotas** sought to deliver himself from excruciation through truth or lies, inasmuch as both true confession and false disquisition held out the identical prospect of an end to his anguish. What he **confessed** was: "You are well aware how friendly my father was with Hegelochus. I mean the Hegelochus who fell in the fighting. He was the source of all our woes. For when first the king commanded that he be called the son of Zeus, he queried quite indignantly, 'Should we therefore recognize this ruler, who repudiates Philip's paternity? We are finished, if we can stand for this. A man who demands recognition as a deity doesn't only look down upon mankind, but also depreciates divinity. We have lost Alexander and are bereft of our king. We have become subject to an insolence that is intolerable either to the gods, to whom he equates himself, or to men, from whom he separates himself. Have we spilt our blood to raise up a god who disdains us and is loath

Book 7: July 330BC – June 329BC

to commune with mere mortals? Believe me, if we be men, we too shall be the chosen of the gods.[37] Who avenged the killing of Alexander, the forbear of the current king, and Archelaus after him and Perdiccas's slaying?[38] But the present Alexander pardoned his father's assassins.[39]'"

7.74 "This was what Hegelochus had to say over dinner and at dawn the next day I was summoned by my father. He was grimfaced and could see that I was troubled, for what we had heard had instilled disquiet into our hearts. Hence in order to check whether he had waffled whilst witless with wine or had imparted some deeper design, we decided to send for him. On arriving he recapitulated the same arguments of his own accord, adding that if we should dare to lead the endeavour, he would stand beside us as our ally, but if we were minded to drop the matter, he would keep the whole conception under wraps. The plot appeared untimely to Parmenion, while Darius were still alive, for we would have been doing away with Alexander rather on behalf of the enemy than to advantage ourselves. However, once we had disposed of Darius, the bounty on the head of the king would be that Asia and the entire Orient should be ceded to his assassins. This reasoning was ratified and relevant vows were exchanged. And though I know nothing regarding Dimnus, I realize that following this confession it shall not avail me that I had no part in his treason." At this they reverted to tormenting him, personally poking at his face and eyes with their javelins so as to compel his confession to that offence as well. Then, when they pressed him for the particulars of the scheduling of the intended outrage, Philotas explained that it had seemed that Alexander would be detained by Bactria for an age, in the course of which he had feared that his father being

---

[37] At this point Hegelochus abandons overt criticism of Alexander's deification and launches into obscurely treasonous innuendo. Ostensibly, "chosen of the gods" parodies Alexander's adoption by Zeus, but in this context there is also an implication that they are to be chosen as instruments of divine retribution against Alexander.

[38] The combined implication of the context and the names themselves is that these are former kings of Macedon, in which case they are Alexander I (reigned c495-c452BC), Archelaus (reigned c413-399BC) and Perdiccas III (reigned 368-360BC). The passage would suggest that the Macedonian nobility had avenged their murders in each case. The mode of death for Alexander I is not known, but Archelaus was slain by his *eromenos* Crateuas, who was then slain in turn (Aelian, *Varia Historia* 8.9). Perdiccas III died in battle against the Illyrians, but hostile writers suggested that his mother, Eurydice, was somehow implicated (NGL Hammond, *The Miracle That Was Macedonia*, p.56).

[39] It has sometimes been assumed that this is a reference to Alexander letting Alexander Lyncestes live, despite executing his brothers as accomplices in the assassination of Philip (Justin 11.2.2). However, Hegelochus must be speaking shortly after the visit to the oracle at Siwa, when Alexander Lyncestes had already been imprisoned on treason charges for a couple of years (Arrian, *Anabasis* 1.25). Hence the criticism that Alexander had pardoned him could not have carried much force in these circumstances. More cogently, it is the alleged involvement of Olympias in Philip's murder that is meant. She is explicitly accused of having arranged horses for Pausanias's getaway in Justin 9.7, but clearly Alexander took no action against her. Hence the sense of this passage is that Alexander was complicit in the murder of hs father and so should be a target for Macedonian nobles avenging regicide rather than the object of their protection.

seventy years old might pass away. Parmenion commanded such colossal forces and was the custodian of so much money that he himself, stripped of such strong resources, would lack the backing to do away with the king. Hence he had hastened to implement his plan, whilst the prize lay to hand. And unless they believed that his father had played no part in the affair, he would not balk at further torture, though it was already more than he could bear.

7.75 On having conferred, they considered that sufficient inquistion had occurred, so they reported to the king, who ordered *at the assembly* the next day that the admissions made by Philotas should be recited and that he himself should be carried in, as he could not walk. After he had acknowledged everything, Demetrius was brought in, having been accused of complicity in the recent treachery. He strenuously denied equally by his disposition, his resolution and his expression that he had entertained any intention to act against the king, even demanding for himself vindication through torture. Whereupon Philotas swept his gaze around to either side letting it alight upon Calis, whom he bade move nearer, though he stood not far away. But when Calis was apprehensive and refused to approach him, he asked: "Will you endorse the deceit of Demetrius and the repetition of my torture?" Turning deathly pale, Calis was speechless and the Macedonians were suspicious that Philotas's intent was to incriminate the innocent, since neither Nicomachus nor Philotas during his torture had named this adolescent. Yet when the king's commanders stood around him in a ring, Calis confessed the complicity of Demetrius and himself in the plotting. Hence **in accordance with their country's custom all who had been named by Nicomachus together with Philotas at a signal suffered extermination** *by stoning*.

7.76 Alexander had been freed from a frightful threat not merely to his wellbeing but even to his existence. For Philotas and Parmenion as the most senior among his Friends could not have been condemned without offence to the entire army, unless publicly shown to be guilty. Hence the outcome hung in the balance whilst the deed was denied and torture was viewed with abhorrence. But following his confession Philotas did not even merit the compassion of his adherents.

7.77 While Philotas's tracks in the treason were still fresh, *the soldiers* judged that he had been justly punished; yet after the object of their detestation had been despatched, their censure switched to remorse. They **were moved both by the illustriousness of the young Philotas and by the venerability of his father**, which was accentuated by the loss of his several sons. It had been Parmenion who had first established a bridgehead in Asia for the king and as his partner in every peril he had in battle always commanded the opposite wing. He had also been the foremost among Philip's Friends and so loyal to Alexander himself that the king had preferred him to any other agent in slaying Attalus. Suchlike rumination grew rife among the army, whose mutinous mutterings were recounted to the king. *Some had said that they themselves could not count on better*

Book 7: July 330BC – June 329BC

treatment from him. But Alexander was unperturbed, since he was well aware that mischief born of idleness is dispelled by actual action and so he announced that everyone should gather in the court of the royal quarters. When he had determined that it was thronged, he strode into this assembly.

7.78 Doubtless by prior arrangement, **it was proposed** by Atarrhias **that Alexander Lyncestes, who had sought to assassinate their sovereign long before Philotas, should be arraigned before them.** He *had been denounced by two informers (as was mentioned above)*[40] *and was currently in his third year of confinement in fetters. It was also considered certain that he had been complicit with Pausanias in Philip's assassination. But since he had been the first to herald Alexander as king, he had been granted immunity from punishment rather than from incrimination. Furthermore, the appeals of Antipater,*[41] *his father-in-law, on his behalf had been staving off the king's righteous retaliation. However, the pain of this ulcer burst out again, since their current crisis called to mind the old threat.* Hence Alexander Lyncestes was led forth from confinement and bidden to speak. Yet *despite having had fully three years to prepare his defence,* he managed shakily and falteringly to pronounce just a few words *of what he had composed, until ultimately not merely his memory but even his mind forsook him. Nobody doubted that his agitation was an indication of a guilty conscience rather than impaired recollection.* Therefore, *whilst he still fought with his forgetfulness,* he was transfixed by the lances of *some of* those who stood nearby.

7.79 His corpse having been carted away, the king commanded that Amyntas and Simmias be led in. For Polemon, who was their younger brother, had fled upon learning that Philotas was being tortured. They had been the closest of all the friends of Philotas and they had been promoted into prominent and eminent offices especially through his sponsorship. The king recalled that he had recommended them with the utmost élan and did not doubt that they had also been participants in Philotas's final plan. He had long viewed them with suspicion on account of correspondence from his mother, which had cautioned him to keep himself safe from them. And although he was reluctant to give credence to defamation, he had been compelled by palpable evidence to command their incarceration. For there was no room for doubt that they had secretly consorted with Philotas the day before his treachery was laid bare. Furthermore, their brother, who had fled upon the news of Philotas's

---

[40] Curtius 7.1.6 refers back to the lost section at the beginning of his account, where the arrest of Alexander Lyncestes probably immediately preceded the episode of the Gordian knot, which opens the surviving parts of his work; cf. Diodorus 17.32 and Justin 11.7.1.

[41] Diodorus 17.80.2 speaks of Lyncestes' "relationship with Antigonus", but this is surely an error for Antipater, who was his father-in-law (Curtius 7.1.7) and rather more influential.

interrogation, had made it quite clear why he had run away from there. Of late, contrary to customary practice yet in semblance of doing their duty, they had removed the rest of his royal retinue to a distance and set themselves at his side for no plausible reason. Alexander had been bewildered that they were attending him out of their turn and alarmed by their nervousness, so he had promptly ensconced himself among his guards, who were trailing just behind them. It was appended to this that when Antiphanes, the clerk of the cavalry, had notified Amyntas the day before the detection of the treachery of Philotas that, as was customary, he should donate some of his steeds to those who were missing their mounts, Amyntas had arrogantly retorted that, unless he ceased his insistence, he would shortly discover the extent of Amyntas's influence. Moreover, the harsh language and rash verbage that had been vented upon the king himself was nothing other than a symptom and attestation of treacherous intent. If these charges were true, then they deserved to share Philotas's damnation. Else if they were false, then the king himself required that they provide a refutation.

7.80 Antiphanes was next led forward to attest to the failure to surrender the horses as well as the accompanying haughty menaces. Then Amyntas was granted the opportunity to speak and said: "If the king has no objection, I request that I should be freed from these fetters, whilst I speak." Alexander bade that both of them be released and when Amyntas also yearned for his guardsman's outfit to be restored to him, the king *even* commanded that he be handed a lance. Amyntas grasped this in his left hand and, keeping off the spot where the corpse of Alexander Lyncestes had lain a little beforehand, he began to declaim: "Whatsoever verdict is fated for us, Sire, we appreciate that we shall owe thanks to you, if it go in our favour; but we shall blame Fortune, if the outcome be graver. We are ourselves uncurbed in body and mind and our defence of the case is heard without prejudice. You have even restored the raiment in which we are accustomed to do our duty in your service. It is impossible that we should mistrust our defence and we shall cease to distrust providence."

7.81 "I crave that you permit me to counter the last of your charges initially. We, Sire, are quite ignorant of having uttered anything that was directed against your majesty. I would say that you long since transcended unpopularity, if there were no risk that you might suspect more malicious murmers were being flushed away by flattery. But even allowing that any of your soldiers might have been heard to mumble worse than a grumble either when wearied and worn out on the march or when imperilled in battle or when wounded and tending to his injuries in his tent, nevertheless we have deserved by our gallantry that you should choose to attribute it to the circumstances rather than to true dissent. When anything awful occurs, everyone is on trial. We turn harmful hands

Book 7: July 330BC – June 329BC

against our own selves, which are certainly not objects for revulsion.[42] Parents, in restraining their offspring, are met with both ingratitude and indignation. Conversely, when we are honoured with rewards and we come back laden with prizes, who can bear us? Who can contain such elation? In soldiering neither exasperation nor exhilaration exists in moderation, but we are quickly carried away by every emotion. We scold, we praise, we pity or we rage as we are swayed by our current mood. At one moment we are looking to leave for India and the Ocean, but in the next we are checked by the recollection of our wives, our children and our own nation. But such reflections and such chatter amongst the men are curtailed by the peal of the trumpet, when we each rush to our station in the formation. Then whatever resentment has been pent up in our tents is poured down upon the heads of our opponents. Would that Philotas's transgression had been confined to conversation!"

7.82 "And so I return to the basis of the allegations against us: our friendship with Philotas, which I am so far from refuting that I confess that through it we both cultivated and reaped a great fruiting. Are you truly surprised that we have pursued the patronage of Parmenion's son, whom you saw fit to set next in rank to yourself, exceeding almost all your Friends in distinction? By Heracles! You, Sire, if the truth be told, are the cause of our present predicament. For who else instituted that he must treat with Philotas who would make you content? It is through his sponsorship that we have risen to our current rank in your fellowship. He stood so high in your estimation that we needed both to curry his favour and to fear his vexation. If not quite in your own words, have we not all recited the oath you have dictated that we should share as friends and foes the same such men as you propose? Bound by this pledge of loyalty, could we really turn against him whom you promoted above everybody? Hence if this is an offence, you have few men who can claim innocence. By Heracles! None in fact has any defence. For all coveted the friendship of Philotas, although not all who wished it could have it come to pass. Thus, if you do not distinguish between his accomplices and his companions, neither will you separate his associates from those that have sought such associations."

7.83 "So what evidence is offered that we were in the know? I suppose, it's that he had a cosey conversation with us on the preceding day without being overheard. Yet I'd be unable to exculpate myself, if on that day my lifestyle or habits had altered. So in fact, as we behaved the same way as on every other day upon that day in question, our adherence to routine relieves us of suspicion."

7.84 "Be that as it may, we did not hand over our horses to Antiphanes, and this just the day before Philotas's exposure. This shall be a case between Antiphanes and me. If he wished to incriminate us, because we did not

---

[42] This appears to be a reference to the Greek habit of self-disfigurement to express severe mourning or mortification – an example would be Alexander scratching his own face after killing Cleitus: see Section 9.12 below and Curtius 8.2.5.

surrender our steeds that day, he himself cannot evade suspicion, since it was just then that he wished to take them away. Indeed it is ambiguous where the blame lies between the gripper and the grabber, except that his cause is nobler who hangs on to his own than his who would claim what is owned by another. As it happens, Sire, I had ten horses, out of which Antiphanes had already allocated eight to those who were bereft of theirs, so that two were all I had left. When this most insolent man - at any rate the most unjust - sought to commandeer these last, unless I were willing to fight on foot, I had to hold fast. I'll not deny that I spoke in the spirit of a free man addressing one of the most craven and a person who possesses the sole military role of assigning the steeds of others to fighting men. We are quite beset by adversities, when I must simultaneously excuse my words to Alexander and to Antiphanes!"

7.85 "But, by Heracles, your mother has denounced us in her letters as your enemies. Would that more prudence had tempered her fretting for her son and that her troubled mind had not evoked vague fantasies. Why indeed does she not impart the reason for her unease? And, finally, why does she not reveal her source? What deeds or words of ours prompted her to pen you such a fearful discourse? How dire a dilemma confronts me, since perchance it is less risky to hold my tongue than to speak plainly. But whatever the outcome may be, I would rather that my defence should displease you than have you doubt my fidelity. You yourself will confirm what I am going to relate, since you will recall that, when you sent me to fetch forces from Macedonia, you did intimate that there were many fit young fellows who were hidden on your mother's estate. Hence you instructed that I should pay heed to none save you, but rather bring to you those shirking soldiering service. Which is exactly what I did, executing your command with more willingness than was in my best interest. Thence I recruited Gorgias, Hecataeus and Gorgatas, who have been serving you with success. What, therefore, could be more unjust than that I, who would justly have been punished had your orders been betrayed, should now die for having obeyed. For the only cause your mother has for spiting us is that we favoured your acquisition over a woman's appreciation. I led hither six thousand Macedonian infantry and six hundred cavalry, some section of whom would not have followed me, had I been willing to collude with those who fought shy of service in the military. Therefore, since it is on this account that we are objects of her rancour, it follows that you should mollify your mother, since it is you who have exposed us to her anger."

7.86 Whilst Amyntas was stating his case, there chanced to arrive those who had given chase to his brother, Polemon, who having fled, as has been said, they were bringing back in shackles. Their hackles raised, the seething assembly could scarcely be restrained from instantly stoning him to death, as was ordained by custom *in such cases*. But he, entirely unterrified, said: "I do not ask forgiveness for myself, but beg only that the innocence of my brothers should not be impugned by my desertion. If this be deemed indefensible, mine is the culpability. Their own cause is actually the better for the fact that my flight

Book 7: July 330BC – June 329BC

diverts suspicion onto me personally." Yet by these words he won the approbation of the entire assembly. All were moved to shed a tear and they were so abruptly converted in their estimation that what had most undermined him became his sole source of salvation. He was a youth in the first flower of adolescence, who, when the cavalry was rattled by the torture of Philotas, had been carried away by others' consternation. Forsaken by his comrades and wavering between his options of desertion or reversion, he had been overtaken by his pursuers. Now he began to wail and thrash his face, not distressed for his own sake, but on behalf of his brothers, whose jeopardy was of his making. By this point he was also garnering the king's compassion, as well as the assembly's sympathy, but his brother alone was implacable and, glaring at him menacingly, he exclaimed: "When you spurred your steed in flight, cretin, that was the time that tears were due as the deserter of your brothers and the sidekick of deserters too. Whither did you think you'd flee and whom were you evading, villain? You have laid a capital charge against me on behalf of the prosecution."

7.87 Polemon lamented that he had let himself down, but repented that he had betrayed his brothers even more grievously. Then indeed those at the assembly neither withheld their tears nor the acclamations whereby such crowds express their favour. With one voice they collectively called upon the king to pardon these blameless and valiant fellows. Being afforded an opportunity to be merciful, his Friends too welled up as one and weepingly besought their acquittal. Having hushed them, Alexander announced: "I myself share the view that Amyntas and his brothers should be acquitted. To these young men I say that I would rather that they obliterate the memory of this kindness than ruminate upon their jeopardy. Amyntas, let you and your brothers favour me with the same loyalty with which I return you to favour with me. Failing having confronted you with these accusations, my furtiveness might have festered foetidly. It is better that you are vindicated than treated suspiciously. Be mindful that no one can be acquitted unless he states his case judicially. Now let you, Amyntas, pardon your brother, which shall also signify that you are unreservedly reconciled with me."

7.88 Thereafter **the king** dismissed the assembly and **bade that Polydamas be called.** He was by far the most familiar of Parmenion's associates, customarily fighting beside him in battle. And despite counting on his clear conscience in coming to the king's quarters, his assurance switched to nervousness and he began to fret when he was bidden to present his brothers, who, being juveniles, were as yet unfamiliar to the king on account of their age. He became more fixated by what could tarnish their good name than how they would shield themselves from such shame. By now the guards, who had been detailed to bring his brothers, were leading them forward, and Alexander, whilst waving everyone else away, ordered Polydamas, pale with apprehension, to draw nearer in order **to say:** "We have all equally been targets for the treachery of Parmenion, but especially you and I, whom he duped by masquerading as our companion. But see how much I trust in your loyalty: I have arranged to employ your services to **seek Parmenion out and impose our penalty.** Your brothers shall serve as surety, whilst you discharge this duty. You shall leave for Media carrying letters written by my own hand to my prefects there. **Speed is of the essence, so as to outrun rumour.** I wish you to reach the place at night and to implement what is written the next day. You shall also bear letters for Parmenion: one from me and the other written in the guise of his son. I have at my disposal his signet ring. If his father thinks the letter was sealed by Philotas, when he sees you, he will suspect nothing."

7.89 Freed from his frightful fretting, Polydamas promised his best efforts even more vehemently than they had been requested. Lauded and laden with reciprocal promises, he adopted Arab dress, his own being divested. **Arab guides,** whose wives and offspring were kept by the king to bind their loyalty, **were assigned as his company. They attained their destination on the eleventh day by riding racing camels across waterless desert territory**, *a journey of thirty or forty days normally.*[43] Ere his arrival were heralded Polydamas resumed his Macedonian attire and got to the pavilion of Cleander, one of the king's commanders, in the fourth watch *of the night*.[44] His letter being delivered, they arranged that they would go in company to Parmenion at first light, since Polydamas had brought royal mail for the rest as well. They were about to visit Parmenion, when he heard tell of the arrival of Polydamas. Whilst gratified to be able to greet his friend, he was simultaneously keen to learn what the king might intend, since he had received no message from him for a lengthy interlude, so he bade that the whereabouts of Polydamas be pursued.

7.90 The lodges in that land possess picturesque parks with grandiose groves planted by hand, which were the particular pleasure of their satraps and kings. Parmenion was pacing about in one such grove amidst those officers, who had been commanded to kill him by the king's written orders. They had scheduled the deed to be done during the time when he had begun to read the letters that Polydamas had brought. Parmenion perceived the approach of Polydamas from afar, scurrying forward to embrace him, his countenance portraying some semblance of delight. After they had greeted one another, Polydamas delivered to him the letter written by the king. Whilst fiddling with its fastening, Parmenion asked what things the king was doing? Polydamas responded that through the letter itself he would learn everything. On perusing it, Parmenion commented: "The king is readying a campaign against the Arachosii. Such a forceful fellow and quite unrelenting! But it is time he spared himself for the sake of his wellbeing, having already gleaned so much glory." Next he read the

---

[43] The distance from Prophthasia (Farah) to Ecbatana (Hamadan) is around 600 miles, so the rate of travel would have been in excess of 60 miles per day, which is just barely feasible on camels. Strabo 15.2.10 points out that it should normally have taken thirty to forty days to make this journey.

[44] Probably a few hours before dawn, as the Greeks usually divided the night into four watches.

Book 7: July 330BC – June 329BC

Figure 7.3. The assassination of Parmenion (from a French translation of Curtius by de Vaugelas, 1696)

other letter, ghostwritten in the name of Philotas, with obvious pleasure as could be judged from his expression.[45] At this Cleander cleaved his sword into his side, then slashed his throat and the rest also stabbed him, though he had already died.

7.91 But the guards stationed at the entrance to the grove became aware of the killing and, being ignorant of its cause, they reached the camp and roused the troops to riot with their riveting reports. The soldiers seized their arms and marched en masse to the grove where the killing had occurred, threatening that, unless Polydamas and his accomplices in the crime were surrendered, they would demolish its encompassing wall and expiate the liquidation of their leader with the blood of all. Cleander commanded that the chief men among these troops be admitted and read aloud a letter to them from the king's own hand, in which were combined an account of Parmenion's machinations against Alexander with the king's invocations for vengeance to be planned. Consequently, recognizing the king's intent, their mutiny was suppressed, though not their sense of discontent. Though many of them drifted away, a few sought to stay, begging that they might be permitted to bury the body of Parmenion anyway. Warrant was withheld for a long while, on account of Cleander's anxiety not to offend the king. Then, when they pleaded more vehemently, reckoning that reasons for insurrection should be removed, Cleander consented to their interring the decapitated corpse, its head being conveyed to the king.

7.92 Thus Parmenion perished by assassination, having been an outstanding stalwart *of the regime* in war and peace. He had accomplished much without the king, whereas the king had achieved nothing significant without him. He ably served a most successful sovereign, who insisted that everything should match up to his own exalted condition. In his seventieth year he still discharged the duties of a youthful officer and often even those of a common trooper. A skilful strategist and forceful fighter, he was popular with his officers and even more so among the lower ranks of his soldiers. Whether this popularity impelled him to covet the kingship or simply subjected him to such suspicions may be deemed unresolved, since it was uncertain, even when the affair was fresh and could more readily have been clarified, whether Philotas, broken by dire excruciation, spoke the truth about things that could not be verified or sought the termination of his torment through fabrication.

7.93 Alexander had learnt that some among the Macedonians had openly deplored the death of Parmenion *and had made malign remarks about him*, moaning that he had disowned the legacy of his father, Philip, and the customs of his country. **Reckoning that these should be separated from the rest of his**

---

[45] Although it is not explicitly stated, there is a strong implication that the letter seeming to come from Philotas contained some treasonous message and that the officers had been alerted to watch Parmenion's reaction as he read it. This would be why they awaited its reading before killing him.

Book 7: July 330BC – June 329BC

forces, he sequestered them into a single company, which he called the Disorderly Division, *setting it under the leadership of Leonidas, who was himself a former close colleague of Parmenion*. This was more or less made up from those of whom the king had for various reasons formed a low opinion. *Alexander was concerned particularly that their criticism might be promulgated even unto Macedonia, sullying his glorious conquests with the stain of tyranny.* **Wanting to test attitudes among the troops, he alerted those who had penned letters to their loved ones in Macedonia to tender them to men he was sending back** *from among his Friends*, **who would faithfully convey them thither.** *He warned that such opportunities would diminish as they went on further.* **They had written frankly to their relatives revealing their true feelings. Most were willing warriors, but some considered their soldiering service onerous.** Thus their sovereign *secretly* secured sight of the sentiments of *both the gratified and* the aggrieved *among the correspondents.* **So the men who happened to have complained of weariness with the campaigning in their letters were ordered as a company to pitch their tents apart from the rest** *on account of their ignominy. Alexander would exploit their boldness in battle, whilst* **isolating their loose tongues from the ears of the gullible.** *He planned to dispose of them either by the attrition of the campaign or by settling them as colonists in some distant domain.* This stratagem, though it might have appeared rash in that the bravest of young men were nettled by its slur, like everything else, the king's fortune caused to prosper. For none proved more dashing in war than these fellows. It was from a desire to diminish their disgrace that their valour arose and because small numbers necessarily expose bravery.

7.94 Having dealt with these matters and settled the situation among the Drangians *by appointing Arsaces*[46] *as their satrap,* Alexander bade that a march be made against the people once known as the Arimaspians, but now called the Euergetae.[47] They were renamed on account of that Cyrus, who propelled the primacy of the Medes into the hands of the Persians. For he was once warring in the wastes, where his warriors were worn out for want of warmth and rations, so that they were resorting to cannibalism in their desperation. Whereupon the Arimaspians manifested themselves with thirty thousand wagons weighed down with provisions. Preserved from perdition, Cyrus granted them exemption from taxation together with other tokens of his recognition and, spurning their previous appellation, preferred to know them as his Benefactors. Likewise, when Alexander led his columns into their country, they received him hospitably. *On the fifth day after he had arrived in that*

---

[46] The name/region is corrupted (*arianiorum*) at Curtius 7.3.1, but Arsames (*arsami*) is replaced by *tamsonor* (Stasanor?) as governor of the *dramearum* (Drangarum?) at Curtius 8.3.17; however, this is likely to be a mistake for Arsaces, who was also Satrap of Aria (Arrian, *Anabasis* 3.25.7 & 4.7.1).

[47] Which translates literally as the "Benefactors".

region, he discovered that Satibarzanes, who had defected to Bessus, had surged back into Aria with a colossal corps of cavalry, renewing the revolt among its populace. Therefore the king dispatched a task force against him under Erigyius *and Caranus supported by Stasanor, Artabazus and Andronicus. They led contingents of six thousand Greek infantry and six hundred cavalry. He himself devised government for the Euergetae in the space of sixty days and showered his funds upon them, since their superb service to Cyrus had earned his praise.* Alexander founded a town in their territory on the route into India, which he named Alexandria.[48] *He left Amedines, who had been the Darius' secretary, to preside over them. Their neighbours, the Kedrosians, also proffered the king their fealty, so they too were rewarded with fitting generosity. Tiridates was made the marshal over both of these peaceable peoples.*

7.95 Thereafter, *in a few days,* **Alexander subdued the Arachosii,** *whose territory extends to the* River Indus.[49] The army that had been commanded by Parmenion caught up with him in Arachosia. It comprised six thousand Macedonians and two hundred knights; and five thousand Greeks with six hundred cavalry. They were without doubt the cream of all the king's chivalry. Menon was made governor of the Arachosii and a garrison of four thousand infantry and six hundred cavalry were left with him.

7.96 The king himself with his army invaded a nation not well known even to its neighbours, since it had no commerce to cultivate communion. They are called the Paropamisadae, a rude race of men, benighted even among the barbarians, the harshness of their habitat having hardened the habits of its inhabitants. Most of their landscape faces into the very wintry northern celestial pole, so it is snow-clad and inaccessible due to the cold. Westwards it borders on Bactria and to the south it verges upon the Indian Ocean. They construct their cottages with brick from their bases, but since their territory is timberless, even the lee of the mountains being bare, they extrapolate the same brickwork to the crest of each lair. That is to say, their build is broader at the base and gradually grows narrower as the structures rise, meeting much like ship's keels at the crests, where central apertures are left to vent smoke and let in light from the skies. *These homes afford sufficient shelter to those that reside in that land, being walled on every side to withstand the weather, since deep snow keeps them indoors most of the year with their stores at hand.* Those vines and trees that are able to survive in such icily

---

[48] Possibly this records the foundation of Kandahar, since *Metz Epitome* 4 is clear that it was within the Arimaspian territory.

[49] The manuscripts of Curtius 7.3.4 read *ponticum mare* meaning the Black Sea, which is complete nonsense. It is clear from Strabo 11.10.1 that ancient geographers asserted that Arachosia extended to the River Indus (cf. Curtius 8.13.3, 9.7.14 & 9.10.7). The inference must be that the Greek word for a river (*potamos*) has somehow been corrupted to give Pontic in the Latin.

solid soil, they heap up earth around leaving them buried throughout the winter and restoring them to air and sunlight only when the thaw begins to free the ground. Indeed the snow lies so deep across this land, which a perpetual hard frost keeps fast bound, that not even traces of birds and beasts are anywhere to be found. The overcast skies, like dusk, more truly shade than light a concealed landscape, where even the foreground almost slips out of sight. *Marooned amidst this solitude, then devoid of human activity,* the army endured *every evil that it is possible bear, including scarcity of supplies, perishing cold,* exhaustion *and despair. Being unaccustomed to the numbing paralysis of drifts, many were frozen to death, whilst many others got frostbitten feet and* an enormous number suffered snow-blindness, due to the glare of the snow and the harsh radiance of the reflected glow. It was particularly pernicious for those that were flagging, *for, when they collapsed, they splayed themselves upon the very ice and when they had ceased to move, the power of the cold so paralysed them that when they tried once more to rise they found themselves immobilized. But their comrades shook them from their torpor, since there was no other remedy but to be made to march on. Only then did any energy return to their limbs, when the warmth of exertion came on.*

7.97 *Those Macedonians that managed to reach the cottages of the natives were rapidly revived, but* the murk was so dense that the only feature that revealed the presence of the buildings was their smoke, even when they were stood upon them, *since they were steeped in a snowy cloak. The inhabitants had never before seen outsiders in their territory, so when armed men suddenly hove into sight, being breathless with fright, they proffered aught that they had in their habitations, beseeching the Macedonians to spare their persons. The king did the rounds of his columns on foot, setting some on their feet that he found lying and saving others that were struggling to keep up from dying by bearing them up with his own body. At one moment appearing in the van, in another at the center or tail of the column, he compounded his personal exertion. But eventually they reached more cultivated regions with ample supplies, whereby the army was revamped and at the same time the stragglers arrived where they were encamped. Soon the king had stamped his authority upon that nation.*

7.98 Thereafter the army advanced into the Caucasus Mountains, *a continuous chain of ranges that divides Asia, among those particular ridges* that some call **Mount Paropamisus.** The sea lapping Cilicia, the Caspian Sea and the River Araxes[50] together with the wastes of Scythia are all likewise

---

[50] Probably the modern River Aras with its headwaters in Armenia and emptying into the Caspian Sea.

overlooked by this Caucasus. The Taurus Mountains rise up in Cappadocia, skirt Cilicia and merge into the mountains of Armenia, meeting up with the Caucasus, though they are lesser in size. Thus interconnected these ranges are arranged in an uninterrupted chain, from which almost all the rivers of Asia arise and empty into the Pontic or else the Caspian or Hyrcanian or else the Red Sea. **In the midst of that range there is a rock ten stades around and four in height, on which the natives denoted a cave as the immemorial site of the chaining of Prometheus** *as well as the eyrie of the eagle and the furrows of the fetters as in the fable.* **Alexander selected a location for founding a city** *at the foot of the range on the side of the pass that leads down into India.*[51] *The king also created additional settlements within a day's march of this city. Seven thousand natives, three thousand from the army's retinue and volunteers from among the mercenary soldiers unfit for active service the king consented to settle in the new foundations, the chief of which was named* by its inhabitants *Alexandria.*[52] **Then he advanced his forces towards Bactria, since he received word of enrolment of an army and assumption of the diadem by Bessus. By the sixteenth day thereafter the army had traversed the width of the Caucasus.**[53]

7.99 These were the concerns of Alexander *in the seventh year of his reign.*

---

[51] The manuscripts of Diodorus 17.83.1 read *Media*, which must be an error. According to Strabo 15.2.10, the city was on the Indian side of the mountains, where Alexander wintered in 330-29BC.

[52] Alexandria-in-the-Caucasus: Arrian, *Anabasis* 3.28.4; Strabo 15.2.10.

[53] Strabo 15.2.10 has 15 days, Diodorus 17.83.1 has 16 days and Curtius 7.3.21 has 17 days.

4. Book 8: July 329BC – Autumn 328BC

Alexander's Advance to the River Oxus; Bessus Betrayed to Alexander; The Fate of the Branchidae; Alexander Wounded near Maracanda; The Revolt of Spitamenes; Alexander's Advance to the River Tanais; Annihilation of a Macedonian Column by Spitamenes and Alexander's Counterattacks; Capture of the Rock of Ariamazes

KEY
<u>**Underlined bold text for attributed Fragments of Cleitarchus**</u>
Bold text where there is overwhelming evidence
Bold italic text where there exists direct-firm evidence
Normal text where direct-weak evidence applies
Italic text where the evidence is conjectural
Grey text for connecting passages, if Cleitarchus' version is indeterminate

8.1 *At the beginning of the eighth year of Alexander's reign,* **Bessus had had it heralded that he had become the king.** ***Being absolutely alarmed by Alexander's dynamism*** **and having performed the sacrificial rites for the gods of his fatherland in accordance with the customs of his countrymen, he was consulting with his comrades and the commanders of his contingents concerning the conflict in the context of a banquet.** ***Well the worse for wine, they began to boast about their own potency and duly to disdain the audacity and then the paucity of their opponents. Above all, having become so conceited by a sovereignty won through wickedness as hardly to have kept his head, Bessus began with wilful words to denounce the indolence of Darius. This had fuelled the fame of their foes, for he had happened upon them in the most constricted confines of Cilicia, when a withdrawal would have drawn them unwarily into naturally defensible sites, where divers rivers ran across their route and there were so many crannies amidst the crags from which the ambushed enemy could not even have escaped, let alone opposed, their opponents.***

8.2 ***It would please Bessus to retire towards Sogdiana. By way of a wall he would waylay their foes with the Oxus River, whilst hefty reinforcements*** were mustered from the neighbouring nations. The Chorasmii would come as well as the Dahae & Sacae, the Indians and such of the Scythians as were settled on the far side of the Tanais River.[1] Not a man among these was so short that his shoulders were not at least level with the scalp of a Macedonian man-at-arms! His sozzled supporters yelled in unison that this was their sole sane strategy and Bessus bade that yet more pure wine be poured out for them as he devised the defeat of Alexander upon his dining table.

8.3 Among the men at that meal there was a Mede named Bagodaras.[2] Though he meddled in magic arts (if indeed they are arts and not the shams of the sharpest shysters), he was more famous for his pretentions than his expertise, yet otherwise honest and mild-mannered. He introduced himself with the observation that he knew it to be more sensible for a servant to follow orders than to offer advice, since followers suffer no worse a fate than their fellows, whereas advisors particularly imperil their own persons. *But* **Bessus** *advised him that he should make his counsel clear and* even handed him the goblet in his own grip.[3] On accepting it Bagodaras began to speak: "It is in the nature of mortals that they may be called capricious and contrary on this account also, that each of them is less effective in furthering his own affairs than in handling those of others. Those who advise themselves devise deranged designs. They are driven by dread, else distracted by desire or sometimes by a natural fondness for their own fancies, actual arrogance being unconscionable in your case, Sire. Your background leads you to believe at least that what you have yourself devised is either the only or the optimum approach. You bear a heavy burden upon your head, the symbol of sovereignty, which must be upheld with restraint, lest - may the fates forfend! - it should cause you to be crushed. Thus there is need for due deliberation instead of an instinctive stampede." Then he appended proverbs in common use among the Bactrians: that a cringing cur barks more vigorously than it bites and that the deepest rivers run least raucously.

8.4 By these words Bagodaras had his hearers holding their breath and thereupon he unveiled his advice, which was beneficial for Bessus rather more than gratifying to him: "Upon the doorstep of your domains stands a most dashing king, who will fling his forces against you whilst you are still stowing that table. So now you would summon up an army from the Tanais and parry his arms with rivers. Obviously, you are fearless of your foe following wheresoever you may go, though the course is common to

---

[1] The Tanais is the Cleitarchan name for the ancient Jaxartes, identical with the modern River Syr-Darya: this stems from geographical confusion with the River Don (the Tanais proper).

[2] Bagodaras in the manuscripts of Diodorus, but Cobares in Curtius.

[3] Possession of the goblet symbolized that he had formally taken the floor.

Book 8: July 329BC – Autumn 328BC

you both, yet more secure for the conqueror. Though you may deem that dread drives hard, hope is yet hastier. Why not ingratiate yourself with the greater power by devoting yourself to his cause? For, however affairs fall out, your fortunes shall fare more favourably as his devotee rather than as his enemy. A realm you have reaped from another may be relinquished all the more readily. Perchance you would arise as a rightful ruler, when he himself had raised you up, who can either confer a kingdom upon you or wrest your realm away. You have heard out devout advice that it would be vain to belabour at more length. A pure breed of steed is steered sheerly by the shadow of the lash, but even the spur cannot stir a mount of trash."

8.5 Bessus, being bilious both by temperament and intoxication, came so close to boiling over that he was barely held back from butchering Bagodaras by his friends, since he had already unsheathed his sabre. At any rate he burst forth from the banquet beside himself with rage, whilst Bagodaras slipped away under cover of the confusion and swathed by night to switch his allegiance to Alexander. *The sanctuary that he received and Alexander's promises of presents were a temptation to the topmost captains of Bessus's battalions.*

8.6 Bessus had eight thousand Bactrians under arms. So long as they imagined the Macedonians would be moved to head for India instead by the wildness of their weather, they obeyed Bessus's bidding. But once they were wise to Alexander's approach, they vanished into their various villages, thus abandoning their boss. With a handful of his adherents whose loyalty had not lapsed, he got across the Oxus River, burning his boats to forestall their ferrying his foes. Then he sought to assemble substitute soldiers among the Sogdians.

8.7 Actually, Alexander had already clambered across the Caucasus, as related earlier, though he had come close to starvation through scarcity of grain. They barely kept *their gullets* greased with the sap squeezed from sesame as an inferior form of oil, but each amphora of this juice cost two hundred and forty drachmae, whilst each such jar of honey fetched three hundred and ninety drachmae and three hundred was charged for an amphora of wine. Little or no wheat was winkled out, for the barbarians keep caches that they call "siri", which they cunningly camouflage in such a way that none save those that dug them can discover them. Hence in these their harvests stayed hidden away. Faced with such famine, the soldiers subsisted on freshwater fish and greens. But when even these provisions were vanishing, they were commanded to kill the beasts of burden that carried their encumbrances. They eked out their existence on this meat until they met with the Bactrians.

8.8 The territory of the Bactrians has many and motley natures. One area is thick with trees and vines that nurture an abundance of soft fruits with widespread springs drenching the rich soil. They sow their grain in the more sheltered spots and the rest they render up to the foraging of their flocks.

Beyond, a great stretch of the same land is taken up by desert sand. By dint of its dreadful dryness this region does not nurture either men or agriculture. When indeed the wind whistles in from the Pontic Sea, it sifts what sand is strewn about the land into dunes, which, when fully formed, appear from afar like huge hills, obliterating all trace of former tracks.[4] Hence, those that transit these tracts study the stars by night, on which they base the bearing of their course in the mode of mariners. Thus the shade of night comes close to being clearer than the day's light. Therefore they find those parts impassable during the days, since they lack a lead from any landmarks and the lustre of the stars is hidden in haze. Furthermore, if any be engulfed by a gale sprung in off the sea, then the sands smother them utterly. Yet, where the land is lusher, it accounts for a multitude of men and mounts. Therefore the host of the Bactrian horse formed a thirty thousand strong force. Bactra itself, the regional capital, sits beneath Paropamisus' mountain wall. The Bactrus River, which runs past its ramparts, gave its name to the city and surrounding parts.

8.9 Whilst Alexander was sojourning at Bactra news was announced from Greece regarding the revolt of the Peloponnesians and the Spartans[5] *(for they had not yet been decisively defeated, when those who were to announce the outbreak of that insurrection had set forth.)* And another cause for alarm was heralded to be at hand: that the Scythians that subsisted beyond the Tanais were on their way to bolster Bessus' band. **In the same period the accomplishments of Caranus and Erigyius in the region of the Arians were reported. The Macedonians had fought a battle with the Arians, in which the turncoat Satibarzanes had been the boss of the barbarians, since he was striking in his strategic virtuosity and valour. The Macedonians had encamped close to their foes, so that there arose repeated scattered skirmishes for a time with a multitude of tiny tussles. Then their full formations were engaged and became deadlocked in stalemate. Stirred by this state of affairs, Satibarzanes rode into his front ranks, raised his hands and removed his helmet so as to be recognized. After staying his missile chuckers, he challenged any Macedonian captain who cared to contest the outcome to duel with him in single combat, adding that he would give battle bareheaded.**

---

[4] The view that Bactria lay just to the east of the Pontic Sea (the Cleitarchan name for the Euxine, the modern Black Sea) is a Cleitarchan misunderstanding of the geography, which is also reflected in his concept that the Syr-Darya river was the Tanais (see note in Section 8.2); Alexander was actually >1000km east of even the Caspian Sea.

[5] This may indicate the arrival of the Spartan envoys/hostages, whose departure from Greece had been delayed until the summer of 330BC (Aischines 3.133). It is scarcely credible that Alexander was still unaware of Antipater's triumph over Agis at the Battle of Megalopolis some two years after it took place. However, Megalopolis may not have been recognized at the time as the end of hostilities, since this passage seems to be saying that the envoys who had announced it to Alexander had not been able to confirm that the Macedonians had won the whole war.

Book 8: July 329BC – Autumn 328BC

8.10 Erigyius could not tolerate the taunting of the barbarians' boss. Though virtually of venerable age, he would not be believed less robust in body and spirit than any of the youths. Doffing his helm to bare his greying hair, he declared: "The day has dawned for me to demonstrate either by predominating or else most dauntlessly dying just what sort of soldiers and friends Alexander possesses!" Then without additional eloquence, he steered his steed towards his opponent's, so a courageous contest could commence. *The impression given was that both battle-lines had been bidden to sheathe their weapons, for they fell back at once, forming a free space. They were fixated upon a fight that would not only allot their leaders' fates, but their own as well, since they too must fall who followed whichever of them fell. The barbarian began by launching his lance, which Erigyius dodged by a slight nod of his head, and then spurring his steed he sped his sarissa straight through the throat of his foe, so that it poked out of the nape of his neck. Though he hurtled from his horse, still the barbarian battled on. But having levered his lance out of the wound, Erigyius aimed it again into the face of his foe. Then Satibarzanes seized it in his grasp so as to speed his last gasp by guiding his enemy's blow.*

8.11 *The woebegone barbarians, being bereft of their boss, whom they had backed more out of kinship than for his own sake, and even then not unmindful of the rewards from Alexander, ceded themselves to Erigyius to seek their safety in surrender.* Whilst rejoicing in this success, the king, though not at all flippant concerning the Spartans, yet tolerated their revolt with magnanimity, saying that they did not dare to lay bare their designs until they knew him to have reached the rim of India.[6] Then he mobilized his men in pursuit of Bessus and was met on the way by Erigyius exhibiting the head of the barbarian as his spectacular spoil from the fray.

8.12 Accordingly, having entrusted the Bactrian tracts to Artabazus, **Alexander** left the luggage and the baggage there with a garrison. He himself **entered the desert spaces of Sogdiana** with a disencumbered contingent and he led this force forward by night marches. The aforementioned want of water fires a thirst, firstly through despair of its relief, even ere men are actually driven to drink. For four hundred stades not the merest modicum of moisture emerges. The searing summer sun incinerates the sands and when they are simmering, it

---

[6] This is not the outrageous anachronism that it might seem, because in Cleitarchan geography India began in southern Afghanistan in the region of the Helmand River, where Alexander had been during the previous year (cf. Curtius 8.9.10, who mentions the River Ethymantus, which seems to mean the Helmand, as being part of India). Some modern translations have interpreted this passage as Alexander being "not free of anxiety" about the Spartan revolt, but he must at this point have known that it had ended, so it is more apt that Curtius/Cleitarchus was defending him against a charge of flippancy. That such flippancy was an issue is shown by Plutarch, *Agesilaus* 15, where Alexander says of the Battle of Megalopolis: "It seems, my friends, that while we have been conquering Darius here, there has been a battle of mice in Arcadia."

is as though everything is cooked by a continuous conflagration. Thereupon, a haze evoked by the vicious heat of the terrain distorts the daylight, so that in vision the plain has a vast and boundless sheen like an ocean main.[7]

8.13 They noticed that nocturnal travel was tolerable; due to the dew and dawn chill recharging their bodies. But with the radiance itself the roasting resumed and their very saliva was sapped as they marched, so that their mouths and innards grew greatly parched. Consequently, firstly their verve and then their vigour began to flag: it perturbed them either to push on or to lag. A few, forewarned by those familiar with this land, had furnished themselves with water beforehand, which for a while withheld their thirst, but then their wish for wetness was rekindled when the heat reached its worst. Therefore, whatever wine and oil there was about was for each and all poured out and they were so besotted by this booze that their fear of thirst they were later to lose. After wine enough to be well the worse for wear, their arms were more than they could bear nor could they press on anywhere. Thus it was they came to think that they were happier who had had no drink, when those who had drunk without refraining were forced to spew forth all they were retaining.

8.14 Beset by such blights an anxious Alexander was encircled by his Friends, who begged him to bear in mind that his inspirational spirit was the sole succour for the failings of his forces. Thereupon, he was met by two scouts, who had gone ahead to select a site for the camp. They were lugging skins of water to support their sons, who were serving in the same sections and were understood to be suffering severe hardship from the shortage. When they came across Alexander, one of them unbound one of the bladders, filled a cup he was carrying and proffered it to the king. In accepting it, his sovereign asked for whom he had brought the water and discovered that he was carrying it for his sons. Then returning the brimming beaker, just as it had been handed to him, Alexander declared: *"Lest I pain my companions,* I cannot bear to drink alone and neither can I share such a trickle among all. So chivy along to your children and hand over to them what you have hefted for their sakes."[8]

---

[7] Anyone who feels that the Cleitarchan descriptions of the terrain are vague or exaggerated would do well to examine the route between Bactra (modern Balkh at Google coordinates 36.768352,66.901674) and the River Oxus (modern Amu-Darya at Google coordinates 37.359242,66.869316) on Google Maps in the Satellite images view. The overall distance is about 70km corresponding closely to the 400 stades mentioned by Cleitarchus. The last 30km just south of the river is a band of enormous dunes, some of them 100's of metres long and therefore tens of metres tall. On their leeward edge they would have been too steep to be negotiated by men in armour or carrying heavy packs, which would have compelled them to wend a winding course. Progress would have been terribly slow and the place a great trial for men on foot.

[8] A similar story is told by Arrian, *Anabasis* 6.26.1-3, in the context of the Kedrosian march, though he concedes that some accounts had placed it earlier in the general vicinity of the Paropamisus. However, Cleitarchus seems to have attributed the Kedrosian disaster to a shortage of food rather than lack of water, stressing that wells had been dug in advance along the army's route. It may be that Alexander regularly made a point of refusing water, if his men had to go

Book 8: July 329BC – Autumn 328BC

EXERCITVS ALEXANDRI PENVRIA AQVARVM LABORANS LIBERATVR.

Figure 8.1. Alexander refuses a drink, whilst his army suffers from lack of water (from a 1696 edition of Curtius)

8.15 *Eventually, the king reached the River Oxus* at around dusk, but the greater part of the army had not managed to keep up with him. Hence he bade that beacon fires be lit upon a crag, so that those struggling to follow should know that they were not far from his camp. Those in the foremost formations being rapidly restored by food and drink, he had some of them fill skins and others any vessels to hand that could hold water in order to carry aid to their comrades. *But those troops that drank too drastically choked and gave up the ghost in numbers that far exceeded the king's casualties in any conflict.*[9] As for Alexander himself, he stood, still encased in his cuirass and having tasted neither food nor drink, waiting beside the way by which his soldiers straggled in. Nor did he stand himself down to pander to his own

---

without: Plutarch, *Alexander* 42.3-6, has him do so during the pursuit of Darius, although his otherwise resembles the Cleitarchan version in Curtius 7.5.9-12. Frontinus, *Stratagemata* 1.7.7, even places such an incident in Africa, but perhaps he was following Trogus and mistook the location.

[9] The circumstances were a classic case history for death through hyponatremia (loss of body salt) and "water intoxication". It is seriously dangerous to drink too much fresh water after severe, sweaty exercise, because the consequential sudden dilution of body salts can cause cells to swell, leading to death through seizures and coma. Such overindulgence is common, since there is a lag between the physical act of drinking and the psychological alleviation of thirst.

person until his entire force had passed before him. And he spent that whole night in sleeplessness with his mind in a mighty turmoil.

8.16 Nor was Alexander less dour the next day, since he lacked any launches and neither could a bridge be erected, by reason of the area around the river being bare and utterly devoid of timber. Therefore he implemented the only plan that could be devised to meet his need. He distributed a great many skins stuffed with straw so that reclining upon these they could paddle their way across the river with the vanguard standing guard whilst the rest came over.[10] Eventually, by the sixth day he had been able to convey his whole host across to the opposite side.

8.17 At this point Alexander had resolved to continue to prosecute the pursuit of Bessus, when he heard what had occurred in Sogdiana. **Bessus held Spitamenes in the highest honour relative to the rest of his comrades, but treachery cannot be traded away by any manner of meed,** *though it could be deemed less damnable in his case, since it seemed that no sinful deed could be done against Bessus, the murderer of his monarch.* **And so Spitamenes vaunted the avenging of Darius as a** *meretricious* **motive for betraying his lord,** *but it was Bessus's ascendancy rather than his villainy that he truly abhorred.* **Prompted by the news that Alexander had crossed the River Oxus, Spitamenes invited Dataphernes and Catanes,** *in whose lasting loyalty Bessus believed,* **to be his accomplices in the plot he had conceived.**

8.18 *To these and others who had been close to Darius he declared that the time had come to curry Alexander's favour by seizing Bessus and surrendering him as soon as they could to the king. They were no sooner told than enrolled, since day by day their desire to have Darius back grew, as an abomination of Bessus took hold. Rallying eight of their lustiest lads, they duly deployed a devious deception. Spitamenes went to Bessus and asked that the guards should leave, then in strict privacy averred that he had discovered that Dataphernes and Catanes had conspired to hand him over alive to Alexander. He, however, had forestalled their fickleness by fastening them in fetters.*

8.19 Bessus, *being obliged by such a superb service as he supposed it to be, was both thoroughly thankful and passionately impatient for their*

---

[10] The use of such floats in crossing rivers was a standard tactic in Alexander's repertoire: Arrian, *Anabasis* 1.3.6, has him filling the leather tent covers with hay in order to cross the Ister (Danube) in 335BC. The straw/hay was necessary, because the skin bags could not be made completely airtight and so would have collapsed under the pressure of their load in the absence of stuffing. Furthermore, the hollow cores of the strands would have retained air, even if the skins became partially waterlogged. The floats were necessary not merely as buoyancy aids, but in order to get the soldiers' armour and baggage across. For this purpose and also because Curtius literally has the troops resting athwart them, they must have been quite large – perhaps half a cubic metre or more in volume.

punishment, so he bade that they be brought before him. *Their collaborators in the conspiracy then dragged them in with their arms voluntarily tied. Bessus sprang up, scowling scarily and unable to withhold his hands from them. At this* they shed their shamming and engirded him, frustrating his struggles by strapping him in bonds, ripping the royal coronet from his brow and rending the raiment that he had assumed from among the suits of his assassinated sovereign. *Bessus avowed that the divinities were visiting vengeance upon him for his villainy, but added that, though they were not opposed to Darius in so avenging him, they were especially well disposed towards Alexander, even whose enemies ever aided his victories. It is unclear whether the multitude might have militated for Bessus to be set free, except those that had fettered him feigned they had done it by Alexander's decree, thus intimidating them in their dubiety.* Then the plotters plonked Bessus on a horse and led him to be relinquished to Alexander.

8.20 Also at this time Alexander nominated nine hundred men due for discharge and donated two talents to each cavalryman and three thousand drachmae to each of the foot, then set them heading off homewards after goading them to beget offspring.[11] He gave his thanks to the rest, who had signed up to serve in all his coming campaigns with zealous zest.

8.21 *Whilst Bessus was leading him a merry chase,* Alexander came upon an inconsequential citadel. *Its populace comprised* the Branchidae,[12] who had migrated from Miletus at the bidding of Xerxes, *when he was on his way back from Greece. They had set themselves up it this seat, since they had profaned the sanctuary called the Didymeon to appease Xerxes. In the interim they had hardly lapsed from the habits of their homeland, though they were now bilingual, having little by little been lured from their own languange by the local lingo. Therefore they were greatly gratified to greet Alexander and to set their city and themselves at his service.* Then the king commanded that the Milesians who were serving in his forces should assemble. *They nursed the ancient enmity against the Branchidaean folk. Hence he allowed those whom they had betrayed freely to judge whether they wished to recollect the kinship or the crime of the Branchidae. Then, having received various views from them, he himself undertook to weigh up what had best be done.*

8.22 *The next day, when the Branchidae came before him, he called upon them to accompany him and, when they had come to the city, he himself got through its gate with a designated detachment. The phalanx he*

---

[11] A silver talent comprised 6000 drachmae, each weighing about 4.2g on the Attic standard.

[12] The important references on Alexander's destruction of the Branchidae are: Curtius 7.5.28-35; Diodorus, *Contents* of Book 17; Plutarch, *Moralia* 557B; Strabo 11.11.4 & 14.1.5; Suda (Aelian fragment 54) s.v. *Branchidae* (Adler number: Beta 514).

instructed to ring the ramparts of the fortress and to tear down the town at a given signal, since it was an asylum for quislings and *these should be mown down to a man. Being defenceless they were massacred everywhere and neither their shared speech nor the beseeching of the suppliants with olive branches and prayer could curb the cruelty. Ultimately they undermined the foundations of the walls so that they could be cast down in order that no vestige of the town should stand. And in order to leave naught but wiped out waste and lifeless land with even its roots eradicated, they not only felled the copses and sacred groves, but also extirpated the stumps. Had this been contrived against the traitors themselves, then it would have been vindicated as valid vengeance rather than rated as ruthlessness. As it was, the descendants suffered for the sins of their ancestors, though they had not even seen Miletus and hence never had the ability to betray it to Xerxes.*[13]

8.23 *From there Alexander progressed to the Tanais River, whither* Bessus was delivered *not just strapped* in chains *but also stripped of every scrap of his raiment. Spitamenes led him by a leash and collar of links, a sight that gratified the Persians as much as the Macedonians. Then Spitamenes spoke: "I have wreaked revenge on behalf of both Darius and yourself, my successive sovereigns, by leading this liquidator of his lord before you, after overmastering him in a manner for which he himself set the example. Would that Darius could awake to witness this spectacle with his own eyes! Would that he should arise from the Underworld, for his fate was unfitting and he deserves such solace!"* At this unexpected exposition, **Alexander specially praised Spitamenes, then turned to address Bessus directly:** *"Of what crazed creature did the insanity seize your soul that you could firstly bear to bind then butcher the sovereign who was your best benefactor? And yet you actually bribed*

---

[13] By modern standards the destruction of the Branchidae was an atrocity. By the standards of Alexander's era, the issue is far more complex. It appears that contemporary religious law, which then enjoyed genuine respect, dictated that the descendants of serious religious criminals inherited the guilt (Plutarch's dialogue *On Delays in Divine Vengeance* in his *Moralia* attacks the application of this religious law through various examples, including the case of the Branchidae, but it nevertheless treats it as axiomatic that such a law was applied and even cites an attack upon the same principle by Euripides at *Moralia* 556E). It was a sacred duty of Alexander to uphold religious law, but he would probably have been conscious that this particular tenet was controversial and that the passage of 150 years could be seen as a major mitigation. It was probably his sense of a dilemma that led him to seek a sentence from his Milesians. Curtius is usually translated to the effect that these Milesians could not decide, so Alexander took the decision instead, but actually he need not mean more than that Alexander imposed a punishment in accordance with the preponderance of the varied views of the Milesians. Translations that make Alexander override his own policy of consultation are unnecessarily implying irrationality and vindictiveness on the part of the king, which is not substantiated by the actual words of Curtius. Among the ancient sources Aelian and Strabo seem to endorse or accept the justice of Alexander's treatment of the Branchidae, whereas Curtius and Plutarch express doubts.

yourself to commit monarch-murder with the pretended title of king!" Bessus did not dare to deny the misdeed, but said he had usurped the sovereignty in order to be able to surrender his society to Alexander, since some other would have seized the state, had he hesitated.

Figure 8.2. The punishment of Bessus (André Castaigne, 1899)

8.24 ***But* Alexander** felt he had himself formed a friendlier foe for Darius than this supposed comrade, so he **bade Oxathres, the brother of Darius, whom he had incorporated among his bodyguards, to come forward and then he handed Bessus over to him together with the task of torturing the traitor by attaching him to a cross and mutilating his ears and nose, so that the Persians could pierce him with arrows.** *Yet Alexander also prescribed that his person be preserved even from the attentions of the birds. Oxathres averred that he and his family would assuredly take care of everything, adding that none other than Catanes could keep the birds at bay, since he desired to display and show his exceptional skill with a bow, for he shot so sure at anything that he even downed birds on the wing. It was a massive marvel for those that saw it in effect, which reaped Catanes real respect.* **Thereafter *ere they were dismissed*** presents were provided to all those who had delivered up Bessus. *But his execution was deferred, so that he should be slain in the same place, where he himself had done Darius to death.*

8.25 In the meantime, some Macedonians who had fared forth on a foraging expedition in fragmentary formation were surprised by the natives, who careered down upon them from the contiguous crags. More of the Macedonians were captured than were killed and the barbarians harried their hostages into hurrying before them as they headed back into the highlands. These marauders amounted to twenty thousand men, who fell upon their foes with slings and bows. Whilst Alexander was blockading them with himself among the most prominent combatants, he was struck by an arrow, which left its head embedded in the middle of his shin.[14] The frantic and fretful Macedonians conveyed the king back to their camp, but it did not evade the notice of the natives that he had been freighted away from the front line, for they surveyed all the sights from their lofty heights.

8.26 Therefore the next day they sent emissaries to Alexander whom he instantly bade be admitted. Unbinding his bandages and making light of the largeness of the lesion, he showed his shin to the barbarians. On being bidden to settle down, they maintained that the Macedonians were not more miserable than they themselves in being made aware of the wound. Had they been able to ascertain who had inflicted the injury, they would have handed him over, since solely the sacrilegious waged war against the gods. Furthermore, they offered him the fealty of their folk, being overwhelmed by his wound. Having promised them his protection and recovered his captured colleagues, the king accepted their surrender. Then the Macedonians struck camp and Alexander was lifted upon a military litter. The entire infantry and cavalry corps contended as to who should carry it. The cavalry, with whom the king customarily cantered into combat, considered it their prerogative. Conversely, since they were accustomed to carrying their incapacitated comrades, the infantry complained that a function that formally fell to them was being usurped most specifically when Alexander was to be borne about. Perceiving the two parties to be at loggerheads and reckoning a decision between them to be a dilemma and liable to be loathed by the losers, the king bade them take turns to bear him.

8.27 From there on the fourth day they reached the city of Maracanda,[15] which is a matter of *six* days' journey from the River Tanais. This city is both sumptuous and secure, being bordered by the wide waters of its river and entirely encompassed by an uninterrupted rampart seventy stades in circumference.[16] A wall also surrounds the citadel inside. Alexander left a garrison *of one thousand soldiers* in the city *and emptied and incinerated the nearby shantytowns.*

---

[14] Curtius 7.6.3: this was a severe wound, as is confirmed elsewhere in the sources (Arrian, *Anabasis* 3.30.11; Plutarch, *Moralia* 327A-B & 341B and *Alexander* 45.3); splinters of one of the lower leg bones (most probably the tibia, but alternatively the fibula according to Arrian) are stated to have emerged from the wound.

[15] Samarkand.

[16] Both Curtius 7.6.10 and Metz Epitome 7 agree that Alexander arrived at Maracanda "on the fourth day", that the circumference of its wall was 70 stades and that the king left a garrison. These are strong indications that the two authors had the same (Greek) text before them, despite the vast differences in scale, style and purpose between their respective Latin versions.

Book 8: July 329BC – Autumn 328BC

8.28 Thereafter the envoys of the Scythian Abii appeared in order to place themselves at Alexander's disposal, though they had been independent since the death of Cyrus. They were generally judged the most just of the indigenous peoples, for they forbore from making war unless molested and the highest and the humblest persons had been put on a par by their balanced and leveling liberty. Alexander addressed them graciously and then dispatched Derdas from among his Friends to those Scythians who inhabit Europe. He was to instruct them not to stray across the Tanais River save at the king's command. This emissary also had the mission of scouting out the terrain as well as visiting such of the Scythians as were settled above the Bosphorus.[17] *Having arrived at the river and encamped beside it,* the king had selected a site for a city on the banks of the Tanais to act as a bulwark on which to belay both those already subdued and those he had determined duly to bring to bay.[18] However, his designs were delayed by news of insurrection among the Sogdians that also embroiled the Bactrians. The example of seven thousand horsemen by whom it was instigated, all the rest imitated.

8.29 Alexander called for Catanes and Spitamenes, who had surrendered Bessus, to be summoned, not doubting that the rebels might be reconciled to his rule through focusing their efforts upon the fomenters of the affair. But being in fact the ringleaders of the revolt that he had invoked them to avert, they published the report that the king was calling up the cavalry from all over Bactria in order to kill them. But they said that they themselves could not stomach executing such an instruction, lest they should commit an inexcusable crime against their countrymen. And so they asserted that they could no better bear the beastliness of Alexander than the regicide by Bessus. Thus they readily incited armed insurrection from those already driven by dread of doom to such a reaction.

8.30 On becoming fully informed of the defection of these deserters, the king commanded Craterus to besiege Cyropolis. He himself took another town in that country by cordoning it off. The signal was issued that the adult men should be slain, but that the rest were to remain as the reward for their captor. That town was torn down, so that others might through the example of its extirpation stay steadfast to the crown. However, a powerful people called the Memaceni had resolved to sustain a siege as being not just more respectable but actually safer. Alexander sent ahead fifty cavalrymen to soften their stubborn stance by flourishing the king's clemency for those that capitulated whilst also

---

[17] This means (north of) the Cimmerian Bosphorus (the modern Strait of Kerch off the eastern tip of the Crimea in the the Black Sea); Cleitarchus mistakenly thinks his Tanais is the River Don, so he seems to believe that the Scythians beyond its northern bank are Europeans.

[18] Although it is nowhere explicitly stated in the sources, the circumstances and analogy with the reaction of the Scythians to the foundation of the same city (Curtius 7.7.1 and 8.33 below) suggest that it was this decision to embed the Macedonian presence in the territory that instigated the renewed rebellion among the natives.

brandishing his implacable displeasure towards those he had to subdue. They responded that they were in no doubt concerning either the king's clemency or his reliability and they directed the riders to rig their camp outside the fortifications of their town. Then they hosted them hospitably, but in the dead of night they sallied forth and slew them, when they were sleeping and sluggish from feasting.

8.31 Being suitably incensed by this incident, Alexander encircled the city with a cordon of troops, since it was too finely fortified to be taken at first onset. Hence he enjoined Meleager and Perdiccas to invest the place, *whilst he himself continued on to Craterus at* Cyropolis, which was already besieged as has been said. However, he had ordained that this city established by Cyrus should be spared, since there were no other persons from their peoples that he admired more than that king and Semiramis: he believed the two of them far to have surpassed the rest both in the vastness of their vision and the distinction of their deeds. Yet the obduracy of its denizens left him so annoyed, that when it had been captured he had it destroyed. On having wiped it away and feeling, not unreasonably, riled regarding the Memaceni, he returned to Meleager and Perdiccas. But no stronghold ever withstood a siege more stoutly, since the most resolute of his soldiers succumbed and the king himself endured dire danger. For the nape of his neck was struck by a stone so smartly that his vision was veiled and he tottered over hardly wholly conscious. Indeed the army moaned as if they were already bereft of him. But being unconquerable in confronting things that unnerve others, he pursued the siege all the more insistently whilst his wound had not yet wholly healed, aroused to redoubling his regular rapidity. Therefore, having undermined its defences to broach a broad breach, he broke through into the town and as its captor he commanded that it be torn down.

8.32 *From this place Alexander despatched Menedemus to the city of Maracanda* with three thousand foot and eight hundred horsemen. **Having made Maracanda's Macedonian garrison forsake the city** *for its royal citadel,*[19] **the turncoat Spitamenes had ensconced himself within its walls** without its denizens having endorsed his design to defect, although afterwards it appeared as though they had, as they proved unable to inhibit him in any respect. Meanwhile **Alexander returned to the Tanais River and encompassed the countryside that had contained his camp with a wall, such that the circumference of this incipient city, which he commanded should be called Alexandria,**[20] **was sixty stades.** Its founding was accomplished so swiftly that seventeen days after the fortifications were

---

[19] To agree with Arrian, *Anabasis* 4.3.6-7, *Metz Epitome* 9 (which is somewhat corrupt) might mean "the Greek force, which went to the garrison left in the royal citadel"; Curtius 7.6.24 is clear that the garrison had been ejected from the main part of the city, but says nothing of its citadel.

[20] Alexandria Eschate ("the Farthest") at modern Khujand: cf. Arrian, *Anabasis* 4.4.1; Justin 12.5.

Book 8: July 329BC – Autumn 328BC

erected its dwellings had also been perfected. *Since the work was apportioned piece-by-piece, considerable competition had arisen among the teams of troops over who would be the first to release his completed project.* The king selected captives *from the three cities founded by Cyrus* to populate his pristine town, *freeing them by paying off their worth to their masters.* They continue to be recognised among their countrymen as a monument to the memory of Alexander.

8.33 Yet the Scythian sovereign, *whose rule then ranged beyond the Tanais, reckoned that this riverbank foundation of a fortified city by the Macedonians amounted to a halter around their necks. Hence he* sent his brother, named Carthasis, with a huge hoard *of horsemen to eradicate it and to remove the Macedonian forces far beyond the river.* The Tanais sunders the Scythians that are dubbed European from the Bactrians, since it is the same as separates the edges of Asia and Europe by its course.[21] Moreover those Scythian people settled not far from Thrace range right from the Orient to the North and are not the neighbours of the Sarmatians as some suppose, but rather a part of them.[22] Straight on from there they inhabit a further region ranging beyond the Ister[23] and reaching to the ends of Asia by Bactra. Their settlements occupy the nearer North, beyond which dense forests and wide wastes are encountered. On the other hand, their land hardly differs from farmed places, where they verge upon Bactra and the Tanais.

8.34 Being about to conduct an unplanned conflict with this people, given that they aggressively galloped before his gaze, Alexander convened a council of his Friends, though still troubled by the trauma that had especially spoilt his speech, neck-ache and meagre meals having mutually muted his voice. Yet it was not these foes that he feared, but the terrible times. The Bactrians had rebelled and the Scythians too were inciting him to action, whilst he himself could neither stand upon his feet nor bestride a steed nor even direct and exhort his men. Perched between pincers of peril and even blaming the gods, he bemoaned that he, from whose velocity nobody had previously been able to flee, lay thus languishing, such that his own men hardly held that his ill health was not a hoax. Consequently, though he had ceased to consult seers and diviners after his defeat of Darius, he relapsed into superstition, that mockery of the mind of mankind, and required Aristander, to whom he had consigned his credulity, to enquire by sacrifice as to what was going to transpire.

8.35 It was the practice of such prophets to examine their entrails in the absence of the king, then to regurgitate what they were portending. As Alexander waited while they investigated the guts of livestock to learn about

---

[21] Reiteration of the >2000km confusion between the Tanais/Don and Jaxartes/Syr-Darya.

[22] Strabo 11.2.1 agrees in making the Sarmatians a species of Scythian.

[23] The River Danube.

obscured outcomes, he called upon his comrades to sit nearer him than normal, so that he should not rupture his raw lesion by straining his voice. Hephaistion, Craterus and Erigyius in the company of the Bodyguards had been admitted to his pavilion and *the king counselled* them *thus:* "This crisis has enmeshed me at a moment that is more opportune for my opponents than for me. But necessity supersedes careful calculation, particularly at the point of a lance, which rarely allows you leeway to pick and choose your chance. The rebellious Bactrians, on whose jugular we remain, mean to measure our mettle through a proxy's campaign. There is no doubt where our best interest lies. If we fail to answer the Scythians, when without prompting they have taken up arms against us, then we shall be contemptible in the eyes of the rebels when we turn back. *If,* however, **we transit the Tanais and vaunt our universal invincibility by slashing and smashing the Scythians, who will hesitate to obey us** when even Europe yields us the field? He errs who stints our accolades according to the breadth of the tract that we are about to traverse. A single stream intervenes, on passing over which, we shall have carried our conquest into Europe. And how much it must be admired that, in the course of capturing Asia, we should have made memorials to our might in what is almost another world. That which Nature has evidently divided by such substantial distinctions would all at once have become conjoined in a combined conquest."

8.36 "Yet, by Heracles, if we should faintly falter, the Scythians shall be harrying our backsides. Is it only we that can swim across rivers? Many stratagems that have availed us of victory will recoil upon us. It is the fate of warfare even to school those it scuppers in its skills. Having lately set them the example of traversing a torrent on stuffed hides, even if the Scythians cannot conceive how to copy it, the Bactrians shall be their guides. What is more, only the first force from these folk has yet arrived – others are to be anticipated besides. Hence by shunning a showdown we should simply aggravate the aggression and, when we might have seized the initiative, we would be forced onto the defensive."

8.37 "The sense of my plan is plain, but I worry whether the Macedonians will permit me to implement what I please, since, as a result of receiving this wound, I have neither been able to ride around on horseback nor get about on foot. But, if you will volunteer to follow me, I am revitalized, my friends, and well enough to endure what I have proposed. Or else, if the end of my days be now nigh, in what such exploit were it better to die?" This was whispered in a waning and quavering voice that was barely audible to those beside him, whereupon everyone sought to dissuade the king from so cavalier a course. Erigyius was especially insistent, but when his own influence failed to reduce his ruler's resolution, he sought to subvert him with superstition, which Alexander was powerless to resist. Hence he declared that even the deities disapproved of the plan and the king would be exposed to potent peril if he should traverse the river. On entering the royal pavilion Erigyius had encountered Aristander, who had said that the signs in the offal were awful. Thus Erigyius was but announcing what he knew from the augur.

8.38 Having hushed him, Alexander was disconcerted not just due to annoyance but also by embarrassment that there were now revealed the superstitious ceremonies that he had concealed, but he bade that Aristander be called before him. When he had come, the king glared at him, complaining: "It was as a private client that I commissioned an augury rather than in my capacity as king. Why therefore did you disclose what was foretold to another rather than to me? Your indiscretion has exposed my private and confidential business to Erigyius, and, by Heracles, I am sure that he has extrapolated the entrails in the image of his own apprehensions. Yet you, who hedge in what you can, let you testify to me myself and publicly avow what the entrails have taught you, such that you may never gainsay what you say now."

8.39 Pastily pallid, Aristander stood as if stupefied, even his voice stilled by consternation, but finally the same fear prompted him not to protract the king's expectancy, so he responded: "I foretold an impending turning point of titanic yet not futile toil and it is not my art but my goodheartedness that discomfits me. I witness the weakness of your well-being and I know how much relies upon you alone, so I am apprehensive of whether you can cope with the present pressures." But the king bade him: "Let you find faith in my famous fortune, for it is for further feats that the gods have ceded me such celebrity." Thereafter, whilst he was weighing up with these same stalwarts by what recourse they could cross the river-course, Aristander reappeared reporting that he had never otherwise witnessed such wonderful offal, it being besides quite at odds with the former insides. Then, cause for concern had been evident, but now, purely auspicious signs had been sent![24]

8.40 But the news that was announced to the king not long afterwards blotted his unblemished succession of blessings. As already related, **Alexander had sent Menedemus to besiege Spitamenes, the abettor of the rebellion of the Bactrians.** Being informed of the approach of the foe and so as not to become confined within the fortifications of the city, **Spitamenes concealed his soldiers by the wayside whereby he perceived his opponent must pass**, confident that he could catch Menedemus unawares. The way was swathed with woods as is apt for an ambush. Here he hid his Dahae, a duo of whose warriors ride upon each steed, disconcertingly dismounting in alternation, so as to sow confusion among the columns in a cavalry combat. The dash of these men matches the motion of their mounts. Having been bidden by Spitamenes to surround the woodland way, they managed all at once to appear at the front and the flanks and the rear of their enemy. Though boxed in on all sides and outnumbered, Menedemus long battled on, yelling that having been tricked by a treacherous trap no other option arose but a distinguished death through the solace of the slaughter of their foes.

---

[24] In the tradition followed by Arrian, *Anabasis* 4.4.3, (Aristobulus?) Aristander's signs stayed bad.

8.41 Menedemus himself bestrode a hugely hefty horse, which he repeatedly rode in a rush against wedges of barbarians that he disintegrated with great carnage. But when all assailed him alone and a lot of lesions left him blanched of blood, he exhorted Hypsides, who was one of his friends, to alight upon his steed and save himself by flight. This being gasped out, he gave up the ghost and his corpse slid from his horse to the turf. Hypsides could indeed have fled, but having lost his comrade he resolved to die instead. His sole concern was that he should not perish unavenged, so, spurring on his horse with his heels, he hurtled into the heart of the hostile host and after faring famously in the fighting he was felled by a hail of missiles. On seeing this, **the survivors of the massacre ensconced themselves upon a hillock** a little loftier than the rest, **where Spitamenes beleaguered them**, looking to compel their capitulation through starvation. There fell in that fray two thousand foot and three hundred horsemen. Alexander disguised this disaster with shrewd intent, designating death for those delivered from the debacle, if they divulged the event.

8.42 Moreover *when* **the king could not** *any longer* **keep up his confident countenance in contradiction of his true feelings of uncharacteristic inadequacy,**[25] he retired into his tent, *which he had intentionally sited beside the bank of the river*. There *without witnesses* he weighed up his decisions one by one, whilst whiling the night away in wakefulness and worry over his woes. *Often, he lifted the skins of his tent in order to survey the fires of his foes, from which he could suppose how multitudinous their men were. But he persisted in perceiving his previous proposal as the most profitable one, so he determined to press on with what he had begun.*

8.43 *Presently* day dawned, whereupon he donned his cuirass and went forth to his troops *for the first time since receiving his recent wound. So vast was their veneration for their sovereign, that his mere presence readily eradicated the rumination upon the risks that had rattled them. Exultant therefore and shedding tears of joy in deploying their salutes, those that had formerly fought shy of the* forthcoming *fight now boldly beseeched him for a battle*. **Their monarch announced that he would ferry the phalanx and the cavalry upon rafts,** *but he bade the more lightly armed men to swim with the support of* stuffed *skins. The matter did not demand that more be spoken, nor could the king say more by dint of his debilitation. Yet* **such was the enthusiasm of the soldiers by whom the craft were fabricated that within three days towards twelve thousand rafts had been created.**[26]

8.44 Presently everything had been readied for the river transit, whereupon a score of Scythian emissaries careered through the camp upon their high horses,

---

[25] Alexander's feelings are derived by conflation of *Metz Epitome* 9 with Curtius 7.8.1.

[26] *Metz Epit.* 10 read *duo milia*, perhaps an error for *duodecim milia* given *XII milia* in Curtius 7.8.7.

Book 8: July 329BC – Autumn 328BC

since such are the manners of their nation, bidding that it be announced to the king that they desired to deliver a decision to him in person. On their admission to the royal pavilion and having been bidden to be seated, each of them riveted his gaze upon the king's countenance[27] and the eldest of them delivered this speech: "If the gods had willed that your physical size were on a par with your avaricious aspirations, then the world would not contain you. You would touch its sunrise rim with one hand and its sunset brim with the other, and following upon nightfall, you would wish to know where such a divine shining had shaded itself. Thus too you covet whatever you cannot capture. From Europe you assail Asia and from Asia you launch into Europe. Thereafter, if you have overcome all human races, you will wage war against woodlands, wild beasts, rivers and snowy places. To what end? For do you not know that tall trees take time to grow, yet are uprooted in an hour or so? He is a fool who ogles their fruit, but fails to judge how high they shoot. Watch that you don't dive down with the selfsame branches you seize, whilst trying to reach the tops of those trees. Just as the lion occasionally becomes the meat of the most minute of birds and iron is eaten by rust, nothing is so robust that it is not at risk even from feeble things."

8.45 "Of what concern are we to you? We have never touched your territories. Is it intolerable that the inhabitants of forsaken forests should claim ignorance of who you are and whence you came? It is impractical for us to obey anyone and neither do we desire to have aught to run. So that you may savvy Scythian society, the gifts given to us are the yoke for oxen, the libation bowl the lance and arrows. These we employ for our friends and deploy against our foes. The fruits of the efforts of our oxen we furnish to our friends, with whom we offer wine to the gods with the bowl. With arrows we take a toll of our enemies from far away, whereas with the lance we bring them to bay. So it was that we subdued the sovereign of Syria[28] and later the overlord of the Medes and the Persians, such that the road as far as Egypt lay open to our incursions."

8.46 "Yet you, who vaunt your invasion as a pursuit of pillagers, you are yourself the marauder of every race that you have reached.[29] Lydia lies under

---

[27] Curtius (7.8.9-11) interjects personal comments here, concluding that he will faithfully render the words of the Scythians "just as they have been passed down to us" despite their gracelessness.

[28] It is a specific Cleitarchan idiosyncrasy to refer to Assyria as Syria: e.g. Athenaeus 530A (F2).

[29] The Scythian's speech (from Curtius 7.8.19) has a striking parallel in one of the references to Alexander's audience with the pirate, Aristonicus of Methymne. St. Augustine (*De Civ. Dei* IV, 4. 25) tells this story of Alexander and the pirate, which he probably took from Cicero, *De Republica*, who in turn is likely to have sourced this material from Cleitarchus. St. Augustine has: "Indeed, that was an apt and true reply which was given to Alexander the Great by a pirate who had been seized. For when that king had asked the man what he meant by keeping hostile possession of the sea, he answered with bold pride, 'What thou meanest by seizing the whole earth; but because I do it with a petty ship, I am called a robber, whilst thou who dost it with a great fleet art styled emperor.'"

you, Syria is seized and Persia is possessed by you, the Bactrians are bent beneath your sway and India is an intended target. Even now you are greedily grasping at our herds with ever hungering hands. What is the worth of wealth to you, when it aggravates your appetite? You are the first ever to have procured famine from profusion, such that the more you have possessed, the more obsessively you have coveted all the rest. Does it not strike you that you have lingered long about Bactria? And even while you have been subduing her cities, Sogdiana has commenced hostilities. Indeed, your wars are spawned by your victories. For though you be bravery's boldest incarnation, no one willingly suffers foreign domination."

8.47 "Just let you pass across the Tanais and you will find out how widely the Scythians range about, though you will never overhaul them. In our austerity we shall be swifter than your army, who are lugging the loot from so many lands. On the other hand, when you think we're far in the distance, we shall be seen among your tents. For we both chase and flee with the same rapidity. I hear it said besides that the isolation of the Scythians is satirized in the sayings of the Greeks.[30] But we haunt wilderness and desert strands rather than stalk through cities and lushly farmed lands. Hence hold onto your fair Fortune with a firm grip, since she is slippery and cannot long be kept against her will. Competent counselling shall be recognized more clearly by the future than by the present day. Yet you should curb your successes, so as to make them more manageable *in every way*. Our folk affirm that Fortune is footless, having hands and wings only. When she proffers her hands, also grasp her wings firmly!"

8.48 "In summary, if you be a deity, it is your duty to give gifts to mankind and not strip them away. But if you be a human being, you should bear that in mind day after day. It is folly only to think of those things that make you forget your humanity. Those that you refrain from waging war with, you can engage with in amity. For it is between peers that friendship is firmest and they appear equal who have not put each other's strength to the test. Have a care not to consider those you've conquered to be your comrades, for there can be no camaraderie between a serf and his lord, since even in times of peace a thrall is governed by the sword. And do not suppose that the Scythians consecrate a concord with an oath: their ratification grows from its observation. Such sacred precautions are a practice of the Greeks, who conclude their covenants with divine invocation. The keeping of faith is itself our creed: they, who disrespect their fellows, fail the gods indeed. Neither is a friend of doubtful goodwill of use to you in need. Yet we would be your rangers in both Europe and Asia. But for the intervention of the Tanais, we border on Bactria. Beyond the Tanais, we live in the lands as far as Thrace and rumour reckons that Macedon adjoins that place. With us being at the borders of your domains at both ends, think well on

---

[30] E.g. Aristophanes, *Acharnians* 704: "Cephisodemus, who is as savage as the Scythian desert…"

Book 8: July 329BC – Autumn 328BC

whether you wish us to be your enemies or your friends." So spoke the barbarian.

8.49 In reply **Alexander** retorted that he would rely on his own luck and upon their advice, since he would follow both Fortune, in whom he had faith, and the counsel of any who urged him not to act with rashness and recklessness. And having dismissed the delegation, he **embarked his forces upon the readied rafts** *that had been deployed along a designated stretch of the bank, commanding that they should cast off together at a given signal. He put hypaspists in their prows,[31] bidding them to crouch down upon their knees, so that they should be safer in the face of a hail of arrows. Behind them stood the men who cranked the catapults, encompassed on either flank and ahead by the men-at-arms. Being stationed behind the artillery, the rest of the armed men guarded the rowers, who lacked the cover of corselets, by forming a tortoise shell with their shields. The self-same arrangement was retained aboard the rafts that conveyed the cavalry. Most of these let their steeds swim at the stern trailing by their reins. However, those who skimmed across on skins stuffed with straw stayed sheltered to the rear of the rafts.*

8.50 *The king himself with a crack crew was aboard the first raft to cast off, directing that it be steered straight for the far bank. Advancing over the deep channel they appeared with their vast array of rafts like a phalanx forging forward in formation on a battlefield rather than a river. However,* the Scythians were resolute that the king's rafts should not even reach the land, so they arrayed ranks of riders at the rim of the shoreline with jutting javelins. *But besides the sight of such forces thronging the bank, the pilots were particularly perturbed, since the steersmen could not correct their course, which was canted by the current. Furthermore, in their anxiety to avoid being jettisoned the tottering troops hindered the helmsmanship of the pilots. Neither could the soldiers even poise themselves to cast their javelins, since their priority had to be to keep their footing rather than risk assailing their foes.*

8.51 *Yet upon a signal given at midway the Macedonians gave vent to roars and the men's morale was right then raised by a peal of trumpets, the rhythmic rant of the rowers and the plash of the oars. However,* the Scythians *similarly shouted out and* started to shoot arrows and other missiles at the Macedonians, wounding many and causing some

---

[31] Curtius' term for these troops is *clipeatos*, which means shield-bearing soldiers. This is most probably a literal Latin translation of *hypaspists*. A secondary possibility would be *peltasts*, who were equipped with the smaller circular rimless shield (*pelte*) plus spears and long swords. These might specifically be the Agrianians, who were equipped as *peltasts* and are mentioned in this battle by Arrian, *Anabasis* 4.4.6.

mortality, because, being hemmed in, the men could not elude their lethality. *Their salvation lay in the catapults, which flung their bolts, thus inflicting mayhem amidst the ranks of their compacted opponents who rashly rendered themselves as targets. But* the barbarians *too* rained such a heavy hail of arrows upon the rafts that scarcely a shield was not shot with a shower of shafts.

8.52 Shortly, the rafts were grounded upon the shore, *whereupon the hypaspists rose up in unison and being now sure of their stance took precise aim to volley their javelins from their vessels. As soon as they saw that the Scythian steeds were startled and starting to stampede, motivated by mutual exhortation they sprang ashore and set upon the disordered opposition.* Such squadrons of cavalry as had their mounts bridled broke through the disarrayed ranks of the barbarians. *Meanwhile, the rest readied themselves for combat in the cover afforded by the fighting formations. As for the king himself, what bodily vigour he was through infirmity denied, his resolute spirit supplied. Whilst his rousing words could not be heard, since his neck wound was not yet wholly healed, still everyone witnessed him fighting in the field.* Hence, as the phalanx also followed them forwards, they *themselves delivered their own leadership, each exhorting his fellows, so that they forgot their safety and hurtled headlong at their foes.*

8.53 Then, in truth, the Scythians could not cope with either the growls or the scowls or the arms and armour of the Macedonians, so slickly slackening their reins, for they were an array of riders, they all of them took flight. *Despite that he was unable to ride upright because of the bouncing of his debilitated body,* the king persisted with the pursuit *for eighty stades. And presently, when his spirit had expired, he specified that his men should dog the tracks of the fugitives so long as any light at all lingered. He himself, having exhausted even the resilience of his soul, returned to his base and remained there during the rest of the chase.* And now they went beyond the boundary of Dionysus, which was punctuated by rock pillars at frequent intervals[32] *and by lofty trees, the trunks of which were sheathed with ivy.* But the Macedonians were fired to press further forward by their fury, for it was almost midnight when they came back to camp on the Tanais having slain many, made even more captive and driven off eighteen hundred horses. *Of the Macedonians themselves sixty cavalrymen and around a hundred foot fell with a thousand being wounded.*

---

[32] Perhaps Alexander's expedition observed immense glacially deposited monoliths/boulders in the plain north of the Syr-Darya River. During the Ice Ages an area of glaciation spread forth from the various northern Himalayan Ranges into that region.

Book 8: July 329BC – Autumn 328BC

8.54 It was the repute of so convenient a victory in this excursion that subdued that far-reaching region of Asia, which had sought to secede. They had considered the Scythians to be unbeatable, but, when they were shattered, they conceded that no nation could match the Macedonians in military matters. Consequently, the Sacae sent envoys to proffer the fealty of their folk, being prompted less by Alexander's ascendancy than by his clemency towards the worsted Scythians: for he had repatriated all those taken prisoner without ransom, so as to curry confidence that his contention with the most provocative peoples was a question of chivalry rather than a tantrum. Therefore he welcomed the emissaries from the Sacae and gave them his Greeter,[33] *Bagoas the Eunuch*, as their escort. He was as yet a mere youth and beloved by the king for his cuteness of those years, but, although he was equally as handsome as Hephaistion, he could not match his masculine charm, being barely manly at all it appears.[34]

8.55 *Three days after returning to the Tanais* the king made a forced march to the metropolis of Maracanda in order to surprise Spitamenes, *having bidden Craterus to bring the bulk of the army after him by steady stages*. But when Spitamenes was apprised of Alexander's arrival, he *aborted his beleaguering of the Greeks and* fled *to Bactra*.[35] In consequence, the king covered a considerable compass of the country in four days, reaching that locality where he had lost two thousand foot and three hundred cavalry under the leadership of Menedemus. He ordered that a mound be made to accommodate their bones and gave offerings to the spirits of the dead according to the customs of their country.[36] Presently, Craterus, who had been ordered to follow with the phalanx, caught up with the king. And so, in order that all who had rebelled should similarly

---

[33] The best reading from the manuscripts of Curtius 7.9.19 is *excipinon* (in B, F, L, M & V, whereas P has been read as *escipinon*): despite confusion sown by modern editors, inspired by Hedicke's hugely imaginative emendation to *Euxenippon* and Foss's frankly weird *Elpinicon*, it is clear that this is a reference to the individual elsewhere known as Bagoas the Eunuch; he was the young, unmanly male, who had a sexual relationship with Alexander at this time; Diodorus 17.77.4 has Alexander appointing "Asian born rod-bearers to his court" just at the time that Bagoas had joined his retinue; presumably these officials resembled what we would call court ushers; hence the name/title might derive from *excipio* to greet or *excido* to castrate; it is likely that Bagoas spoke Greek as well as Persian, which is why Nabarzanes used him as his apologist before Alexander (Curtius 6.5.23) and why he would have been an appropriate escort for the Sacae at this point.

[34] The obvious sexual innuendo here accurately reflects the Latin in Curtius, where *lepore* for charm is also the ablative case of the word for a hare, which was a traditional love-gift between an older and a younger man in the ancient world (e.g. depicted on Greek vases).

[35] Presumably the Greek garrison of Maracanda had held out in its citadel for the whole period or (less probably) the survivors of Menedemus' forces were still holding out on their hillock.

[36] Entombment according to Macedonian rites was also later granted to Alexander himself by Ptolemy in Memphis according to Pausanias 1.6.3, which may be sourced from Cleitarchus.

suffer the sorrows of insurrection, he divided his forces, fired the fields and called for the killing of adult men. *It is claimed that over twelve myriad were slain.*

8.56 The most substantial section of Sogdiana is desert. An area almost eight hundred stades wide is occupied by empty waste and that region runs onwards for a vast space, through which the river that the locals call the Polytimetus is traced. There are rapids where it is constricted into a gorge by its banks and then it is consumed by a cavern and courses underground. The only sign of its suppressed progression is the sound from the sloshing of its waters, since the soil itself, beneath which such a torrent has snaked, is not the slightest bit slaked.

8.57 *There were led before the king thirty of the noblest Sogdians, chieftains of rare robustness of body. When they realized through an interpreter that they were being escorted to their execution by command of the king, they started to sing songs as if in celebration and rhythmically to stamp their feet and lewdly to jerk their bodies so as to display a species of spiritual joy. Watching with wonder as they went to meet their death with such magnanimity, Alexander bade that they be recalled and requested the reason for such rapture, when the spectre of extermination stood before their gaze? They confided that they would have been desolated to die by order of any other, but seeing as they were to be reunited with their forbears by so mighty a monarch, the conqueror of every country, they were celebrating with their customary merrymaking and choir a distinguished death, to which heroes might even aspire.*

8.58 *Then, admiring of their gallantry, Alexander responded: "I wonder whether you would wish to live without hostility towards me, in whose gift your welfare lies?" They replied that they had never been inherently hostile towards him, but when goaded into hostilities they were necessarily hostile towards the aggressors. If a person had preferred to approach them with presents rather than provocations, they would have fought not to be surpassed in civility. And when Alexander asked by what pledge their fidelity might be affirmed, they replied that what life were granted to them they would pledge to his cause. They would be at his service whensoever he should call. Nor did they revoke this avowal. For those who were sent home have led their population into alliance by their allegiance and four of them, whom he kept as bodyguards, were no less loyal than any of the Macedonians in their care for the king.*

8.59 Having left Peucolaus in Sogdiana with three thousand foot, since indeed he had no need for a greater contingent, **Alexander relocated to Bactra. Here he had Bessus brought before him and bade that he** *be led to Ecbatana to* **pay through capital punishment for dealing death to Darius.** *There he*

Figure 8.3. The Sogdian prisoners are joyful on their way to execution, leading Alexander to spare them (from a 1696 edition of Curtius)

was killed according to the custom of the Persians by being suspended, split and diced into little bits that were subjected to dispersions.[37]

8.60 During virtually these same days Ptolemaeus and Maenidas brought a thousand cavalry and four thousand foot to serve their sovereign as mercenaries. Asander arrived too with a comparable count of foot and five hundred cavalry. Just as many accompanied Asclepiodorus from Syria and Antipater had sent eight thousand Greeks incorporating six hundred cavalry. With his army thus augmented, the king set forth to pacify those parts that had been convulsed by the revolt and, after having executed the instigators of the disturbances, he arrived at the River Oxus on the fourth day. Due to conveying silt, its current is always cloudy and hence unhealthy to drink. Therefore the soldiers started to sink wells, but, though they dug down deep in the earth, no source was seen to seep forth. Finally, a fount was found right beside the tent of the king himself. Then the men made out that it had only just begun to spout, since they had been slow to scout it out. And Alexander himself was desirous that it be deemed a donative from the deities.

8.61 *On the eleventh day* after leaving Bactra **the king reached and crossed the River Ochus. Subsequently, he traversed the River Oxus** *and reached the city of Margania.*[38] *In its environs Alexander selected six sites for the foundation of citadels: two to its south and four to its east. They were near neighbours of one another, so that mutual aid might be conveyed without being delayed by distance, and all of them were established upon high hills.* To these and six other of his foundations in Bactria their ruler relegated those he regarded as rebels within the ranks. Back then these citadels served as curbs upon those conquered in this land, but now, oblivious of their origin, they serve those that they used to command.[39]

8.62 *And so the king had imposed peace upon all other parts, but impelled by panic a multitude of men from the province had sought the*

---

[37] With slight emendation *Metz Epitome* 14 can agree with Plutarch, *Alex* 43.3 & Diodorus 17.83.9.

[38] A cogent explanation of Alexander's itinerary at this point has been put forward by A. B. Bosworth, "A Missing Year in the History of Alexander the Great", *Journal of Hellenic Studies*, Vol. 101, pp. 17-39, 1981. Bosworth points out that the readings *marganiam* or *marginiam* in the MSS of Curtius should not have been emended to read *margianam* (i.e. Margiana, the modern Merv). The Ochus must be a major tributary of the Oxus in the east of Bactria, which makes it most probably the modern River Surkhab. Hence Alexander travelled east from Bactra until he met the Oxus and continued eastwards along its southern bank (i.e. without crossing). Somewhere north of Kunduz, he crossed the Ochus (Surkhab), and then he headed on into the Kochka region, where he crossed the Oxus heading northwards somewhere near Ai Khanum. Margania must have been an otherwise unknown ancient city in the region to the north of the Oxus, which was the SE part of ancient Sogdiana. It cannot have been Margiana (Merv), since it does not fit the geography.

[39] Cleitarchus was writing half a century after these events, which is a sufficient perspective for Curtius to have found these comments in his text: it would alternatively be surprising, if Curtius, writing some four centuries after their foundation, even knew precisely where these citadels were.

Book 8: July 329BC – Autumn 328BC

protection of a towering pinnacle. This rock was occupied by the Sogdian Ariamazes with *thirty thousand warriors and* previously hoarded provisions*, so as to provide for such prodigious numbers for as long as two years.* The altitude of this pinnacle presented an intimidating sight, for it soars up in excess of twenty stades in height *with a circumference of a hundred and fifty.*[40] *None but the birds may inhabit it, for* it is *thickly forested,* sheer on every side and approached by a *precipitous and pinched pathway.*[41] *At about the halfway point in the ascent* the path passes into a cavern *with a narrow and shadowy mouth,* which is the only way up to the heights. *But bit-by-bit it broadens further in and ultimately even develops deep alcoves. Springs spout virtually throughout the cavern and the waters that course forth collectively source a stream that cascades down the crags.*

8.63 Having observed the obstacles that the place displayed, the king considered that it could not be captured by storm. *He had decided to depart, when he was inspired by a yearning even to harass Nature's art. Nonetheless, before gambling his Fortune on an investment, he sent Cophes, who was a son of Artabazus, to the barbarians to persuade them to surrender their craggy emplacement.* From the supposed security of his surroundings, Ariamazes made many a haughty reply, culminating in the question of whether Alexander could even fly?

8.64 *When this was relayed to* Alexander, *it so fired his spirit that he convened his customary counselors, to whom he reported the arrogance of the barbarian, who had lampooned them for lacking wings.* But he said that he himself in the next night would make the man maintain that Macedonians were even capable of flight, adding: "Let you fetch me three hundred of the fittest young fellows from your respective forces, such as at home herd their flocks up mountain tracks and across crags that are practically impassable." They readily recruited those who were outstanding in both agility and dauntless daring. *Scrutinising them* the king confided: *"It is beside you, O youths that are my comrades, that I have surmounted the palisades of cities, which were erstwhile deemed invincible; that I have passed through peaks perpetually swathed in snow; that I have negotiated the narrows of Cilicia and suffered the fierce*

---

[40] Manuscripts of Curtius have *XXX eminet stadia*, whereas the Metz Epitome had *XX stadiis*.

[41] Polyaenus, *Stratagems* 4.3.29 provides the details that the rock was accessible only to the birds and heavily forested, although it is slightly surprising that neither Curtius nor the Metz mentioned the forest, if it was in Cleitarchus.

frost of India without indolence.[42] *Thus I have presented you with proof of my princeliness and you have provided me with proof of yours!"*

8.65 *"As you can perceive, the pinnacle posesses but one portal, which the barbarians infest, whilst neglecting all the rest. They have set no sentinels, save those that contemplate our camp. You will ferret out a route, if you sedulously seek for fissures to see you to the summit. Nature has set nothing so high that it cannot be conquered by courage. We have taken Asia by attempting what has intimidated others.* Let you soar up to that summit. When you have seized it, issue me a signal with white banners, *which you will wear as belts*. Then I shall shift up our forces to fend the focus of our foes off you and onto us. *The prize for him who first scales the crest shall be ten talents with one fewer for the next to follow and the same again until ten men have met the mission. But I am sure you shall be motivated not so much by my munificence as by my ambition."*

8.66 *They heard out their sovereign with such exultation that it seemed as if they had already seized the summit. When they were dismissed,* in accordance with the king's counsel, **the men made ready rugged ropes and tapering iron pegs to wedge between the slabs. Then their ruler rode around the rock and at its rear,** *where the access seemed least severe and precipitous, bestowing his blessings* **he bade them begin their ascent in the second watch of** the night.[43] **Packing provisions sufficient for two days and armed only with swords and spears, they started their climb. And at first they forged forward on foot, but then** upon reaching the cliffs some *levered themselves aloft by grasping handholds in the rock, whilst others hauled themselves up on ropes with nooses cast ahead* to snag on protrusions. **Still others** wedged the tapering iron pegs *into crevices* between the slabs, **threading their ropes through them, so as to establish a ladder up which they could clamber. And each of them helped out the rest, as step by step they crept to the crest.**

8.67 *A day was taken up between terror and toil. After struggling up hard stretches, still more arduous parts lay ahead and it appeared as if the pinnacle were elevating. It was a really wretched spectacle, when* those that were fooled by infirm footings tumbled down from the rockface, *for their fellows' fate foreshadowed what likewise awaited the watchers.* Yet they fought through these threats to surmount the summit, *all weakened by the weariness of relentless labour and some maimed in some section of their limbs. And there they were simultaneously overcome by night*

---

[42] This is a reference to the blizzard conditions that the Macedonians had encountered in the highlands of central southern Afghanistan as they approached the passes across the Paropamisus Range (Curtius 7.3.12-14; Diodorus 17.82.2-7): Cleitarchus regarded this region as a part of India.

[43] The Greeks usually divided the night into four watches.

Book 8: July 329BC – Autumn 328BC

and slumber. With their bodies stretched and strewn about upon the impassable, jagged rocks, oblivious of their perilous position they dozed until dawn. *And then at last as if stirred from a stupor they studied the concealed vales that were revealed beneath them, uncertain in what part of the pinnacle a foe in such force might be confined, whereupon they spotted smoke coiling up from a cavern below them. Hence they deduced that their enemies' lair lay there, so* they used their spears to raise the white banners *clear of the trees, the manner of signal that had been agreed. Then they counted the climb's cost and found that thirty-two of their number had been lost.*

8.68 *The king spent the whole day peering at the peak of the pinnacle, more anxious about the fate of those that he had consigned to such palpable peril than on account of his ambition to put the place in his power. Not till nighttime, when darkness veiled his view, did he retire for rest and repose. The next morning, whilst day was still dawning, he was the first to behold the banners that signaled the seizure of the summit. Yet the interplay of sunshine and shade from the shifting cloudscape made the king wonder whether it had fooled his eyes. But as brighter light filled the skies, no further doubt could arise,* despite Alexander's surprise that success had come so soon.

8.69 And having called for Cophes, through whom he had *previously* sounded out the resilience of the barbarians, he sent him *back* to them with the warning that they should now as a minimum adopt a stance that was more in their interests. But should they remain resolute in their faith in their fastness, he bade that those that had seized the summit at their rear should be exhibited to them. On being admitted, Cophes commenced urging Ariamazes to relinquish the rock and thereby curry the king's favour through not diverting him in the siege of a single crag whilst he was setting such mighty matters in motion. However he, speaking more haughtily and arrogantly than before, commanded that Cophes should depart. But Alexander's emissary grasped the hand of the barbarian, begging that he come outside the cavern with him. This request being granted, Cophes pointed out the presence upon the peak of the young men and, in a not unjustified jest at Ariamazes' arrogance, agreed that Alexander's warriors were indeed winged.

8.70 At this juncture there were heard from the Macedonian camp trumpet peals and the roar of the entire corps. These things, though vacant and hollow like many other events in warfare, pushed their opponents into capitulation, for being fixated by fear they were incapable of gauging how few were those that threatened their rear. Therefore *out of panic* they promptly recalled Cophes, who had left them in their alarm, sending thirty of their chieftains with him to barter the surrender of the pinnacle for safe passage for their departure. *Though nervous that the* *natives on noticing the negligible numbers of his climbers might annihilate them,* **the king was** *nevertheless* **both riled by the arrogance of Ariamazes and confident of his good fortune, hence he held out for capitulation without conditions.** *In consequence, more out of despair than from his real ruin in the affair,* **Ariamazes was** *escorted by his kindred and the most noble of the natives down towards the king's camp, and they themselves collectively commanded that he be* **scourged and crucified** *at the base of the pinnacle.*[44] **Ariamazes having been killed, Alexander willed that the lives of the rest be spared when they surrendered. A huge host of those who handed themselves over were given as gifts to the settlers in the new settlements together with monies taken in the matter and Artabazus was left in charge of the rock and the region around it.**

8.71 These were the concerns of Alexander *in the eighth year of his reign.*

---

[44] Although the Latin of Curtius implies that Alexander ordered the execution of Ariamazes, this is flatly contradicted by the *Metz Epitome*, which is clear that this was the act of Ariamaze's own men. The latter version is far more likely to be correct, firstly because it is incredible that Sisimithres would have surrendered only months afterwards (as is also related by Curtius) had Alexander been in the habit of executing those that put themselves in his hands; secondly because small tweaks to the Latin of Curtius can reconcile his version with the *Metz Epitome*.

5. Book 9: Autumn 328BC – May 327BC

The Hunt in Basista; The Killing of Cleitus; The Treaty with Sisimithres; The Decapitation of Spitamenes; The Proskynesis Experiment; The Conspiracy of the Pages; The Army Caught in a Blizzard; The Marriage to Roxane

KEY
Underlined bold text for attributed Fragments of Cleitarchus
Bold text where there is overwhelming evidence
Bold italic text where there exists direct-firm evidence
Normal text where direct-weak evidence applies
Italic text where the evidence is conjectural
Grey text for connecting passages, if Cleitarchus' version is indeterminate

9.1 *At the beginning of the ninth year of his reign,* having acquired more notoriety than admiration through putting in his power the pinnacle *of Ariamazes*, Alexander strewed his strikes in answer to his errant enemies by splitting his army into three columns. He entrusted the command of one to Hephaistion, of another to Coenus and led the last himself. But the barbarians were not all of like mind: whilst some were subdued by force of arms, yet more submitted to his sovereignty ere a contest could occur. And he ordered that the latter be allotted the land and lodging-places of those who had proved dogged in their defection. But the Bactrian evictees in league with eight hundred horse of the Massagetae laid waste to the surrounding settlements. Aiming to thwart them, Attinas, the prefect of that province, led forth his three hundred cavalry quite ignorant of the trap that was being contrived for him. For their enemies ensconced armed troops within the forest that chanced to verge upon the meadows, where a few foes drove forth livestock, such plunder as to entice Attinas unaware into the snare. Therefore he charged after the chattels in fractured and fragmented formation and as he wended his way past the woods those who waited within unexpectedly sprang out upon him, so that he perished with his whole host.

9.2 Repute of their ruin rapidly reached Craterus, who came upon the place with his complete corps of cavalry. Though the Massagetae had already fled, a thousand of the Dahae were left dead and their extinction extinguished the insurrection in that entire region. Having crushed the Sogdians afresh,

Alexander the Great in Afghanistan by Andrew Chugg

Alexander too returned to Maracanda.[1] There Derdas, whom he had sent to the Scythians dwelling beyond the Bosphorus, met him with emissaries from that people.[2] Additionally, Phrataphernes, who presided over Choras, which was contiguous to the territories of the Massagetae and the Dahae, had sent representatives to proffer his allegiance. The Scythians petitioned that Alexander should wed a daughter of their king or else, if such nuptials were beneath his dignity, that he should allow the Macedonian nobility to forge marriage alliances with the aristocracy of their people. They further affirmed that their king would presently appear in person. **Alexander** listened to both delegations with courtesy whilst in quarters awaiting Hephaistion and Artabazus. When they had rejoined him, he **proceeded to the region called Basista.**

9.3 There is no vaster evidence of the affluence of the barbarians in those bounds than their aggregations of grand and brutal beasts enclosed within great groves and parklands. For this purpose they reserve wide woodlands lushly laved by lots of ever gushing springs. They ring these woods with walls and they have havens to harbour the hunters. One such forest infiltrated by **Alexander** with his full force had lain undisturbed for four successive generations when he **ordered an assault from every side upon its savage beasts.** Amidst this slaughter it chanced that Lysimachus (he that later reigned) stood beside Alexander when a lion of singular size careered towards the king. Hence he aimed to thrust his hunting spear into the crazed creature, but his ruler shoved him aside and said he should back off, adding that he himself had as much skill as Lysimachus to liquidate a lion at a stroke.

9.4 Indeed, once when they had been prowling for prey in Syria, Lysimachus had single-handedly slain just such an exceptionally sizeable beast, but had had his shoulder sheared through to the bone, so that he had nearly lost his life. This was the reason for Alexander's reproach to Lysimachus, but the king's actions spoke louder than his words, for he not only confronted the colossal cat, but also slew it with a single puncture.[3] But despite Alexander achieving a choice outcome in this instance, the Macedonians nevertheless let it be known that in accordance with the customs of their country he should neither hunt on foot nor *alone* without the company of a select band of officers and Friends.[4]

---

[1] Samarkand.

[2] See 8.28 above: this means the Cimmerian Bosphorus, lying off the eastern tip of the Crimea; so these Scythians were thought to dwell in the Ukraine, but were actually beyond the Syr-Darya.

[3] Curtius 8.1.17 comments that he thought this incident the basis for the story that Alexander exposed Lysimachus to a lion. His comment was probably not taken from Cleitarchus, since Pliny, *Natural History* 8.16.21 accepts the exposure story as true, despite also being a source of Fragments of Cleitarchus. NB. *Basista* in Diodorus, but *Bazaira* in Curtius.

[4] I doubt that it is sensible to read into this (as some translators have) that the Macedonian Assembly voted on the matter there and then. Rather this looks like an existing custom to which they drew Alexander's attention: it explains why Alexander & Philip in the mural on the façade of

Book 9: Autumn 328BC – May 327BC

Figure 9.1. Alexander slays the lion in Basista (Antonio Tempesta, 1608)

9.5 Alexander returned thence to Maracanda, where, having agreed that Artabazus might retire on grounds of age, he assigned his satrapy to Cleitus, who was a veteran trooper of Philip and famed for his prolific exploits in warfare. Whilst keeping the king in the shelter of his shield as Alexander fought bareheaded at the River Granicus, it was he who had hewn off the hand of Rhosaces with his saber, when the man had menaced the king's life. Furthermore Hellanice, *the sister of Cleitus, who had reared Alexander as his nurse, the king cared for no less than for a mother.* These were the accounts on which he committed to the conscientious care of Cleitus the most powerful part of his empire.

9.6 Then, having been bidden to prepare to set forth on the morrow, *Cleitus and others among the Friends were summoned by their sovereign to celebrate a festival at an opportune party. There the king, glowing with much unmixed wine and waxing uninhibited in his self-esteem, commenced commending what he himself had accomplished, which grated on the ears even of those who could vouch for the validity of his reminiscences. Nevertheless the elder veterans held their peace, until he ventured to disparage the deeds of Philip, bragging that the brilliant victory at Chaeronaea had been his own work, but that such a superb*

Tomb II at Vergina and Alexander, Abdalonymus & Hephaistion in the hunt scene on the Alexander Sarcophagus are all mounted.

success had been stinted him by the stinginess and jealousy of his father. What was more, when a brawl had broken out between the Macedonian troops and the Greek mercenaries, being incapacitated by a wound, Philip had flung himself to the ground, lacking any other recourse than to play dead. Then Alexander had kept his carcass in the shelter of his shield and had slain his assailants with his own hand. But this Philip could never acknowledge with equanimity, being unwilling to owe his safety to his son. Also after Alexander had launched a victorious expedition against the Illyrians in his father's absence, he had written that his foes were in full flight, for Philip was nowhere to be found. Let not those be praised, asserted Alexander, who had beheld the ceremonies of Samothrace when it would have been becoming to burn and batter Asia, but instead exalt those the magnitude of whose deeds defied belief.*

9.7 To this and the like the lads listened with alacrity, but it was odious to their elders, most of all concerning Philip, under whom they had the longer lived. Whereupon Cleitus, not being himself soundly sober, slewed towards those settled beyond him and recited a song of Euripides, such that only his tone rather than his text could be distinguished by the king. Its gist was that it was a perverse practice of the Greeks that solely the names of their sovereigns were inscribed upon their trophies, for thus these kings were commandeering the glory gleaned by the blood of others.[5] Hence Alexander, since he suspected that the murmuring had been malicious, began to query those about him as to what they had heard Cleitus mutter. Whilst they remained resolutely silent, little by little Cleitus declaimed louder and louder, recounting the campaigns and wars waged by Philip in Greece and accounting them all a cut above their current conflicts. This gave rise to recriminations between the younger and older soldiers. And the king had conceived a colossal rancour, despite appearing passively to overhear Cleitus disparaging his reputation. But just when it seemed that the king could keep control of his temper, if Cleitus should stem his impudent invective, he instead abandoned all restraint and greatly aggravated Alexander's anger.

9.8 For now Cleitus even dared to defend Parmenion and extolled Philip's vanquishing of the Athenians over Alexander's obliteration of Thebes, being not only incited by the wine but also inspired by a depraved spirit of provocation. In concluding he complained: "If a man must die for you, then Cleitus is foremost, but when you allot the rewards of victory, the foremost go to those who most mannerlessly mock the memory of your

---

[5] Euripides, *Andromache* 693-698: "Alas, what perverse customs prevail in Greece! Whenever the army sets up a trophy over the foe, men no more consider this the work of those who really toiled, but the general gets the credit for it. He brandished his spear as one man among a myriad others and did no more than a single warrior, yet he gets more praise than they." Cf. Plutarch, *Alexander* 51.5.

Book 9: Autumn 328BC – May 327BC

father. Sogdiana is assigned to me: repeatedly rebellious and not merely unpacified, but even ungovernable. I am being sent among brute beasts, bred for bravado. But I shall pass over my personal predicament. You scorn Philip's fighters, forgetting that if old Atarrhias here had not bellowed the youngsters back into battle when they broke, we should still be hunkered down around Halicarnassus. How therefore have you subdued Asia with such striplings? What your uncle is established to have stated in Italy is valid in my view: that he had to hack his way through men, whilst you had gone up against women.'[6]

9.9 *Among all the ill-advised and unwise words exclaimed by Cleitus, nothing annoyed his monarch more than his respectful reference to Parmenion, but suppressing his resentment Alexander was content to command Cleitus to quit the banquet. And he only added that had he prolonged his prattle, Cleitus might perchance have chided him with having saved his life, a haughty boast he had often trumpeted. Yet Cleitus was still stalling over standing up, so those reclined around him manhandled him, cajoling and cautioning him as they heaved to haul him away. Whilst he was being dragged off, anger augmented his inherent impetuosity, and he yelled that he had defended Alexander's backside with his own breast, but that after such a space of time the recollection of such surpassing service had become abhorrent. Then he even confronted the king with the killing of Attalus, and, finally, he ridiculed the oracle of Ammon, whom Alexander asserted was his father, quipping that he himself had declared more truths than the king's dad had done.*

9.10 *By now Alexander had realized such wrath as he could scarcely have suffered whilst sober. Yet in fact, his senses having long since succumbed to unmixed wine, he suddenly sprang up from his couch. His frantic Friends did not even set down their cups, but, flinging them aside, surged simultaneously to their feet, fixated upon the outcome of an act instigated with such vehemence. Snatching a lance from a guard's grasp, Alexander strove to strike Cleitus, who still ranted with the same reckless rage, but their ruler was restrained by Ptolemy and Perdiccas. They clasped his waist, holding firm as he wrestled against their grip. Lysimachus and Leonnatus also relieved him of his lance. Then Alexander appealed to his loyal troops, for he was beset by his closest comrades, as had but lately befallen Darius, so he shouted for the trumpet peal to be sounded that would gather his guards to the royal rooms.*

---

[6] Alexander of Epirus, the brother of Olympias, had been killed on campaign in Italy in the winter of 331-330BC; Cleitus' quote is also referenced by Livy 9.19.10-11 and Aulus Gellius 17.21.33.

Figure 9.2. The killing of Cleitus (André Castaigne, 1899)

Book 9: Autumn 328BC – May 327BC

9.11 *Then, to be sure, Ptolemy and Perdiccas sank to their knees, pleading that he should not pursue such aggressive anger. Let him spare a space of time to moderate his mind: everything could be effectuated more fairly on the following day. But his ears were impermeable, being filled with fury, so he dashed deliriously into the courtyard of the royal quarters, where he seized a sentinel's lance and lingered in the entranceway where those with whom he had dined must emerge. The rest had retired and Cleitus came out last lacking a lamp. "Who goes there?" the king demanded, even revealing in his voice the severity of the sin that he intended. Then Cleitus, now recalling his ruler's wrath rather than his own, replied that it was he that departed from the party. Even as he uttered this, Alexander lunged the lance into his lungs and was bespattered with the blood of the dying man.* Then he taunted the corpse with Cleitus' praise for the prowess of his father, **crying, "Now, begone to Philip, Parmenion and Attalus!"**[7]

9.12 *Nature has neglected the mind of mankind, for we are wont to weigh repercussions retrospectively. Thus the king, after the anger had seeped from his soul and even his drunkenness had dried out, on reflection realized too late the magnitude of his misdeed. He saw that he had slaughtered a man who had carried candour into calumny on that occasion, but had otherwise been wonderful in warfare and had saved the king's own life, though Alexander were ashamed to admit it. The sovereign had assumed the vile vocation of an executioner, avenging wilful words that might have been ascribed to the wine with an accursed killing. The courtyard was completely covered with the gore of his guest of a moment before and the astonished sentinels seemed stupefied and stood well back from him, so that in solitude his remorse was manifested all the more emotionally.* Weeping and wailing he cuddled the cadaver, wiped its wounds and admitted his madness to it, as if he could be heard. ***And thereupon he levered the lance from the recumbent corpse and turned it upon himself. He had already brought it to his breast when the sentinels sailed in and, though he grappled with them, they grabbed the lance from his grip, heaved him up and hauled him off to his hut. He flung himself down in the dirt and the entire royal residence resounded with his grievous groans and woeful wailing. Indeed he disfigured his face with his fingernails, imploring those around him not to allow him to live on whilst suffering such shame.***

---

[7] Alexander's taunting of the corpse regarding Cleitus' praise for Philip is only reported by Curtius 8.1.52 and Justin 12.6.4, which is a strong indication that Curtius is following the Cleitarchan version. Arrian, *Anabasis* 4.8.9 and Plutarch, *Alex.* 51 recount a variant version where Cleitus is successfully dragged from the hall, but returns reciting Euripides' *Andromache* 693 and is speared in the doorway by Alexander. Arrian states that he found this account in Aristobulus: it is circumstantially more credible than Curtius, who makes Alexander stalk Cleitus in the courtyard.

9.13 *Punctuated by such appeals, the entire night was dragged out.* And in racking his brains as to whether divine retribution might have driven him to commit such an accursed crime, he recalled that he had omitted to make the annual offering to Dionysus on the appointed occasion. It followed that a killing carried out amidst wine and feasting was the unfolding of the fury of the god of those things. *But he was more upset because he was conscious that his comrades were cowering from him. None now would venture to converse convivially with him, but he must live a lonely lifestyle like a brute beast: sometimes instilling terror; at others times itself terrorised.*

9.14 *At first light he commanded that the corpse should be carried into his quarters, though it was ghastly with gore. When it was deposited before him, his tears welled up and he wailed: "This is how I reimburse my nurse, whose two sons gave their lives for my glory at Miletus: her sole solace in this sacrifice, her brother, I have butchered at my banquet. Where now shall she come by comfort in her misery? Of all those close to her, I alone survive, who alone she cannot look upon lovingly. For I, the assassin of my saviours, when I get home to my own country, shall never be able even so much as to proffer my right hand to my nurse without conjuring up her calamity!" And when his weeping and wailing continued uncurtailed, his Companions commanded that the corpse be carried away.*

9.15 *For three days the king confined himself to his quarters. When* by the fourth day he had not yet fed, *his Courtiers and Bodyguards realized that he had resolved to die,* so *they burst as one body into his hut and, though for ages he parried their pleas, through persistence they prevailed upon him to finish his fast.* They begged him not to allow his sorrow for a single soul to sink them all, for after piloting them to the furthest of foreign fields, he would be forsaking them amidst perilous peoples already roused to waging war. He was particularly persuaded by the entreaties of the philosopher Callisthenes, for they were fast friends from studying together under Aristotle and he had been commissioned by the king to record his accomplishments. ***To lessen Alexander's shame for the killing of Cleitus, the Macedonians ordained his death to have been lawful and would even have debarred his burial had it not been commanded by the king.*** *And indeed, Alexander deserves recognition for having regretted his error and repented his wrath, for,* **if you defend your misdeeds, you will double your disgrace.**[8]

---

[8] Fragment 49 = Antonii Melissa I 13 p. 805 D, considered doubtful by Jacoby, but apposite here: with exactly this sentiment Arrian, *Anabasis* 4.9.6, concludes a passage giving the Cleitarchan stories of Alexander's attempted suicide, his guilt regarding his nurse and the omitted sacrifice to Dionysus. He may well have been inspired in all this by Cleitarchus.

Book 9: Autumn 328BC – May 327BC

Figure 9.3. The philosophers console Alexander regarding Cleitus (Pinelli, 1821)

9.16 Thence, having tarried ten days at Maracanda mainly to shake off his shame, **Alexander** sent Hephaistion into the territory of Bactria with a section of his soldiers to secure supplies for the winter. The province he had previously consigned to Cleitus, he handed over to Amyntas, whilst he himself **proceeded to Xenippa.**[9] This region verges upon Scythia and is settled with many teeming townships, since the fertility of its farmland not only sustains its own society but is also a magnet for migrants. It had been the bolthole of the Bactrian renegades who had rebelled against Alexander, but when it was discovered that the king was coming, the people of those parts expelled them. There were two and a half thousand of them amassed, all of them mounted and habituated to banditry even in periods of peace. At that time their innate brutality had been brought out not just by the warfare but also by despair of pardon. So they launched a surprise assault upon Amyntas, Alexander's commander, and the battle long trembled in the balance. But eventually, with seven hundred of their side out of action, of which three hundred had been seized by their foes, they turned tail to their vanquishers, though the victors were scarcely unscathed, since eighty Macedonians had been slain and a further three hundred and fifty were wounded. Yet even after such a second insurrection they negotiated an amnesty.

---

[9] *Xeinipta* or *Xemipta* were read in the *Metz Epitome* 19 before its destruction in 1944.

9.17 After accepting their allegiance, *the king* accompanied by his entire army *entered the country that is called Nautaca*, a part of Bactria.[10] *Its satrap was Sisimithres, who had sired two sons* and three daughters *born from his own mother, since in that society there is sacred sanction for sexual violations between parents and their offspring.* He had armed his populace and protected the pass into his territory with firm fortifications where it became most constricted. A turbulent torrent tore past and the backside was blocked by a rockface, through which the inhabitants had hacked a passageway. Although the entrance to this tunnel let in light, unless lit by a lamp its core was cloaked in darkness. An endless warren known to none save the natives afforded access to the fields.

9.18 Notwithstanding the natural invulnerability of the narrows, which were guarded by a strong garrison of the barbarians, Alexander deployed his battering rams, demolished the manmade barricades and downed most defenders with archers and artillery. When they had been scattered and were scuttling away he scurried across the wreckage of the ramparts and fed his forces forward towards the rockface. But the river rent his route where the waters from the peaks ran together in a gorge and it seemed a titanic task to fill such a vast fissure: yet still he felled timber and aggregated rocks. And the barbarians, being unwitting of such wondrous works, were terribly terrorstricken when they witnessed a causeway suddenly summoned up. The king reckoned as a result that they could be driven by dread to surrender, so he sent Oxartes of their own nation but sworn beneath his sway to coax their captain into conceding the crag. *And Alexander asked Oxartes ere he went what manner of man was the master of this mighty mountain and, on being told he was entirely timid, retorted, "We shall have it then, for he lacks the strength to struggle against us."* Meanwhile to compound their consternation he both sent siege-towers towards them and bombarded them with bolts fired from torsion catapults. Therefore they fled to the crest of the crag, despairing of any other defence. But now Oxartes began to beg Sisimithres, who was disturbed and discomfited by his predicament, to elect to experience the good faith rather than the forcefulness of the Macedonians, lest he should impede the impetus of an all-conquering army that was aiming its aggression against India. For whosoever got in its way would bring down upon his own head the mayhem meant for others.

9.19 Sisimithres himself was reluctant to reject submission, but his mother with whom he mated made known that she would rather perish than pass into the power of another and she steered the mind of the barbarian towards what was more reputable rather than less risky. So he was ashamed that their ladies loved liberty more than their men. Hence he expelled the apostle of peace and resolved to suffer a siege. But thereupon, on pondering the power of his opponent compared to his own, he began to repent pursuing the policy of a

---

[10] Nautaca may be Shakhrisyabz near the headwaters of the Kashka-Darya.

Book 9: Autumn 328BC – May 327BC

woman that he reckoned reckless rather than irresistible. So he promptly recalled Oxartes and said that he would put himself in the king's power, pleading only that Oxartes should not advertise the attitude and advice of his mother in order that he might the more readily appeal for her pardon too. Therefore, sending Oxartes on before him, he followed in his footsteps together with his mother, his children and a coterie of his kindred, without even waiting for the confirmation of safe conduct offered by Oxartes. The king sent a rider to require them to return and await his arrival. Then he himself overhauled them and, upon sacrificing creatures to Athena Nike, he restored his realm to **Sisimithres**, instilling high hopes of still larger lands, if he faithfully **fostered alliance with Alexander.** And Sisimithres consigned his two sons to the king, who assigned them to serve him as soldiers.

9.20 Following this he forsook the phalanx and continued in the company of the cavalry in order to reduce the *rest of the* rebels. Their path was precipitous and blocked by rocks, though at first they managed to cope. Later, however, not only were the horses' hooves worn down, but the beasts were on their last legs. Many fell behind and their ranks gradually grew thinner as, typically, intolerable toil overcame their sense of shame. Yet the king, occasionally switching steeds, rode on relentlessly after the retreating rebels. All the noble youths who customarily escorted him had relinquished that role, with the sole exception of Philip, the brother of Lysimachus, who had reached the threshold of manhood. As was readily evident, he was a character of uncommon capabilities. Incredibly, he flanked his mounted monarch on foot for over five hundred stades, despite wearing a cuirass and bearing arms. Although Lysimachus often looked to lend him his horse, he could not be coaxed from the king's side.

9.21 When they went through woodland in which the barbarians had hidden, this selfsame youth made a famous fight of it, safeguarding his sovereign in hand-to-hand engagements with the enemy. But when the barbarians broke out of the woodland in full flight, the spirit that had inspired the youth in the heat of battle melted away and all of a sudden he perspired profusely from every pore and slumped against a nearby treetrunk. Then, when even that prop failed to bolster him, he collapsed into the king's embrace, wherein he fainted and expired. And the monarch in his mourning was met with another and not lesser sorrow. Just before he got back to his camp he learnt that Erigyius, one of the king's *most* accomplished commanders, had passed away. The funerals of both these fellows were conducted with every honour and utter splendour.

9.22 At winter's end **Alexander aimed to direct his army against the Dahae, for he had heard that Spitamenes was with them.** Yet in this undertaking, as in endless others, Fortune, who never failed in favouring him, arranged everything in his absence. **Spitamenes felt a far too fervent infatuation for his wife, so he hauled her along with him in conjugal jeopardy, though she could scarcely cope with their continual escapes from successive sanctuaries. Harassed by these hardships, she persistently sought to**

persuade her spouse with womanly wiles finally to renounce flight and to make his peace with Alexander, since his clemency in victory had been vindicated and he could not be outrun. *She was the mother of three grownup offspring by Spitamenes that she now ushered into their father's arms as she implored him to pity them at least – and her appeals were the more potent, since* she had heard that *Alexander was not far away. But Spitamenes thought that she sought to forsake rather than forewarn him, supposing that her faith in the power of her beauty had inspired her desire to be given up to Alexander as soon as possible. Hence he drew his sabre and would have struck her down had her brothers not streaked to her defence.*

9.23 *Nevertheless, he ordered her to get out of his sight on pain of death should she stray within his gaze again and to alleviate his lust for her he started to spend his nights amidst mistresses. But his lingering long-term love for her was relit by repugnance for these partners. Hence he reverted to devoting himself to her alone, but never ceased saying that she should refrain from suggesting surrender and tolerate whatever eventualities Fortune might fling at them, since for him perishing was preferable to prostration. Then she excused herself for what she had appraised as profitable proposals, but were perhaps womanish whims, though urged by loyal intentions. Henceforth, she would submit to the mastery of her man.*

9.24 *Being conquered by her counterfeit compliance,* Spitamenes demanded that a daylit banquet be served, at which *with his wife waiting upon him* he washed down wine *and victuals* in surfeit and was carried semi-comatose to his bedchamber. As soon as she was sure that he had sunk into insensible *and silent* slumber, his wife *arose from the bed, slid the pillow from below his head and* slashed *his extended gullet* with a sword that she had hidden in her robes, hacking his head off. Bespattered with blood she handed the head to a slave *who was complicit in the crime.* In his company and still in her gory garments she came into the camp of the Macedonians and called for the king *to be told that she alone should make a matter known to him. Then Alexander's guards conveyed her to the king, since she seemed decent, despite the bloodstains, due to her dignified demeanour and dress.* He ordered that the barbarian be admitted *at once, but the sudden sight of her bespattered with gore gave him pause. Who was she or more to the point why was she there? He supposed that she had come to complain of an assault, so he bade her state what she sought. But she craved that the slave, whom she had had stand in the lobby, should be led within.*

9.25 *Having* the head of Spitamenes *veiled within his vestments*, the slave was suspected and bared *it before his scrutineers. Pallor had suffused the*

Book 9: Autumn 328BC – May 327BC

Figure 9.4. Spitamenes' wife presents his head to Alexander (1696)

features of its anaemic countenance, so it could not be recognized. Hence Alexander, *on hearing that a human head had been brought to him, emerged from his pavilion to ascertain the nature of the thing, which he verified from the vouching of the slave. "Oh, most mutinous Spitamenes," the king exclaimed, "finally you have paid the penalty for your perfidy!" Then he held the hand of the wife whilst thanking her. But thereupon he pondered the connotations of the case and was caught in a perplexing dilemma. He perceived that it was a huge help to him personally that a deserter and defector had been destroyed, who, had he lived, would have delayed Alexander's prodigious designs. Conversely, he was revolted by the vast villainy of her surreptitious slaughter of a husband who had deserved her devotion, the father of her own offspring! So in the end the savagery of her sin vanquished his thankful feelings for her and he* banished her from his base, *lest by her lesson in barbarity the morality and mellow mettle of the Greeks should be compromised.*

9.26 The Dahae, on discovering the killing of Spitamenes, fettered Dataphernes, his fellow defector, and surrendered both him and themselves to Alexander. *On this account the king concluded that he did not need to field his forces against their stronghold.* Being thus unburdened of the bulk of his current cares, he turned his attentions to avenging the grievances of those oppressed by the avarice and arrogance of his governors. Therefore he assigned Hyrcania and the Mardians together with the Tapurians to Phrataphernes, and charged him with sending Phradates, who was the incumbent, to the king in custody. Stasanor succeeded Arsaces, the satrap of the Drangae, whilst Atropates[11] was sent to Media in order that Oxydates might be removed. Due to the demise of Mazaeus, Babylonia was placed under the direction of Ditamenes.

9.27 *At this juncture* with everything in hand, *he reckoned the time was ripe for a contorted concept conceived some time before*, so he set about considering how he might commandeer divine honours for himself. He not only desired that it were said he was the son of Zeus but even wished it were widely believed, as though he might master men's minds as well as their tongues. Hence *he bade the Macedonians to honour him by greeting him with the Persian practice of prostrating their persons upon the soil,* instead of simply saluting him. To fuel such aspirations he never lacked for flagrant flattery, the constant curse of kings, whose power is more often overthrown by fawning than by foes. Neither was it the Macedonians who were delinquent, for none of them would tolerate the least compromising of their country's customs, but rather it was Greeks who perverted the pursuance of the graceful arts with prejudicial practices. For example: there was Agis the Argive, who composed poorer poems than any, save Choerilus; then Cleon of Sicily, a

---

[11] MSS of Curtius had Arsaces, but this is clearly corrupted, cf. Diodorus 18.3.3 & Justin 13.4.13.

Book 9: Autumn 328BC – May 327BC

flatterer not just from a flaw in his own character but from the character of his country; and also the scum of sundry other cities. These the king favoured before even his kinsmen and the commanders of his mightiest contingents, for these were then paving his pathway to Heaven, proclaiming that Heracles, Dionysus and Castor & Pollux would give way to the new deity!

9.28 Accordingly, the king convoked a feast furnished with profusion upon a festal day, to which were invited not merely those Macedonians and Greeks who were the foremost of his Friends, but even any man of rank. When the king was reclining amongst them, after feasting for a little while he quit the banquet. Then, as had been prearranged *by Hephaistion*, Cleon embarked upon a speech celebrating the successes of Alexander and counting their consequential blessings. There was but one way they could give thanks: if, since they had deduced his divinity, they were to acknowledge it, recompensing such benefactions at the paltry expense of incense. Indeed, the Persians were not purely pious, but also rational in reverencing their rulers along with the gods, for it was the awesomeness of the empire that secured their safety. Neither Heracles nor Dionysus had been deemed deities until they had overcome the envy of their contemporaries and posterity perceives only so much of a man as his own time testifies. If the rest were irresolute, he himself would prostrate his person upon the ground when the king came back to the banquet. The others owed it to him to do likewise and those endowed with wisdom foremost, for they should provide the precedent for reverencing their ruler.

9.29 This declaration was undisguisedly directed against Callisthenes. The self-importance and outspokenness of this man were irritating to the king, as though he had single-handedly held back Macedonians who would have settled for such servility! So, in the ensuing silence, all the rest regarded **Callisthenes** expectantly and he **began to speak**: "Had the king experienced your speech himself, then verily there would be no need for anyone to voice a response, since he himself would have solicited that you not incite him to sink into foreign and outlandish habits nor diminish his most productive deeds with the odium of such obsequiousness. But since he is absent, I say to you on his behalf that no fruit can both last long and ripen over-early. You are not heaping heavenly honours upon our sovereign, but seducing them from him. It takes an interval of time to trust in immortality; hence it will forever be posterity that offers this favour to famous men. But I pray that Alexander's apotheosis be delayed, so that he may both live long and enjoy eternal eminence. Divinity sometimes ensues upon a man's demise, but never attends him in his lifetime."

9.30 "You referred to Heracles and Dionysus just now as cases of consecration to immortality. Do you suppose that their deification was decided by a single supper-party? Nay, for Nature seized them from the sight of men before their fame ferried them to Heaven. O Cleon, of course you and I can confer godhead and the king can accrue credentials for his divinity from us! And yet I would wish to put your powers to the test. Let you make a monarch of someone, if you are able to gift godhead. Is it any easier to hand over the heavens than to reassign realms? ***May the gracious gods*** have heard without hatred what Cleon exclaimed, but let them allow matters to move on in the same manner as till now. Let them ***consent that we be content with our own customs.*** I am not ashamed of my homeland and nor do I hanker for coaching by the conquered in the way in which I should pay homage to my monarch. In fact, I am ready to recognize them as our conquerors, if we learn from them the laws by which we live.*"*

9.31 Callisthenes was heard with open ears as if he were the keeper of their communal liberty. He had elicited not just tacit assent but also vocal vindication from the veterans in particular, since the supplanting of their ingrained customs by those of foreigners was discomfiting. Nor was ***the king*** ignorant of aught that was uttered on either side, since he had drawn up behind the drapes that he had caused to curtain the couches. ***In consequence*** he sent word to Agis and Cleon to terminate the debate and ***averred that none but the barbarians in accordance with their customs should perform prostration when he entered.*** Then a little later, as if he had been occupied by more important matters, he came back to the banquet.

9.32 When the Persians performed their venerations of the king, Polyperchon, who was reposing up past Alexander, poked fun at one among them, who had grazed the ground with his chin, by goading him to scrub the floor more forcefully. Hence he reaped the rage of his ruler, who had been unable to contain his temper for some time. The king enquired: "Do you then refuse me reverence? Do we seem solely to yourself to be deserving of derision?" Polyperchon responded that his monarch did not merit mockery, but neither did he himself deserve disdain. At that Alexander wrenched him from his bench and flung him flat upon the floor and when Polyperchon had fallen face down he queried: "Don't you see that you've done what you derided in another just now?" Then he commanded that Polyperchon be placed in custody and he put paid to the partying.

9.33 Actually, ***Alexander*** eventually pardoned Polyperchon after protracted reproof. But his wrath ***was*** more ***resolute against Callisthenes***, whose insubordination had made him suspect for some while. An opportunity to sate his ire was soon to transpire. *It was the custom as already recorded for the main men among the Macedonians to cede their sons into the king's care on their coming of age for duties not distinctly different from the services of slaves. They took turns to keep watch each night just outside an access to the quarters in which the king slept. They used to convey concubines within by a different door than the gangway guarded by the men-at-arms. Similarly, when their monarch meant to mount, they got the steeds from the grooms and led them up. They comprised his company both in the chase and in battle, being diligently indoctrinated in all the noble arts. They enjoyed the outstanding honour that their sovereign consented for them to sit beside him to sup. And none had the power to punish them with a whipping save the sovereign himself.*

Book 9: Autumn 328BC – May 327BC

Among the Macedonians this coterie of Royal Pages was a kind of crèche for commanders and commissioners and some subsequently became kings.

9.34 *So it happened that* Alexander ordered that Hermolaus, a highborn lad from the band of Royal Pages, be lashed, since he had skewered a wild boar earmarked by his monarch for his own spear. Hermolaus began bitterly to bewail his shaming to Sostratus, who was his fellow bandmember and fervent lover. When he beheld the body, for which he burned, so badly lacerated, being perchance already sore with his sovereign on some other account, Sostratus convinced the youth, who was vexed of his own volition, to exchange vows and to conspire with him in killing the king. Nor did they effect the affair with callow incaution, since they shrewdly selected those they would include as their partners in perfidy. They elected to enlist *Nicostratus,* Antipater the son of Asclepiodorus and Philotas and through these Anticles, Elaphthonius and Epimenes were recruited. But no easy way to perpetrate the plot was at all apparent. It was a prerequisite that the entire cabal be keeping watch on the same night, so as to prohibit hindrance by those who had no hand in their intrigue, but it happened that they were all on duty on different nights. Hence thirty-two days were dedicated to shuffling their shifts and to other preparations for implementing their plan.

9.35 The night had come, on which the company of conspirators was due to keep watch, and they were celebrating their solidarity, demonstrated by so many days during which none had wavered through fear or foreboding, so sheer was their shared rage against their ruler or else their faithfulness to their fellows. Thus they were stood by the door of the salon, in which the king was feasting, in order to escort him to his bedchamber when he quit the banquet. But by Alexander's own good fortune as well as the fellowship of the feasters, all of them grew more immoderate with their wine and time was also taken up with festal fun and games. At first the plotters were pleased at the prospect of assaulting an insensible king, then later grew alarmed lest the revelry last till it were light, since substitutes were due to deliver them from their duties at dawn. It would be seven days before the rota returned to them and they could not expect over that span of time that the faith of all their fellows would hold firm.

9.36 But as day was duly dawning, the banquet broke up and the conspirators collected the king, cheered that a chance to commit their crime had been created. Whereupon a woman out of her wits (or so it was supposed) who was wont to frequent the royal quarters since she appeared possessed and able to foretell the future, did not merely meet the monarch as he emerged, but even set herself in his way. In her countenance and her gaze she displayed a disturbance of mind as she cautioned the king to return to his feasting. Alexander playfully replied that the gods gave nice advice and, recalling his comrades, he continued the carousal until almost the second hour of the day.

9.37 By now other youths from the royal band had relieved the guard-posts before the bedchamber door of the king, but the conspirators still stood by though their term of duty had expired: such is the hold exerted by hope once it is harboured in the human mind. Addressing them more kindly than in other cases, the king commanded that they should stand down and have a care for their own persons, since they had stood on station for the entire night. He gave each of them fifty drachmae and commended them, because they had continued on guard even after the duty had devolved upon others. And they, deprived of such high hopes, betook themselves to their billets. While the rest of them awaited the night of their next watch, Epimenes abruptly repented his participation, either because of the courtesy of the king in relieving him along with the other conspirators or because he believed that the gods were obstructing their objective. Hence he revealed what had been arranged to his brother Eurylochus, whom he had previously preferred to keep clear of the conspiracy.

9.38 Everyone had the fatal fall of Philotas in view, so Eurylochus instantly seized his brother and arrived at the royal quarters, and having roused the Bodyguards, he assured them that what he had to say concerned the safety of their sovereign. Ptolemy and Leonnatus, who were on watch at the threshold of the king's bedchamber, were galvanised both by the hour of their arrival and by their countenances, which hardly heralded settled souls, not to mention the sorrow exuding from the second of them. Flinging wide the doors and leading a lamp within, they woke the king from the stupefied slumber of strong wine. He gradually gathered his wits and asked what they wished to divulge. Without demur, Eurylochus declared that the gods could not completely have forsaken his house, because his brother, despite daring to dabble in faithless foul play, was nevertheless both remorseful and personally proposed to expose the conspiracy. The plot had been planned for that very night that was now vanishing and the perpetrators of this treachery were such as their sovereign would least suspect.

9.39 Then point-by-point Epimenes gave vent to everything he knew including the names of the conspirators. It is established that Callisthenes was not named as a participant in the perpetration of the plot, yet he was wont indeed to offer an affable ear to the youths when they ranted and raved against their ruler. And certain persons assert that when Hermolaus bewailed his whipping in his hearing, Callisthenes confided that it was incumbent upon them to recall that they were now men. But whether this was said in consolation for suffering the lashing or to rouse rancour among the youths remains in doubt.

9.40 When the king conceived what a dire danger he had dodged, losing his lethargy in mind and body, he at once rewarded Eurylochus with fifty talents and the prosperous property of a certain Tiridates. He also gave his brother back to him before he even begged for his deliverance, but ***the authors of the outrage, and among them Callisthenes, the king commanded to be kept***

Book 9: Autumn 328BC – May 327BC

in fetters.[12] When these persons had been pulled into the palace quarters, wearied by wine and waiting up the king rested right through that day and the next night. The following day the king convened a mass meeting intermingled with the fathers and family of those accused. Neither were these kindred confident of keeping themselves safe, for according to the killing custom of the Macedonians the lives of all were liable to be lost who were related to those arraigned. The king commanded that all the conspirators save Callisthenes be brought forth and they confessed without hesitation what they had been hatching. Then, when the crowd growled at them, the king himself grilled them as to what he had done to deserve the devising of such damnable designs against his person.

9.41 The rest being totally tongue-tied, Hermolaus replied: "As you ask as though you did not know, we did indeed design your death due to you beginning to bully us as if we were slaves rather than ruling us as your countrymen." His own father, Sopolis, reacted most rapidly among them all, moaning that he was morally the murderer of his dad and barging forwards to muffle his son's mouth with his hand, declaring that they ought no longer to listen to a man made mad by malice and misfortune. But, restraining his parent, Alexander told Hermolaus to tell them what he been taught by his tutor Callisthenes.

9.42 Hermolaus retorted: "I shall capitalize on your kindness by telling what I have been taught by our catastrophes. Not many Macedonians remain as a result of your ruthlessness! Not many at all, excepting those of most servile descent! Attalus and Philotas and Parmenion and Alexander Lyncestes and Cleitus as far as our foes have fathomed still thrive; still stand in fighting formation, their shields sheltering you, enduring injuries for your glory and for your victory. To these you have rendered remarkable requital. One garnished your table with his gore; another did not even die a clean death. The commanders of your contingents were racked in torment for the entertainment of Persians over whom they had prevailed. Parmenion, through whom you had exterminated Attalus, was hacked down without a hearing. Truly in turn you utilize the hands of unhappy people to perpetrate your purges, then you unexpectedly order others to annihilate those who have just served as your assassins."

9.43 At this the whole host howled at Hermolaus and his father drew his death-dealing blade and would undoubtedly have dispatched his son had his ruler not restrained him. Of course, the king called for Hermolaus to carry on and appealed for patience in hearing him out, as he was compounding the case for his condemnation. When with difficulty they had been calmed down, Hermolaus continued, "How courteously you consent for boys inexperienced in speaking to spout forth. Yet the voice of Callisthenes is kept in confinement,

---

[12] Strabo 11.11.4 locates the arrest of Callisthenes in Cariatae in Bactria.

since he alone is adept at discourse. Why else indeed is he not appearing, when even those who have confessed are granted a hearing? Doubtless you dread to hear free speech from a spotless speaker or even to look him in the face. However, I hold that he had no hand in anything. Those who devised the dashing deed are here with me. There is none among us who alleges that Callisthenes was in league with us, though each has been doomed to die by the most tolerant and righteous of rulers. Such therefore are the rewards of the Macedonians, whose blood you squander as if it were squalid and expendable. Thirty-thousand mules convey your captured gold, whilst your troops will traipse home with naught save the scars from uncompensated injuries."

9.44 "Still we could have stood all this before you abandoned us to the barbarians and as a novel vogue set the victors under the yoke. You revel in the rites and robes of the Persians and revile the customs of your own country. Hence we wished to do away with a Persian potentate rather than a Macedonian monarch and we meant to molest you under martial law as a deserter. You desired the Macedonians to kneel before you and to venerate you as a god. You spurn Philip's paternity and, were any god exalted above Zeus, you would actually disdain *the kinship of* Zeus himself. Are you amazed that autonomous men cannot tolerate your arrogance? What hope can we have in you, if we must either suffer a sinless death or else survive in servitude sadder than death? You shall indeed owe much to me, if you can mend your ways. For from me you have begun to ken what cannot be borne by freeborn men. For the rest, be moderate and do not pile punishments upon those made childless in old age. But order us led forth to be liquidated, so that what we sought to gain from your death we may attain through our own." So said Hermolaus.

9.45 But Alexander responded: "It is patent from my patience how ridiculous the defendant's testimony is as taught to him by his tutor. For though he has confessed to the foulest of offences I have not only heard him out myself, but also had you hear him. For I well knew that when I allowed this delinquent to lecture you, he would manifest the madness that made him mean to murder me, when it was his duty to foster me like a father. Recently, when he behaved impertinently on a hunt, according to the custom of our country and the conduct of immemorial Macedonian monarchs, I ordered that he be disciplined. This is both proper practice and is also perpetrated upon pupils by their pedagogues and upon wives by their husbands. We even suffer slaves to whip boys of his age. Such then was the supposed savagery from me, which he sought to avenge with an insidious assassination. Yet the rest of the youths let me treat them according to my disposition, though my leniency is legendary and beyond suspicion."

9.46 "By Heracles! That Hermolaus disapproves of the punishment of traitors scarcely surprises me, since he has himself deserved the same penalty. Thus indeed he serves his own cause in favouring Philotas and Parmenion with his applause. Actually Alexander Lyncestes I left at liberty despite him conspiring

Book 9: Autumn 328BC – May 327BC

twice against my life by the testimony of two informants. When he was once more implicated in plotting, I still stayed my hand for three years, until you yourselves demanded that he duly die to atone for his duplicity. As for Attalus, you will recall that he posed a threat to my life ere I became king. Concerning Cleitus, I would he had not roused me to such rancour against him! Yet I tolerated his reckless tongue lambasting both you and me with abuse for longer than he would have let me likewise vilify him. The clemency of kings and commanders relies not solely on themselves, but also correlates with the characters of those they command. Compliancy cushions compulsion, but when deference dies in men's minds and the highest are jumbled with the humblest, then force must needs fend off force."

9.47 "But why would I wonder that the defendant has denounced me as a despot, when he has the audacity to accuse me of covetousness? I would not wish you to bear witness one by one, for fear of forcing my generosity to rebound on me, if I make it undermine your modesty. But behold our whole army: those that a bit beforehand had nothing but their arms now slouch on silver couches, burden their benches with gold, lord it over loads of slaves and cannot transport all the spoils they chose from our foes."

9.48 "But he states that the Persians stand high in my esteem, though we have vanquished them. In fact it is the surest sign of my clemency that I do not even dominate the defeated with disdain. For I did not enter Asia intending utterly to dispossess its peoples nor to wipe out half the world, but rather conceiving that those I overcame in conflict should cease to resent my victory. And so they serve as soldiers beside you, shedding their blood to shield your empire, whom harshness would have roused to rebellion. Possession secured through the sword is never lasting, whereas gratitude for graces is everlasting. If we wish to win over Asia, rather than just journey through it, we must convey our compassion to these people. Their loyalty to us shall establish a stable and enduring empire. And in reality we have more territory than we can occupy. Indeed, it is insatiable greed to keep on filling what is already overspilling. Yet I am reproved for pressing the practices of the Persians upon the Macedonians. Certainly, I see in many peoples aptitudes that we should not blush to emulate and such an immense empire cannot correctly be ruled other than by both handing habits to its inhabitants and assimilating some from them."

9.49 "As for Hermolaus' assertion that I should spurn Zeus, whose own oracle acknowledged me, that almost merited mirth. Is it even in my power to determine what deities ordain? Zeus presented me with the sobriquet of son. Nor was accepting it at odds with the activities in which we are engaged. Would that the Indians should believe me to be a god, for warfaring feeds on fame and often even a false faith has gained the tribute of truth. *Do you imagine that I am having your arms emblazoned with silver and gold to suit my sense of extravagance? Actually, I wish to show to those used to nothing meaner than these metals that the Macedonians, who are invincible in everything else, cannot even be beaten in gold. Therefore from the first I shall* *amaze the gaze of those that expect to see a wholly meek and meager host, inculcating that our coming is not due to our desire for silver and gold but in order to hold the whole world in our hands. Such is the triumph, traitor, that you have sought to forestall and by eliminating their king to set the Macedonians at the mercy of the conquered countries."*

9.50 "Yet you exhort me to spare your kindred. It is not really right that you be made aware of my decision on this, so your deaths might be the more distressing, if indeed you have any respect and regard for your relatives. But in fact I long since suspended that particular practice of killing the guiltless kith and kin as well as the culprit[13] and I avow that they shall all now retain the same rank as they formerly merited. Concerning your Callisthenes, who alone sees in you a soldier though you are really a marauder, I well know why you wish him to be brought forth. It is so there might once more emerge from his mouth before this meeting those slurs that you have just slung at me and had earlier heard from him. Were he a Macedonian, I would have had him appear with you, a master most meriting such a student, but as an Olynthian he is not subject to the same jurisdiction."

9.51 After this Alexander dismissed the Assembly and commanded that the condemned be consigned to the custody of their colleagues from the same cohort. These tortured them to death, so that their ferocity might make manifest their faithfulness to the king. **Callisthenes** also **succumbed to torment, despite being spotless in respect of any conspiracy against the king's life.**[14] But his character was not at all compatible with a court and its sycophants. Consequently, no other killing caused greater grievance among the Greeks against Alexander, for Callisthenes was furnished with the finest feelings and faculties and had coaxed back the king's capacity for life when he had determined to die after the killing of Cleitus. Yet Alexander not only slew but also harrowed him without even a hearing. Repentance of this persecution came too late.

9.52 All being settled, **Alexander** *fared forth with his forces* after two months ensconced in winter quarters *and* **headed towards the territory known as Gazaba.** *The first day provided for peaceful progress. The next, whilst*

---

[13] In the context of the conviction of Philotas: Curtius 6.11.20 and Section 7.72 above.

[14] There is considerable diversity in the ancient accounts of the death of Callisthenes: Plutarch, *Alexander* 55 cites Chares for a relatively credible version, which had Callisthenes expire from obesity and infestation by lice after seven months in a cage; Aristobulus broadly concurred and the Cleitarchan account as reconstructed mainly from Curtius 8.8.21-23 is not explicitly inconsistent with Chares & Aristobulus; Justin 15.3.4 expands the caging version with antecedent mutilation and by having Lysimachus assist Callisthenes' suicide with poison, but Alexander's consequential punishment of his Bodyguard by exposing him to a lion appears anachronistic relative to the Cleitarchan version; Ptolemy's suggestion that Callisthenes was hanged (Arrian, *Anabasis* 4.14.3) may be a gloss on the less savoury truth. Callisthenes must have died in privacy for such disagreement to stem from the early sources. But hanging is a mode of execution that implies an audience.

Book 9: Autumn 328BC – May 327BC

not particularly tempestuous and miserable, was nonetheless gloomier than before and did not end without warning of impending blight. Then upon the third day, *in gathering gloom* lightning flashes flamed across the whole scope of the sky, *alternately illuminating and eclipsing the landscape and beginning to sear the souls as well as the eyes of the forces forging forwards.* There were nearly continuous cracks of thunder and bolts of lightning were witnessed to fall far and wide. *Hence* the army, being both deafened and dazed, *dared neither to endure it where they were nor to press on, whereupon* they were *suddenly* hit by a hurricane of hail *that poured upon them with the power of a torrent.*

9.53 At first they deflected the deluge *by sheltering beneath their shields,* but soon *these slippery* safeguards could no longer be held in hands stiffened by the storm. *Nor could they decide which way they should shift themselves, since* they were met on every side by a more tumultuous tempest than they cared to confront. *Therefore* their ranks were ruptured and their formations straggled throughout the forest. *Being fatigued by fear even ere they over-exerted themselves,* many *among them* grovelled upon the ground, despite the fierce frost cohering the hail into hard ice. The troops' tents and textiles too were rendered rigid by the intensifying frigidity. Though some sought shelter under cliffs and overhangs, others still were too stiff to stoop from their steeds. Others *again* entrusted themselves to the trunks of trees, which provided a prop and protection for many. *Yet they knew that they might be choosing a spot to expire, since they would shed the warmth of vitality through inactivity. But dormancy was welcome in their weariness, so they failed to refuse to perish for the sake of being at rest.* In fact the force of this foulness was not just furious but also tenacious, and the light that is Nature's solace was filtered out by the forest shade, which combined with the murk of the maelstrom, leaving it little lighter than night.

9.54 *None but the king was able to cope with such a calamity: by circulating amongst his soldiers, mustering the missing men, lifting up those that were languishing and indicating the smoke that twirled up from huts in the distance, urging each man to requisition the nearest refuge.* Nothing was more crucial to their salvation than that they were ashamed to forsake their sovereign, who was, by redoubling his efforts, overcoming the calamity to which they themselves had succumbed. Furthermore, force of circumstances, which is more effective when in difficulty than cool calculation, discovered a cure for the cold: for they fought to fell the forest far and wide with their hatchets and set fire to the heaps and piles of lumber. It soon seemed as though the woods were an unbroken inferno with scarcely room to range their regiments between the flames. The heat from this blaze revived their numbed limbs and little by little their breath that had been curbed by the cold began to course more freely.

9.55 Some settled themselves in the bothies of the barbarians *that in extremity they had hunted out, though they were hidden in the heart of the forest. Others kept to a camp that they had set up upon sodden soil, since the savagery of the skies was now abating.* That scourge massacred as **many** as thirty thousand **military men** *including also servants and sutlers and* four thousand **beasts of burden.** *Many more men that made it back to camp were incapacitated by exhaustion or injury. Those that had collapsed upon the ground had found that their clothes stuck sound, rendering them helpless and no help to anyone. It is also attested that some were seen attached to the trunks of trees, seeming to be not only alive but even indulging in conversation, yet frozen in that attitude in which death had surprised them.*

9.56 *It chanced that an elderly man of the Macedonian rank and file had managed to reach the camp, though hardly able to hold himself upright let alone his arms. On catching sight of him, Alexander sprang from his seat, despite having just then been warming himself back up close to a fire. He relieved the lethargic and almost insensible soldier of his arms and bade him settle himself in the selfsame seat. For a long while he was unaware of where he was resting and who had rescued him. On eventually reviving to vitality with the warmth, he saw that he was sitting in his sovereign's seat in the king's presence and rose up in trepidation. Regarding him attentively, Alexander queried: "Do you appreciate, soldier, how much more comfortably you live under a king than the Persians? Among them your life would have been forfeit for resting upon the royal throne, yet in fact your life has been saved by it."*

9.57 The following day, having convened his Friends and the commanders of his contingents, the king ordered it to be announced that he would himself make restitution for all that had been lost. And he faithfully fulfilled this undertaking, since Sisimithres delivered loads of pack-mules and two thousand camels as well as flocks of sheep and herds of oxen, which were distributed evenly among the soldiers, saving them from suffering and famine. The king proclaimed his gratitude to Sisimithres for these services and instructed his troops to carry cooked food sufficient for six days in setting out against the Sacae. Having ravaged the whole region, he presented Sisimithres with thirty thousand looted livestock.

9.58 Alexander then pressed on in his progress towards Gazaba and entered the territory that was in the sway of the celebrated satrap Chorienes, who submitted himself to the mastery and magnanimity of the monarch. Alexander restored him to his rule, *requiring nothing more than that two of his three sons serve as soldiers in the king's campaigns. In fact in their friendship the satrap also surrendered the son he had kept into the custody of the king.*

Book 9: Autumn 328BC – May 327BC

9.59 Chorienes[15] convened a banquet equipped with outlandish luxury, to which he welcomed Alexander. Whilst this was being conducted with considerable conviviality, the satrap instructed that thirty thoroughbred virgins should be introduced *as dancers at the dinner. These included the satrap's own maiden daughters as well as those of his friends.* The most remarkably radiant among them was Roxane *and she was also distinguished in her deportment to a degree that is rare among the barbarians. Though she strode among a select band of beauties, yet she garnered the gape of all and most especially* engaged the gaze of Alexander, *who was no longer so much the master of his lust, having been fawned upon by Fortune, whom mortal men too little distrust.*

9.60 *Hence* he *who had beheld with hardly more passion than that of a parent Darius' queen and her pair of virgin daughters, to whom none except Roxane could compare in comeliness,* was *then so* infatuated with feelings for this *little* virgin *of vulgar roots relative to royalty that he at once* asked to know her name and her father. On discovering that she was the daughter of Oxyartes, *also a diner at the dinner,* the king *took up his cup and tipped a libation to the gods, then* began to declaim: "Much that befalls many men and women commonly occurs against expectations. Thus countless kings have sired sons on women won in war *or dispatched daughters to distant domains to seal an alliance with wedlock.* Indeed it is conducive to the durability of my domains that Persians and Macedonians be matched in matrimony, for only so may the humiliation of the vanquished and the vanity of the victors both be banished. And among my own ancestors, Achilles, of course, coupled with a captive wench."

9.61 Then the king focused upon the foreigners: "In my view the Macedonians are not a better breed than you and nor do I believe you to be beneath intermarriage with us too, even though you look for an alliance with us as losers. Therefore to forestall all ill-feeling I would like by lawful wedding to take to wife Roxane and I shall ensure that the other Macedonians act accordingly." He himself having exhorted his Friends with these words, each of them led away a virgin that he wedded at the banquet. Oxyartes and the rest of the foreigners were happy beyond their hopes for this to happen *and Alexander, in the heat of his ardent desire, ordered that a loaf of bread be brought in accordance with his country's customs. This was sliced with a sword and tasted by the two of them, which is the most sacrosanct surety of marriage among the Macedonians.*

---

[15] "Cohortandus" in the manuscripts of Curtius, spuriously altered to Oxyartes by Aldus: the true error in Curtius is to state that Roxane was a daughter of Cohortandus; it is clear from Metz 28-29 that Cleitarchus wrote that Roxane danced among Cohortandus' daughters, but was herself the daughter of one of his friends.

Figure 9.5. The marriage of Alexander and Roxane (André Castaigne, 1899)

Book 9: Autumn 328BC – May 327BC

9.62 *In this fashion, the King of Asia and Europe married a maid who had been paraded as a performer at a feast, so as to breed from the conquered a king to command their conquerors. His Friends were ashamed that Alexander should have decided the parentage of his bride from among the defeated whilst wining and dining, but after the killing of Cleitus freedom of expression was suppressed and assent was expressed by their facial expressions, which are the most submissive.*

9.63 These were the concerns of Alexander *in the ninth year of his reign.*

6. Alexander's Route Through Afghanistan

The problem of Alexander's route is at its most complex and controversial during his Afghan years (see Figure 6.1). A recapitulation, let alone a resolution, of all the issues is beyond the scope of this relatively short review. Rather the objective is to identify some of the key interdependencies between the reconstructed text of Cleitarchus and Alexander's geographical whereabouts. In the rest of this Section, "Engels" means *Alexander the Great and the Logistics of the Macedonian Army* by Donald Engels and "Brunt" means Appendix VIII in Vol. I of P. A. Brunt's Loeb translation of Arrian's *History of Alexander and Indica*.

The *Stathmoi* or Stages of Alexander's journey are of central importance for the geography of Alexander's route in these years, as has been shown in the discussion of the location of Prophthasia in Section 2. The distances between major cities, towns and fortresses on their march seem to have been recorded by Alexander's *bematists* or pacers and some of their data has been preserved in surviving ancient texts, notably Strabo's *Geography* 11.8.9 and Pliny's *Natural History* 6.61-62. A detailed analysis of the *Stathmoi* is also beyond the ambitions of this volume, but the reader may refer to Table 8 in Appendix 5 of Engels and Appendix VIII of Brunt's Loeb translation of Arrian's *Anabasis* and *Indica* for the rudiments of their application to the problems of Alexander's itinerary.

Shortly after the death of Darius, Alexander sojourned at Hecatompylus, which has been associated with the excavated ruins of an ancient city 32km southwest of the modern Damghan at a site called Sahr-i Qumis (Engels p.83; Brunt p.495-6).

Regarding Alexander's subsequent advance into Hyrcania in the late summer of 330BC, Cleitarchus' vivid description of the River Stiboeites provides a promising landmark for determining the king's route. And indeed the Stiboeites has been tentatively identified with the modern Chesmeh-i-Ali about 25km NW of Hecatompylus.[1]

Cleitarchus mentions an Hyrcanian town that housed the palace of Darius at Section 7.31. This might be another reference to Arvae, which had already been mentioned in 7.24. Arvae seems to be identical with Zadracarta in Arrian, *Anabasis* 3.23.6. The best available speculation (Engels p.84; Brunt p.497) is that this should be the modern Sari.

Satibarzanes surrenders to Alexander at Section 7.40. This occurred at Sousia according to Arrian, *Anabasis* 3.25.1-3, which is probably the modern Tus (Engels p.85; Brunt p.498) about 20km north of Meshed. If so, Alexander was

---

[1] P. Pédech, "Deux campagnes d'Antiochus III chez Polybe," *Revue des Études Anciennes*, 60 (1958), 67-81.

Alexander's Route Through Afghanistan

already well on his way eastwards beyond Hyrcania, when the baggage was incinerated.

The next major destination on Alexander's march was the chief city of Aria, which is Artacana in the manuscripts of Curtius 6.6.33 and Artacoana in Arrian, *Anabasis* 3.25.6, but Chortacana in Diodorus 17.78.1. Its location remains unconfirmed. Most authorities have assumed that it lay at or in the close vicinity of modern Herat, but Donald Engels has argued that the "rock" in the nearby mountains was Kalat-i-Nadiri 60km north of Tus.[2] A reconciliation of this with the order of events in the Cleitarchan tradition is not apparent, since, for example, Engels reverses the order of the attack on Artacana and the siege of the rebel stronghold in the mountains; it is easier to accept the traditional view, which would place Alexander on the borders of Bactria near Kushka ~100km immediately north of Herat when he heard of the defection of Satibarzanes and took the major decision to divert his advance southwards instead of marching directly eastwards towards Bactria (although Brunt p.498 thinks that Alexander had always intended to visit Artacana). Hence the Cleitarchan tradition supports the traditional interpretation that Artacana was near Herat, which is also the approximate site of the king's foundation of Alexandria in Aria (cf. Strabo 11.10.1 & Claudius Ptolemy, *Geography* 6.17).

As has already been extensively discussed in Section 2, the Philotas Affair seems to have taken place at Prophthasia, which was founded by Alexander at or close to the modern Farah (Brunt p.499). Afterwards Alexander headed on southwards into central Drangiana (Drangianê). It is overwhelmingly likely on logistical ground that he reached the vicinity of Lake Seistan and then journeyed through the lands of the Arimaspians (a.k.a. Euergetae), following the Helmand River eastwards to the vicinity of Kandahar, which lay at the far edge of the Arimaspian zone (Engels p.91-3).

Metz Epitome 4 records that Alexander founded a town in the territory of the Arimaspians on the route into India, which he named Alexandria. This probably records the foundation of Kandahar, since it is clear that it was a city foundation within the Arimaspian territory and Kandahar is on one of the main routes into India proper. Thereafter, the beleaguering of the army in deep snow (Sections 7.96-97) is likely to have occurred between Ghazni and Kabul, where such conditions are normal in winter, for Alexander reached this region in the winter of 330-329BC.

Arrian, *Anabasis* 3.28.4 and Strabo 15.2.10 as well as Curtius 7.3.23 and Diodorus 17.83.1 confirm the foundation of Alexandria-in-the-Caucasus at the foot of the Hindu Kush probably in the vicinity of Begram and Charikar. The manuscripts of Diodorus 17.83.1 read that the city was founded "in the pass which leads down to Media", which must be an error - perhaps "Media" should

---

[2] Donald Engels, *Alexander the Great and the Logistics of the Macedonian Army*, pp.87-91.

be "India". According to Strabo 15.2.10, the city was on the Indian side of the mountains, where Alexander wintered in 330-29BC (as discussed in Section 2, India incorporated southern Afghanistan in Cleitarchan geography.) Engels p.94-95 believes that Alexander crossed the Hindu Kush into Bactria via the Khawak Pass in the spring of 329BC, rapidly penetrating to Bactra (a.k.a. Zariaspa) as Bessus fled the scene.

Anyone who feels that the Cleitarchan descriptions of the terrain are vague or exaggerated would do well to examine the route between Bactra (modern Balkh at Google coordinates [36.768352, 66.901674]) and the River Oxus (modern Amu-Darya at Google coordinates [37.359242, 66.869316]) on Google Maps in the Satellite images view. The overall distance is about 70km, corresponding closely to the 400 stades mentioned by Cleitarchus 8.12. The last 30km just south of the river is a band of gargantuan dunes, some of them hundreds of metres long and therefore tens of metres tall (as can be seen by zooming in on the Google satellite image). On their leeward edge they would have been too steep to be negotiated by men in armour or carrying heavy packs, which would have compelled them to wend a winding course through these obstacles. Progress would have been agonisingly slow and the place a great trial for men on foot just as Cleitarchus avers.

Thereafter Alexander progressed to Maracanda, which is probably the modern city of Samarkand in Uzbekistan (Brunt p.504-505, Engels p.99 is skeptical about the identification of every site in Sogdiana). A deceptive pacification having been imposed upon Sogdiana, Alexander moved up to the river that his expedition (and Cleitarchus following them) identified as the Tanais (which is actually the Greek name for the River Don). This was in reality the Syr-Darya, more correctly called the Jaxartes by later ancient geographers. Here he founded Alexandria Eschate ("the Farthest"), which has been located at modern Khujand (Khodjend).³ When revolts broke out, Cyropolis was besieged by Craterus (Cleitarchus 8.30). It might be Kurkath (Engels p.103).

After campaigning extensively across Sogdiana in order to quell the widespread revolts, which appear to have flared up in response to his city foundations and the air of permanence that they lent to the Macedonian presence, Alexander eventually returned to Bactra, where he wintered in 329-328BC. En route, as mentioned by Cleitarchus in Section 8.56, he crossed the River Polytimetus, which is probably the modern Zeravshan (see Engels p.100). The direction and course of the next campaign, when he set forth for a second time from Bactra in the spring of 328BC, has been a matter of particular controversy. This is recounted from Section 8.60 onwards in the reconstruction of Cleitarchus. A cogent explanation of Alexander's itinerary at this point, where the king eventually moves back into Sogdiana, has been put forward by A. B. Bosworth,

---

³ Cf. Arrian, *Anabasis* 4.4.1 & Justin 12.5; Engels p. 103 is dubious about the exact location, although Brunt p. 505 embraces Khujand.

Alexander's Route Through Afghanistan

"A Missing Year in the History of Alexander the Great", *Journal of Hellenic Studies*, Vol. 101, pp.17-39, 1981. Bosworth points out that the readings *marganiam* or *marginiam* in the manuscripts of Curtius 7.10.15 should not have been emended to read *margianam* (i.e. Margiana, the modern Merv), thereby diverting the expedition way out to the west across vast desert tracts. Instead, the River Ochus that is mentioned must be a major tributary of the Oxus River in the east of Bactria, which makes it most probably the modern River Surkhab. Hence Alexander travelled east from Bactra (rather than west) until he met the Oxus and continued eastwards along its southern bank (i.e. without crossing). Somewhere north of Kunduz, he crossed the Ochus (Surkhab), and then he headed on into the Kochka region, where he crossed the Oxus heading northwards somewhere near Ai Khanum (where the ruins of a major early Hellenistic town have been excavated not far from the confluence of the Oxus with the River Kochka). Margania must have been an otherwise unknown ancient city in the region to the north of the Oxus, which was the southeastern part of ancient Sogdiana (the hill country of modern Tajikistan). It cannot have been Margiana (Merv), since it does not fit the geography described by Cleitarchus in the least (see also Brunt p.506, who agrees that Alexander never visited Margiana, but wrongly blames Curtius for the confusion, which is actually modern in origin). This results in a site for the Rock of Ariamazes in the mountains on the northern margins of Bactria. It then looks as if the division of the army into several columns in the summer was in order that they should advance in parallel up the various valleys of, for example, the rivers Shirabad, Surkhan, Kafirnigan and Vakhsh, which are tributaries of the Oxus with their sources in the Hissar Range. Perhaps he crossed the mountains via the Anzob Pass and/or the Iron Gate Pass down into the vally of the River Zeravshan, which flows past Samarkand further to the west. Eventually the army was reassembled at Maracanda at the end of the summer.

After the killing of Cleitus at Maracanda in the Autumn of 328BC, Alexander cleared out the rebels from a region called Xenippa (Cleitarchus 9.16) that verged upon Scythia and then overawed Sisimithres (Cleitarchus 9.17) at the end of 328BC at Nautaca, where he seems to have spent most of the winter (Arrian, *Anabasis* 4.18.2). Nautaca may be Shakhrisyabz near the headwaters of the Kashka-Darya as suggested by Bosworth.[4]

In the winter of 328-327BC Spitamenes was slain by his wife and resistance collapsed. Alexander diverted himself with the *proskynesis* experiment and the Conspiracy of the Pages ensued. Strabo 11.11.4 locates the arrest of Callisthenes at Cariatae in Bactria, but we do not know where this was.

Afterwards, Alexander headed for Gazaba and was caught in an horrendous hailstorm en route. The army was rescued from destitution by Sisimithres (so

---

[4] A. B. Bosworth, "A Missing Year in the History of Alexander the Great", *Journal of Hellenic Studies*, Vol. 101, 1981, p. 36.

they had not gone far from Nautaca). On reaching Gazaba, its ruler, Chorienes, surrendered to the king and convened the banquet, which engendered Alexander's marriage to Roxane. The location of Gazaba is unknown, but Alexander was probably heading back southwards into central Bactria on his way to India in the late spring of 327BC.

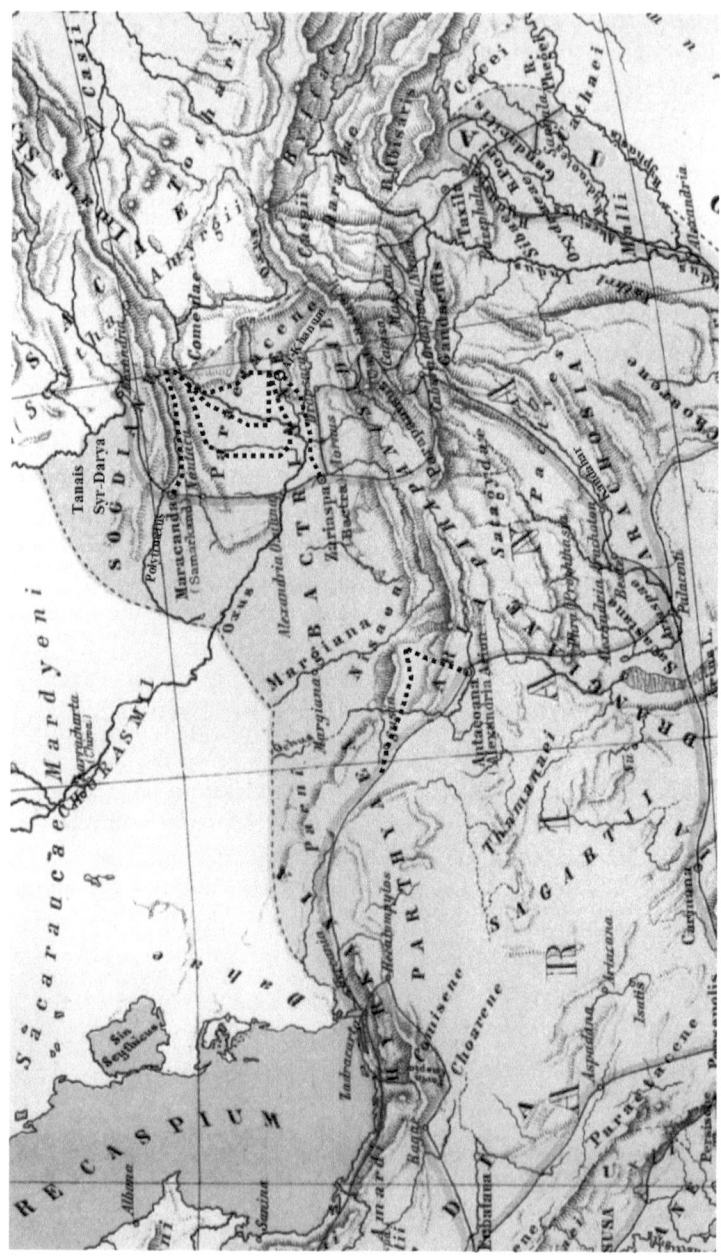

Figure 6.1. Alexander's route in the vicinity of Afghanistan

7. Organisation And Sources

The first column outlines each successive episode in Cleitarchan terms. The second gives the extant sources for each episode. The third cites references to the Cleitarchan nature of the material and the last provides technical comments.

Book 7: July 330BC – June 329BC

Summary	Sources	References	Comment
Advance to Hecatompylus. Persuasion of the army to join in the pursuit of Bessus, who declares himself king and adopts royal regalia as Artaxerxes.	Curtius 6.2.15-6.4.1 Diodorus 17.74.3-17.75.1 Justin 12.3.2-3 (Plutarch 47.1-2) King Bessus: Diodorus 17.74.1 Curtius 6.6.13	(Hammond Sources 80); C6.2.15=D17.75.1 Schwartz	Hammond THA 58 & 134 argues Diyllus as the source for Curtius and Diodorus. But the details are very similar in Justin too, so the common source must be Cleitarchus. Hammond worries that Plutarch has a slightly different order of events and indeed Plutarch attributes his version to a letter from Alexander to Antipater, so it is doubtful whether Plutarch followed Cleitarchus here.
Entry into and description of Hyrcania and the Caspian Sea	Diodorus 17.75 Curtius 6.4.1-22	Hammond THA 58 & 135; C6.4.3-6=D17.75.2 Schwartz; C6.4.18,22=D17.75.3,6 Schwartz	Onesicritus may be the ultimate source of the natural history details – Aristobulus is unlikely despite noting oaks in Hyrcania
Caspian Sea equal to the Euxine (Black Sea)	Pliny NH 6.36-38 Plutarch 44.1-2	Jacoby, Fragment 12 of Cleitarchus Hammond Sources 77	This resembles a comment by Patrocles, a geographer who wrote circa 280BC and was cited by Eratosthenes, but it is possible that the comments are independent of one another or that Cleitarchus inspired Patrocles.
The isthmus between the Caspian and the Euxine is subject to inundation from either sea	Strabo 11.1.5	Jacoby, Fragment 13 of Cleitarchus, Brown, Clitarchus p.140	The "isthmus" in question is the region of the Caucasus Mountains, neither low-lying nor narrow – Brown suggests this was inspired by Polycleitus' error of confusing the Sea of Azov with the Aral Sea
Wonders of Hyrcania: the wasp (*tenthredon*) of the hill-country	Demetrius, De Eloc. 304 Diodorus 17.75.7	Jacoby, Fragment 14 of Cleitarchus	Diodorus has *anthredon*; Tarn (vol 2, Sources, p.90 n.3) notes that Diodorus uses a peculiar phrase μεγίστην ἐπιφάνειαν and a rare verb κηροπλαστεῖν in describing this bee-like creature; the same combination occurs in one other place in Diodorus 19.2.9 in a passage Tarn attributes to Timaeus. Tarn poses the question of whether Cleitarchus is using Timaeus; our answer must be yes, given the other evidence of his doing so.

Alexander the Great in Afghanistan by Andrew Chugg

Summary	Sources	References	Comment
Surrender of Persian commanders (Phrataphernes, Phradates, Artabazus)	Curtius 6.4.23-24 & 6.5.1-5 Diodorus 17.76.1	Hammond THA 135	
Surrender of the Greek mercenaries	Curtius 6.5.10 Diodorus 17.76.2	Hammond THA 135	
Attack on the Mardi: theft and restitution of Bucephalus	Curtius 6.5.11-21 Diodorus 17.76.3-8	Hammond THA 135; C6.5.11-12,18-21=D17.76.3-8 Schwartz	
Surrender of Nabarzanes: entry of Bagoas into Alexander's service	Curtius 6.5.22-23 (Diodorus 17.76.1)	Hammond THA 157	
Visit of Thalestris, Queen of the Amazons, who had journeyed from the River Thermodon to conceive a child by Alexander in Hyrcania	Plutarch 46.1 Strabo 11.5.4 Curtius 6.5.24-32 Diodorus 17.77.1-3 Justin 12.3.3-7	Jacoby, Fragments 15-16 of Cleitarch. Hammond THA 59, 102 & 135 Sources 81 (Jacoby Fragment 32?); C6.5.24-26,30-32=D17.77.1-3 cf. J12.3.5-7 & Strabo11.5.4 Schwartz	The Thermodon is in northern Asia Minor, which anomaly Cleitarchus explained by making the Caucasus region very narrow. The story may have originated with Onesicritus, but could have been embellished by Cleitarchus. (Brown, Clitarchus p.149 suggests Jacoby Fragment 32 was background to the Amazon story)
Alexander's adoption of Persian dress (purple tunic with a vertical white stripe, zona belt, diadem, sceptre) and luxury: 365 concubines from Darius' harem. Macedonian resentments assuaged by gifts from Alexander.	Curtius 6.6.1-12 Diodorus 17.77.4-7 & 17.78.1 Justin 12.3.8-12 Metz 2	Hammond THA 59, 102-3, 136; Pearson 221 (Plutarch, Artaxerxes 27 for Deinon)	Here again is seen the Cleitarchus propensity for making things equal to the days in a year; probably inspired by Deinon - Pearson. The Metz Epitome opens here, replete with Cleitarchan stories. F. Dicaearchus (Athenaeus 13.5 [557]) citing 350 concubines
Alexander burns surplus baggage and wagons to avoid the encumbrance in crossing the mountains into India	Curtius 6.6. Plutarch 57.1-2 Polyaenus 4.3.10	Hamilton Plutarch Alex liii	Plutarch associates this with the invasion of India & Polyaenus likewise; but Curtius is more likely correct. The confusion is probably due to the geographical disparity that Cleitarchus regarded southern Afghanistan from the Helmand River eastwards as part of India. Hence in Cleitarchan tradition this really was the first transit across montains into India.
Revolt of Satibarzanes, who flees to Bactra with 2000 cavalry. Alexander storms a rock occupied by rebels.	Diodorus 17.78.1 Curtius 6.6.20-34 (Justin 12.4.1) Metz 3	Hammond THA 59, 136	The Metz has Ariobazanes and states he fled to India – perhaps this is an error for Barzaentes as at Curtius 6.6.36 (which is suggested by Elizabeth Baynham in Antichthon 29, p.71).

Organisation And Sources

Summary	Sources	References	Comment
Dimnus conspiracy: execution of Philotas	Curtius 6.7-6.11 Diodorus 17.79-80 Justin 12.5.2-3 Plutarch 49	Hammond Sources 87 Hamilton Plutarch Alex liii	Hammond THA 59 argues Diodorus is from Diyllus mainly because he differs from Curtius in saying Alexander "learnt everything" from Dimnus, but Cleitarchus probably said *behaviour* of Dimnus spoke eloquently of his guilt & Diodorus is summarising clumsily. Compelling points of similarity on incidental details between D & C are: Cebalinus hidden in the armoury; Alexander is informed while bathing & Philotas is executed "in the manner of his country, Macedon". Hammond concedes (in Sources) that Curtius must be from Cleitarchus: it is too vividly detailed for a general history, e.g. Diyllus or Duris. Plutarch's version resembles Cleitarchus, but not on Alexander hiding behind a curtain where Plutarch is less likely to be using Cleitarchus than Curtius 6.11.12, who has Alexander not present during the torture.
Execution of Alexander Lyncestes	Curtius 7.1.1-9 Diodorus 17.80.2	C7.1.5-9 =D17.80.2 Schwartz	Hammond THA 138 suggests Diyllus, but his argument about the timing of Lyncestes' arrest being later in Diodorus than in Curtius overlooks the fact that Justin 11.7.1 suggests that the Cleitarchan tradition placed Lyncestes' arrest prior to the march to Gordium (as in Arrian). It looks as if Diodorus mentioned Lyncestes' arrest a few months late, perhaps connecting it with warnings in a letter from Olympias, which might have taken months to reach Alexander. Curtius & Diodorus follow the same source for Lyncestes' execution & the detail in Curtius seems too extensive for sourcing from a general history. (Hammond's view that C & D shared Diyllus as a secondary source is statistically implausible: it implies they independently made the same choice for most episodes between Cleitarchus & Diyllus: it is more likely that matches between C & D means both used Cleitarchus.)

151

Alexander the Great in Afghanistan by Andrew Chugg

Summary	Sources	References	Comment
Assassination of Parmenion: Polydamas' camel trek	Curtius 7.2.11-34 Diodorus 17.80.3 Strabo 15.2.10	C7.2.18=D17.80.3 Schwartz	Detailed correspondence between Curtius and Diodorus implies Cleitarchus was the source for the completion of the story of the downfall of Parmenion
Alexander forms a disciplinary regiment by reading the letters which the troops sent home to Macedonia to identify malcontents	Justin 12.5.4-8 Diodorus 17.80.4 Curtius 7.2.35-38 Polyaenus 4.3.19	Hammond THA 103; C7.2.35-37=D17.80.4 cf. J12.5.4-8 Schwartz	Hammond thinks that the version in Diodorus comes from Diyllus, but its close resemblance to the version in Justin is clear evidence that this material came from Cleitarchus. Hammond THA 139 fails to attribute the corresponding passage in Curtius, but it is Cleitarchus, since it is connected with the execution of Parmenion as in the other accounts.
The march against the Euergetae: origin of the name Euergetae (Benefactors) for the Ariaspi (Arimaspi in Cleitarchus) in their succour for Cyrus' army	Diodorus 17.81.1-2 Curtius 7.3.1-4 Metz 4	Hammond THA 60; C7.3.1,3=D17.81.1-2 Schwartz	From Deinon? Strong correspondences between Diodorus and Curtius
Land of the Paropamisadae	Curtius 7.3.5-18 Diodorus 17.82 Metz 4	Hammond THA 60, 139; C7.3.5-18=D17.82 Schwartz	
Crossing the "Caucasus" (Hindu Kush) in 16 or 17 days; Rock of Prometheus; foundation of an Alexandria; advance into Bactria in pursuit of Bessus	Curtius 7.3.19-23 Diodorus 17.83.1-2 Metz 4 (for the foundation)	Hammond THA 60, 139; C7.3.22-23=D17.83.1-2 Schwartz	Diodorus 17.83.3 has a terminal one-liner, Καὶ τὰ μὲν περὶ Ἀλέξανδρον ἐν τούτοις ἦν ("These were the concerns of Alexander"), which may indicate the end of Book 7 of Cleitarchus. A similar formula ended Bk 6 at 17.73.4 and exactly the same formula ends Bk 12. Similar formulae are used in other books of Diodorus, but this one may echo Cleitarchus, because it contains the title of his history (Περὶ Ἀλεξάνδρου - Pearson p.213).

Book 8: July 329BC – Autumn 328BC

Summary	Sources	References	Comment
Bessus and Bagodaras (D) or Cobares (C) quarrel at a banquet	Curtius 7.4.1-19 Diodorus 17.83.7	Hammond THA 139	Digressions and accounts of events elsewhere often mark a book boundary in Cleitarchus.
Alexander receives news from Greece of the Spartan revolt, of Scythians coming to the aid of Bessus and of the combat between Erigyius and Satibarzanes	Curtius 7.4.32-40 Diodorus 17.83.4-6	Hammond THA 140 Heckel & Yardley on Justin 184; C7.4.33,38=D17.83.4-6 Schwartz	Spartan news is only in C: was this the arrival of the Spartan envoys/hostages in Alexander's camp? Their departure seems to have been delayed (preparing to leave in Summer 330BC - Aischines 3.133).

Organisation And Sources

Summary	Sources	References	Comment
Advance to the Oxus: march through a desert with the loss of many men – anecdote of Alexander refusing water brought in skins	Diodorus, List of Contents for 17 Curtius 7.5.9-12 Front. Strat. 1.7.7		The anecdote being in Frontinus and Curtius tends to confirm that it is Cleitarchan
Betrayal by Spitamenes, Dataphernes & Catanes of Bessus and his dispatch to Alexander as a prisoner	Curtius 7.5.19-26 Diodorus 17.83.8-9 Justin 12.5.10-11 Metz 5-6	Hammond THA 61, 140-141	It appears that Curtius correctly reflects Cleitarchus by breaking up the downfall, torture and execution of Bessus into several mini-episodes. The Metz similarly divides the betrayal to Alexander from the eventual execution
Branchidae	Curtius 7.5.28-35 (in the long lacuna in Diodorus 17, but listed in contents), Strabo 11.11.4, Plutarch Moralia 557B(?)	Hammond THA 141; C7.5.28-35 cf. Dκ Schwartz Aelian, ap. Suidas s.v. Branchidae Strabo 14.1.5	Perhaps Cleitarchus gave the Branchidae story as a doublet with the destruction of Bessus: Persian and Greek traitors similarly destroyed (so Pearson).
Bessus delivered to Alexander in fetters; Alexander hands him over to Oxathres for interim torture but postpones his execution.	Curtius 7.5.36-43 Diodorus 17.83.8-9 Justin 12.5.10-11 Metz 5-6		The handing over to Oxathres is explicit in Curtius, Justin and Diodorus
Alexander wounded by an arrow of which the point remained fixed in the middle of his leg; the rebels sent envoys to apologise the next day; rivalry between the cavalry and the infantry over bearing Alexander's litter	Curtius 7.6.6-9	Hammond THA 142	
Advance to Maracanda – circumference of 70 stades with many rivers flowing around it	Curtius 7.6.10 Metz 7		With Diodorus missing in the great lacuna (and Justin being very thin and episodic here), the Metz Epitome (7-43) provides key corroboration that much of Curtius is from Cleitarchus, wherever there is close correspondence between Curtius and the Metz. This is vital, because it appears that Curtius sometimes resorted to other sources. This applies until the middle of Book 10, where Diodorus resumes.
Plan to found a stronghold on the Tanais to subdue the region	Curtius 7.6.13		News of this plan probably instigated the ensuing revolts.
First news of the revolt of Spitamenes & Catanes	Curtius 7.6.24 Metz 9	Hammond THA 143	Alexander destroys several rebel cities.
Foundation of Alexandria on the River Tanais (Alexandria Eschate) with a circumference of 60 stades in 17 days	Curtius 7.6.25-27; Justin 12.5.12 Metz 8		Hammond THA 142 discusses Aristobulus, but the detailed correspondence of Curtius with Justin is a clear indication of Cleitarchus. Tanais is a Cleitarchan name for this river (through confusion with the Don). Actually the Syr-Darya.

153

Alexander the Great in Afghanistan by Andrew Chugg

Summary	Sources	References	Comment
Emperor of the Scythians sends his brother Carthasis to prevent Alexander crossing the Tanais. Speech of Alexander & augury of Aristander in Curtius. Plan for an attack on the Scythians.	Metz 8 Curtius 7.7.1-29	Hammond THA 143-4	Carthasis is in Curtius and the Metz has "Carcasim"
Insurrection of Spitamenes: routing and destruction of the Macedonian column under Menedemus. (2000 infantry and 300 cavalry are dead.)	Metz 9 Curtius 7.7.30-39	Hammond THA 143	Alexander spends the night sleepless – watches Scythian fires in Curtius, reflecting upon wrongs against him in the Metz
Alexander's attack across the Tanais via 2000 rafts (Metz) or 12000 (Curtius)	Metz 10-12 Curtius 7.8.1-9.16 (Diodorus – contents)	Hammond THA 143-4, Pearson (Lost Histories) 222	X may have been dropped from XII in the Metz. Curtius gives Scythian envoys' words verbatim from his source – arrows, shouts, markers of Dionysus are common; Pearson notes parallels with aphorisms attributed to Cleitarchus
Visit of envoys of the Sacae	Curtius 7.9.17-19	Hammond THA 143-4	Escorted by Bagoas as Alexander's Greeter?
Alexander's return to Maracanda to counterattack Spitamenes who flees; burying of Greek dead and erection of a monument to Menedemus.	Metz 13 Curtius 7.9.20-22	Hammond THA 143	Reached Maracanda on the 4th day – bones covered with mound-monuments in the Metz
Pardoning of Sogdian prisoners (chieftains) who sang on their way to execution	Curtius 7.10.1-9 (Diodorus – contents)	Hammond THA 144; C7.10.4-9 cf. Dκβ Schwartz	
Alexander defeated the Sogdiani & slew over 120,000	(Diodorus – contents)	Hammond THA 61	Hammond notes that Theophylactus Simmocata burnt 120,000 & Goukowsky thought Cleitarchus his likely source
Return to Bactria – orders Bessus to Ecbatana for splitting and chopping up – founds towns (6 or 12?) to curb the conquered nations (in SE Sogdiana near Margania)	Metz 14 Curtius 7.10.10-16 Justin 12.5.13	Hammond THA 103 on Justin; C7.10.15-16 cf. Dκδ Schwartz	Crosses rivers Ochus and Oxus at Metz 14 and Curtius 7.10.15 (Hammond THA 144 thinks this is Aristobulus) – emendations of Margania to Margiana (Merv) are wrong.
Sogdian Rock (Rock of Arimazes in C or Ariobazanen in M or Ariamazes in S or Ariomazes in Polyaenus)	Metz 15-18 Curtius 7.11.1-25 Polyaenus 4.3.29 (Diodorus – contents) Strabo 11.11.4	Hammond THA 144-145	Both Curtius and the Metz Epitome seem to make this a climactic event of the campaigning year in 328BC – hence this should close Book 8 of Cleitarchus as well as Book 7 of Curtius. Curtius 7.11.28 *appears* to differ from the Metz, but this is probably just a transmission error (Hammond THA 144-145 thinks Curtius' account is Aristobulus then Cleitarchus.) Commonalities with the Metz include a cavern on the ascent path, 20 (Metz) or 30 (Curtius) stadia high, 300 climbers signalling with white cloths, iron wedges, ropes.

Organisation And Sources
Book 9: Autumn 328BC – May 327BC

Summary	Sources	References	Comment
Offer of daughter in marriage by the Scythian king. First campaign against Massagetae, Dahae – 3 columns through Sogdiana	Curtius 8.1.1-10	Hammond THA 145	
The hunt in Basista (Bazaira in Curtius) and the abundance of game there	Curtius 8.1.11-19 (Diodorus – contents)	Hammond THA 145; C8.1.11-19 cf. Dκσ Schwartz	Hammond thinks this is Onesicritus (but this is no bar to it being in Cleitarchus)
Killing of Cleitus at Maracanda – Alexander persuaded to forgive himself by Callisthenes	Curtius 8.1.19-8.2.12 Justin 12.6 Arrian 4.9.2-6 (Diodorus – contents)	Hammond THA 104,146 Hammond Sources 242	Arrian has legomena about Alexander's attempted suicide, concern over Lanike's reaction and a forgotten sacrifice to Dionysus
Winter in Bactrian Nautacene (Metz)	Curtius 8.2.13-18 Metz 19		
Treaty with Sisimithres, who had fathered 2 sons and 3 daughters through incest with his mother, after a siege of his rock.	Curtius 8.2.19-33 Metz 19 Plutarch 58.3 Strabo 11.11.4	Hammond THA 146	Hammond Sources is silent on the mention of Sisimthres by Plutarch
Death of Philippus.	Curtius 8.2.34-39	Hammond THA 146-7	Hammond THA thinks Philippus is from Onesicritus (but this is no bar to it being in Cleitarchus too)
Beheading of Spitamenes by his wife assisted by a slave boy – delivery of head to Alexander and his gratitude and her expulsion from camp	Curtius 8.3.1-15 Metz 20-23	Hammond THA 147	
Dahae surrender Daphernes (& Catanes?)	Metz 23 Curtius 8.3.16-17 Justin 12.6.18		Curtius 8.5.2 says that Catanes was subsequently killed in battle. Hammond is unsure of the source for this, but its presence in the Metz suggests Cleitarchus.
The proskynesis experiment	Curtius 8.5.5-24 Justin 12.7.1-3 Val. Max. 7.2 ext 11	Hammond THA 148 says speeches are Curtius' own invention, Alexander hides behind curtain like Agrippina in Tacitus Ann. 13.5.2 (but also like Alexander with Philotas [Plutarch 49], which suggests Cleitarchus) Hammond THA 103-4 for Justin: "most likely Cleitarchus"	This is postponed until the point of departure for India in Curtius. However Cleitarchus evidently placed it here, because Justin agrees with Diodorus by putting the award of silver shields to the hypaspists after Callisthenes' arrest, rather than before as in Curtius. Arrian gave the proskynesis experiment and the arrest of Callisthenes following on from the death of Cleitus, but points out (4.22.2) that the pages' conspiracy occurred at Bactra just prior to the invasion of India. It may be that Cleitarchus was correct in placing the proskynesis experiment at this point and chose to tell the whole story *en bloc*.

Alexander the Great in Afghanistan by Andrew Chugg

Summary	Sources	References	Comment
The conspiracy of the pages and the arrest and execution of Callisthenes	Curtius 8.6.1-8.8.23 Justin 12.7.2 (Diodorus – contents)		Hammond is unsure of the source for Curtius and Justin, but Diodorus' contents list confirms that this material was in Cleitarchus. It is possible that Curtius used other sources as well.
Campaign against the Nautaces and the destruction of the army in a hail storm	Metz 24-27 Curtius 8.4.1-15 (Diodorus – contents)	Hammond THA 147	
Saves a common soldier after the snow storm	Val. Max. 5.1 ext 1a Frontinus, Strat. 4.6.3 Curtius 8.4.15-17	Hammond THA 147	
Visit to (rock of) Chorienes (perhaps a re-visit to Sisimithres, but Cleitarchus now used his title rather than his name – yet it looks as though Cleitarchus believed him to be a distinct individual)	Metz 28 Curtius 8.4.21 has "cohortandus" in MSS wrongly changed to Oxyartes by Aldus		The Metz manuscript read "corianus"; Chorienes is from Arrian 4.21; Brunt & Heckel suggest that Chorienes is an official title of Sisimithres from the name of the area he ruled. Justin 12.6.18 mentions the surrender of the "Chorasmians"
Marriage to Roxane	Metz 28-31 Curtius 8.4.20-30 (Diodorus – contents)	Hammond THA 146	Metz & Diodorus mention marriages of Alexander's companions – hence probably from Cleitarchus

8. An Update On The Organisation And Structure Of Cleitarchus And The Date Of Accession Of Alexander the Great

Introduction

The history of the reign of Alexander the Great composed by Cleitarchus of Alexandria ranks as perhaps the most influential of all the many accounts of the King's career, despite the loss of the original text of Cleitarchus' work and the paucity of the attributed fragments collected by Müller and Jacoby. Cleitarchus was evidently the principal source for the authors of the so-called Vulgate tradition of Alexander historiography, which survives in the works of Diodorus, Curtius and Justin as well as in the anonymous *Metz Epitome*. Even Plutarch's writings on Alexander incorporate substantial Cleitarchan elements, and there are recognisable, though unattributed, fragments of Cleitarchus in a host of other ancient sources, such as Pliny, Aelian and Polyaenus.

The most important structural issues regarding Cleitarchus' work are the questions of the number of books into which it was divided and the periods that were covered by each book. Prior to the present research, no clear answer had been proposed even on the matter of the number, although it is apparent that there were at least twelve, since Jacoby's Fragment 6 of Cleitarchus is attributed to his twelfth book. Pearson thought that there were "two or three books more" beyond Book Twelve, whilst Bosworth has commented that there were "perhaps as many as fifteen" and Heckel has speculated that Cleitarchus' work was published "in 15 books?"

It is the purpose of this discussion to present a revised analysis of the structure of Cleitarchus' work and to propose a specific book structure that is consistent with all the available evidence. This will proceed in the first instance through a fresh look at the Fragments of Cleitarchus with a focus on resolving the problem that it has not been precisely clear where all of these Fragments, including some of those with Book Numbers, fit into the overall history. Secondly, it will be argued that echoes of many of the Book termini of Cleitarchus exist within the text of the seventeenth book of Diodorus. The combination of these two types of evidence will then be shown to imply a thirteen-book structure for Cleitarchus' work corresponding to one book for each year of Alexander's reign. This in turn will permit some pertinent observations on Cleitarchus' organisational principles as well as his quality and fidelity as an historian. Furthermore, it transpires that Cleitarchus located his book termini at the anniversaries of Alexander's accession at least as far as his fifth book and this has enabled me to propose a date for the assassination of Philip II of Macedon for the first time. It now appears that Alexander the Great

Alexander the Great in Afghanistan by Andrew Chugg

acceded to the throne of Macedon on 27th September 336BC and that the duration of his reign was 12 years 8 months and 14 days in the Julian calendar.

The lines of argument that are employed in fitting the fragments of Cleitarchus back together to discover the overall structure of his work are very much analogous to the methods employed by archaeologists to reconstruct fragmentary ancient vases and pots. Such reconstructions are necessarily guided by an hypothesis of the overall form in their early stages, but there is continual testing and sometimes adaptation of this hypothesis as the individual pieces are placed. The tension is whether the small-scale fitting of the individual sherds is consistent with the large-scale form and any design painted or impressed upon it. If such self-consistency between the various fitting criteria can be established, then that constitutes overwhelming evidence for the correctness of the reconstruction. The fitting requirements are so stringent and multi-faceted in practice that there will rarely be more than one viable reconstruction. If any scholars were to suggest that the evidence for the validity of the reconstruction derived from the self-consistency of the reconstructed object itself amounts to a circular argument, then there are thousands of reconstructed vases in museums around the world to demonstrate the fallacy in their position. So too, in the reconstruction of Cleitarchus, it is necessary to find a structure that accommodates a very large number of Fragments and other pieces of evidence. If such a structure can be established, then it gains much credence from the fact that it is extremely statistically improbable that so many strands of evidence could by chance all be found to fit to an incorrect structure.

A successful reconstruction of a vase should also be expected to reveal additional design features that fit the object yet more intimately within the cultural and archaeological context in which it was discovered. So too the reconstruction of Cleitarchus presented here reveals many additional triangulations with the rest of the source evidence on Alexander. For example, the date of 27th September 336BC implied by the reconstructed structure of Cleitarchus' work for Alexander's accession turns out to be the autumnal equinox. (There is a five-day offset between the Julian and Gregorian calendars in Alexander's epoch, so 27th September in the Julian is 22nd September in the back-projected Gregorian calendar.) We know from the sources that Philip II was assassinated at a great festival of the gods to which he had invited delegates from around the Greek world.[1] Holy festivals at the equinoxes are particularly common and likely, because of the traditional linkage between astronomy and astrology. For Philip it served the additional purpose of providing a clear way of communicating the date of the event around Greece at a time when every city-state maintained a slightly different calendar system.

---

[1] Diodorus 16.91.4-6.

Connecting the Timespan and the Number of Books

Relative to his fame and influence, the attributed fragments of Cleitarchus are surprisingly sparse.[2] Nevertheless, it will prove relevant to note by way of introduction that we are well-informed on the matter of the title of his history of Alexander, which is his sole attested work. Athenaeus thrice mentions that it was known, albeit blandly, as Περὶ Ἀλεξάνδρου or Περὶ Ἀλεξάνδρου Ἱστορίαι, which I translate as *Concerning Alexander*.[3] Since Athenaeus is corroborated in this matter by the *Florilegium* of Stobaeus[4] and the Scholia on Apollonius Rhodius,[5] there is little doubt that he is correct.

Only six of Jacoby's Fragments preserve any mention of the book numbers whence they were abstracted. The key evidence for the total number of books is presented by the last and latest of these: Fragment 6 describes the disdain for death professed by the Indian gymnosophists and is attributed to Book 12 by Diogenes Laertius.[6]

There are only two occasions when this topic is at all likely to have been discussed by Cleitarchus: either in the context of Alexander's meeting with the gymnosophists in India or else at the ceremony for the self-immolation of Calanus (a gymnosophist, who is erroneously called Caranus in Diodorus[7]), which took place in Susianê early in 324BC. The estimate of a total of as many as 15 books for Cleitarchus, which is countenanced by some modern experts,[8] might be justified on the assumption that Fragment 6 refers to the meeting in India, but actually the suicide of Calanus is inherently more likely, because there is a detailed account of Calanus' end in Diodorus, which makes specific reference to the theme of his indifference to his death (note however that this event falls within a large lacuna in Curtius):

---

[2] F. Jacoby, *Die Fragmente der griechischen Historiker*, Part II B (Berlin 1929) no. 137.

[3] Jacoby (above, n.2) 137 F1, F2, F30 (Athenaeus, *Deipnosophistae* 148D-F, 530A, 586CD).

[4] Jacoby (above, n.2) 137 F3 (Stobaeus, *Florilegium* 4.20.73).

[5] Jacoby (above, n.2) 137 F17 (Scholia on Apollonius Rhodius 2.904).

[6] Jacoby (above, n.2) 137 F6 (Diogenes Laertius 1.6).

[7] Plutarch, *Alexander* 64.3 explains that Calanus was the nickname of the gymnosophist Sphines, which was derived from his use of the Indian greeting "Kale"; Caranus was the name of one of Alexander's Friends, who was killed by Spitamenes (and also of an apocryphal son of Phillip II in Justin 11.2.3); Arrian, *Anabasis* 3.5.4 has the inverse error of Calanus for Caranus.

[8] E.g. L. Pearson, *The Lost Histories of Alexander the Great* (Philological Monographs XX: Am. Phil. Ass. 1960) 213 recognises that Book 12 is the suicide of Calanus, but thinks there were "two or three books more"; A. B. Bosworth, "In Search of Cleitarchus: Review-Discussion of Luisa Prandi: Fortuna è realtà dell'opera di Clitarco, Historia Einzelschriften 104 (Steiner Stuttgart, 1996)," *Histos* 1 (August 1997) notes that there were "at least 12 books and perhaps as many as 15"; J.C. Yardley & W. Heckel, *Justin: Epitome of the Philippic History of Pompeius Trogus, Vol I, Books 11-12, Alexander the Great* (Oxford 1997) 34 speculate that Cleitarchus' work was published "in 15 books?"

True to his own creed, Caranus cheerfully mounted the pyre and perished. Some of those who were present thought him mad, others vainglorious about his ability to bear pain, while others simply marvelled at his fortitude and contempt for death.[9]

In fact the vocabulary of Diodorus (θανάτου καταφρόνησιν) and that of Diogenes Laertius (θανάτου καταφρονεῖν) in Fragment 6 are identical.

It is also notable that, were the total 15, the effect of the distribution of the other Fragments that possess book numbers would be to concertina the first half of Alexander's reign into the first third of Cleitarchus' books. For instance, Fragment 4 mentions the 50 Spartan hostages surrendered after the defeat of the rebellion of King Agis, which occurred in the late fifth or early sixth year of Alexander's reign and is attributed to Book 5 of Cleitarchus.[10] Conversely, placing the first half of 324BC in Book 12 engenders a total of about thirteen books up to the point of Alexander's death, which results in an even distribution of Alexander's regnal years across Cleitarchus' books. Furthermore, a 13-book total has the particular attraction of giving virtually exactly one regnal year per book, since the total reign was only months short of 13 years. It will be shown below that the other book-numbered fragments are all broadly consistent with the hypothesis of one book per year. Later in the reign Cleitarchus may slightly have expanded the duration of some books and contracted others to suit the pattern of events or perhaps because the precise chronology of events in Bactria and India was mysterious even to him. However, it will be shown that the Cleitarchan book termini were consistently located in the early autumn in the first five years of the reign. They only seem to have shifted into the summer from the death of Darius onwards. In general terms, this scheme is not very different from the book-divisions at the end of each campaigning season as seemingly adopted by Thucydides, Xenophon and Hieronymus.[11] More specifically, the book termini in the first half of the work will be shown to coincide closely with the anniversaries of the accession. It may also be added that there is evidence from his fragments that Cleitarchus had a fondness for associating things with calendar values: for example, he made the walls of Babylon 365 stades in circumference[12] and also seems to have asserted that Darius' harem comprised 365 women (Curtius 3.3.24 & 6.6.8; Diodorus 17.77.6; cf. Justin 12.3.10). In this trait he may be emulating his father, Deinon.[13]

Implicit in this discussion is the view that Cleitarchus' work opened with Alexander's accession, currently generally dated to October of 336BC, and

---

[9] Diodorus 17.107.5 (trans. C. Bradford Welles).

[10] Jacoby (above, n.2) 137 F4 (Harpocration, s.v. ὁμηρεύοντας).

[11] Jane Hornblower, *Hieronymus of Cardia* (Oxford 1981) 101.

[12] Jacoby (above, n.2) 137 F10 (Diodorus 2.7.3-4).

[13] Deinon gave 360: Pearson (above, n.8) 221 & 228-229; Plutarch, *Artaxerxes* 27.

closed with his death, which Plutarch dates to the early evening of 10th June 323BC (Julian Calendar) on the basis of his reading of the official journal compiled by Eumenes. This timespan for the work is relatively orthodox and appears in general to be supported by the evidence. For example, it seems that Diodorus mainly used the universal histories of Ephorus and Diyllus as his sources for his sixteenth book, which proceeded as far as the assassination of Philip.[14] He only switched to the considerably more detailed account of Cleitarchus at the beginning of Alexander's reign in Book 17, then he began to use Hieronymus of Cardia from early in Book 18.[15] Furthermore, although his first two books are lost, the indications are that Curtius opened his main account at Alexander's accession. In fact Jacoby's first fragment of Cleitarchus shows that the destruction of Thebes was described in Book 1, so it is unlikely that there was space for a fully detailed account of Alexander's youth.[16] Since Thebes fell no earlier than mid-September 335BC, it is clear that the first book must have incorporated the entirety of the first year of the reign. Nevertheless, Hammond may well be correct in believing that Cleitarchus also treated Philip's last summer.[17] This would be vaguely consistent with an overall plan of describing the events of thirteen years across thirteen books, since Alexander died in early June. Furthermore, we will find that there are some indications that Cleitarchus introduced his history with an outline of Alexander's birth and ancestry, because Plutarch was probably utilising Cleitarchus in his introductory account of Alexander's descent from Achilles and Heracles (Plutarch, *Alexander* 2.1). Finally, there are good indications that Cleitarchus gave a detailed account of the events in Babylon in the aftermath of Alexander's death down to at least the First Division of the Satrapies in late June or July and that he may also have outlined the transport of Alexander's corpse to Egypt and its eventual transfer to Alexandria.

Locating Jacoby's Fragments and the Book Boundaries

The next step is to assign Jacoby's book-attributed fragments of Cleitarchus to their correct contexts within each book.

Fragment 1 (Athenaeus 148D-F), which is attributed to Book 1,[18] self-evidently relates to the fall of Thebes in September of 335BC. This date is relatively well

---

[14] E.g. Diodorus 16.76.6, though the Philip mentioned there is probably Cassander's son.

[15] For example, the account of Alexander's catafalque in Diodorus 18.26-27 is a fragment of Hieronymus, because Athenaeus 206E attributes it to him: see Jacoby (above, n.2) 154 F2.

[16] Jacoby (above, n.2)137 F1 (Athenaeus, *Deipnosophistae* 148D-F).

[17] N. G. L. Hammond, *Three Historians of Alexander the Great* (Cambridge 1983) 92-93; for the chronology of Alexander's accession see N. G. L. Hammond, "The Regnal Years of Philip and Alexander," *Greek, Roman and Byzantine Studies* 33 (1992) 355-373.

[18] Note that the attribution to Book 1 only occurs in the full manuscript of Athenaeus brought to Venice from Constantinople by Aurispa in 1423 (St Mark Codex A); the Epitome manuscripts

fixed, since both Plutarch, *Alexander* 13.1 & *Camillus* 19.6, and Arrian, *Anabasis* 1.10.2, mention that news of the fall of Thebes became known in Athens just after the celebration of the Great Mysteries had begun in Attica. These are known to have taken place between 15th-23rd of the Attic month Boedromion (roughly corresponding to early October in the Julian Calendar).[19] This Fragment mentions the wealth of Thebes as having amounted to just 440 talents. The same sum is mentioned by Diodorus 17.14.4, who states that Alexander sold the Theban prisoners and realised a sum of 440 silver talents. Bosworth has pointed out that it is not strictly necessary to read Diodorus as stating that the sale of the prisoners raised the entire sum.[20] Rather Diodorus may be abbreviating a longer account, which had listed further resources realising the total. It is anyway clear that the first book of Cleitarchus extended to early October of 335BC, which just antedates the first anniversary of the accession.

Fragment 2 (Athenaeus 530A), which mentions the death of Sardanapalus[21] and derives from Book 4, almost certainly belongs to a visit by Alexander to the Assyrian king's tomb at Anchiale near Tarsus in October 333BC, which is attested elsewhere in fragments of Aristobulus and Callisthenes.[22] It can easily be fitted into the 13-book annual scheme, since it occurs at the beginning of the fourth year of Alexander's reign. Cleitarchus is probably echoing this story from his father Deinon's *Persica*, which might in turn have followed Ctesias' *Persica*.[23]

Fragment 3 (Stobaeus, *Florilegium* 4.20.73) from the fifth book tells of Theis Byblios' passionate love for his daughter, Myrra, which is a legend of Byblos, a city on the Lebanese littoral, where Adonis, the son of Theis and Myrra, was worshipped and which Alexander reached in about January of 332BC.[24] This is

---

from Paris and Florence published by S. P. Peppink, *Athenaei Dipnosophistarum Epitome: Pars Prima* (Leiden 1937) 45 attribute the matter to Cleitarchus but omit the Book number.

[19] A. B. Bosworth, *Commentary on Arrian's History of Alexander* I (Oxford 1980) 92; Boedromion probably began near the New Moon on 19th September (Julian) in 335BC, hence Athens heard of the fall of Thebes perhaps as early as 5th October 335BC and the event may have occurred a day or so earlier.

[20] Bosworth (above, n.8).

[21] Cf. Plutarch, *Moralia* 326F & 336C.

[22] Jacoby (above, n.2) 139 F9a (Athenaeus 530A-B); Jacoby (above, n.2) 139 F9b (Strabo 14.5.9); Jacoby (above, n.2) 139 F9c (Arrian, *Anabasis* 2.5.2-4); Jacoby (above, n.2) 124 F34 (Photius & Suidas s.v. *Sardanapalos*) - this mention is attributed to Callisthenes' *Persica*, but it may be a garbled reference to his history of Alexander; see Pearson (above, n.8) 26; Jacoby (above, n.2) 122 F2 (Amyntas the Bematist in Athenaeus 529E-530A).

[23] Ctesias, writing in the early 4th century BC, had described the reign of Sardanapalus (see Diodorus 2.23); Cleitarchus seemingly contradicted Ctesias on certain points - see L. Pearson (above, n.8) 230, probably in consequence of his father Deinon having written a *Persica* to rival Ctesias' work on the same theme.

[24] See T. S. Brown, "Clitarchus," *American Journal of Philology* 71 (1950) 149.

An Update On The Organisation And Structure Of Cleitarchus

some nine months ahead of the start of the fifth year of Alexander's reign, which is the context implied by the 13-book scheme. There are also strong indications that the epic siege of Tyre, which was so protracted as to extend into the second half of 332BC, was entirely accommodated within the 4th book of Cleitarchus with Book 5 opening after its conclusion. However, the concept of one book per year can be rescued by the observation that Alexander passed along the Levantine littoral *twice*. Logically, the only way to reconcile Fragment 3 with its placing in Book 5 is to suppose that it pertains to Alexander's *return* to Syria in the summer of 331BC. From this we may learn that Alexander was probably in Byblos some time in the late summer of 331BC. The sources are clear that Alexander lingered at Tyre at this time, for he held athletic and musical contests there from around mid-June to early July of 331BC. He subsequently crossed the Euphrates at Thapsacus (circa early August) – see Arrian, *Anabasis* 3.6.1-4, Curtius 4.8.16 and Plutarch, *Alexander* 29. Engels has noted, "There were essentially two routes the Macedonians could have followed to the Euphrates: through Coele Syria via Damascus, Homs, Hamah, and Aleppo, a region which was much more agriculturally productive in antiquity than at present; or up the Phoenician coast to Seleucia, the port of Antioch, and inland by the route essentially followed by Cyrus the Younger, Crassus, Trajan, and Julian through the Amuq Plain to the Euphrates. The latter route would, of course, simplify the army's logistic organisation by utilizing sea transport."[25] We now have an independent argument from the third fragment of Cleitarchus to show that Engels was correct to prefer the coastal route, since that was the one that passed through Byblos. Admittedly the inland route has been the orthodox assumption and will be found marked as the reality on most modern maps of Alexander's itinerary. However, it is actually inspired by the thinnest of textual evidence: specifically, Arrian, *Anabasis* 3.6.4 speaks of Alexander "starting inland towards Thapsacus" immediately after discussing his sojourn at Tyre. In the absence of anyone previously having noticed the evidence of the Cleitarchus Fragment on the matter, this seems to have been held to imply the inland route from Tyre onwards. But of course, Arrian's statement is actually in no way inconsistent with the coastal route either, since it would eventually have been necessary for Alexander to move inland in order to reach Thapsacus at all. In fact, it emerges that Cleitarchus Fragment 3 is the only *solid* textual evidence on the road taken from Tyre northwards and it supports the more practicable coastal route. However, the possibility cannot be excluded that Alexander made an otherwise unreported expedition to Byblos during his second visit to Tyre, even if the army subsequently took the inland route to Thapsacus, since Byblos is only 70 miles north of Tyre (just a couple of days by ship). Therefore this Fragment is indisputably consistent with the one book per year scheme for Cleitarchus, despite the superficial contradiction.

---

[25] D. W. Engels, *Alexander the Great and the Logistics of the Macedonian Army* (California 1978) 65.

Fragment 4 (Harpocration s.v. ὁμηρεύοντας), which is also attributed to Book 5, mentions the fifty Spartan hostages received by Antipater after he quelled the rebellion of King Agis.[26] This revolt against the Macedonian Hegemony in Greece took place in the summer of 331BC, which is the later part of Book 5 according to the 13-book scheme. The implication is that Fragment 4 is drawn from a digression on the fighting back in Greece, which perhaps closed Book 5 of Cleitarchus.[27] Now Diodorus 17.62-63 precisely gives just such a digression on this rebellion in the aftermath of Gaugamela, although Curtius and Justin postpone mentioning the matter until after the death of Darius, which fitted in better with their book structures: Curtius 5.1.1-2 actually states this intention, evidently at the point that he found the account of the rebellion in Cleitarchus.[28] The date of Gaugamela is fixed to 1st October 331BC (Julian Calendar) by a lunar eclipse mentioned as having occurred eleven days before the battle that can be calculated to have happened on 20th September. It looks as though Gaugamela was the climactic event of Cleitarchus' fifth book and it closed with the digression on events in Greece immediately afterwards. This is strongly supported by a comment in Justin 11.14.6, which places Gaugamela within the fifth year of Alexander's reign. Since Cleitarchus via Trogus (and perhaps Timagenes) was the ultimate source of most of the material in Justin, if Cleitarchus had one book per regnal year, then a comment referring an event to the fifth year of the reign should also place the event in the fifth book of Cleitarchus. It is hardly likely that Cleitarchus could be the source of such a comment unless the battle was in his fifth book.

Fragment 5 (Scholia on Aristophanes Av. 487): the greatest conundrum among the fragments with book attributions is presented by the fifth, which assigns a comment about the law that permitted only the Persian monarch to wear the tiara upright to the tenth book of Cleitarchus. According to the 13-book scheme, this cannot have been related earlier than the middle of 327BC and should fit between the summer of 327BC and the summer of 326BC. The most obvious context for such a comment would be an account of a rebellion against

---

[26] The number of 50 is not present in the text of Harpocration (*Lexicon of the Attic Orators*), but is restored from the epitome of Harpocration used by the author of the Suda, of which only the best manuscript has 50 as the numeral ν' (in agreement with Diodorus), whilst others have eight as either the numeral η' or the word ὀκτώ.

[27] The departure of Spartan envoys to Alexander to ask forgiveness for the rebellion seems to have been delayed until the next year, since Aeschines 3.133 records that they were preparing to leave in the Summer of 330BC; their departure from Greece may have been recorded by Cleitarchus at the end of his 6th book, which prompted Diodorus 17.73.5-6 to mention the matter; their arrival with Alexander may be reflected by the comment in Curtius 7.4.32 that Alexander received announcements out of Greece about the Spartan rebellion in about July 329BC.

[28] Apart from Diodorus 17.62-63 the main digressions on the revolt of Agis in the Vulgate authors are: Curtius 6.1.1-20; Justin 12.1.4-11; Diodorus 17.73.5-6.

Alexander's rule of Persia, for Alexander did not himself wear the tiara.[29] However, this occurs too late in Cleitarchus to be associated with the revolt of Bessus, who had been dead for two years. Nevertheless, we do know of a more obscure, subsequent rebellion in Persia led by a certain Baryaxes. Arrian specifically relates that he assumed the title of King of the Persians and Medes and wore the tiara upright. This rebellion evidently occurred whilst Alexander was in India, since Baryaxes was arrested by Atropates, the satrap of Media and presented to Alexander for punishment upon his return in early 324BC according to Arrian, *Anabasis* 6.29.3. The outbreak of this rebellion is the probable context of Fragment 5. A corollary is that Cleitarchus probably did not write that Bessus wore the tiara upright. Bessus' assumption of the upright tiara was reported by Arrian (from Ptolemy?)[30] But Curtius 6.6.13 writes more generally of his adoption of "regal attire" and Diodorus 17.83.3 notes that he "had assumed the diadem". Many points suggest that Cleitarchus usually adopted the tidy principle of placing digressions on events elsewhere at either the start or the end of a book (the matter of the rebellion of Agis as related in the discussion of Fragment 4 is a case in point), so these are the two alternative placements for this fragment. The end is preferable, since Baryaxes probably waited for Alexander to become safely embroiled in his Indian campaigns. This conclusion reveals the history of Cleitarchus in a startling new light, for it provides evidence that his work treated events elsewhere in more detail and in a more chronologically correct order than did Arrian.

Fragment 6 (Diogenes Laertius 1.6): as has already been argued, the sixth and final book-attributed fragment comes from Cleitarchus' account of the self-immolation of Calanus when Alexander was progressing towards Susa in the spring of 324BC. It was reported in Book 12 of Cleitarchus and falls in the middle of Alexander's twelfth regnal year. Hence it is precisely consistent with the one book per year scheme.

Vestiges of Cleitarchus' Book Structure in Diodorus

It is an important axiom for the discussion in this section that the seventeenth book of Diodorus' *Bibliotheke* is largely an epitome of Cleitarchus' account of Alexander's career. This concept had its origins in the application of the so-called *Einquellenprinzip* (single source principle), which was pursued by German scholars, such as Schwartz and Jacoby and has more recently been reasserted by

---

[29] Fragment 30 of Eratosthenes in Jacoby (above, n.2) 241; Arrian, *Anabasis* 4.7.4 seems to be mistaken on this point, for which see P. A. Brunt, *Loeb Classical Library: Arrian, History of Alexander and Indica* 1 (Harvard 1976) Appendix XIV.2 533; the Vulgate sources refer only to the diadem without mention of the tiara (*kitaris* or *kidaris*): *Metz Epitome* 2; Diodorus 17.77.5; Curtius 6.6.4; Justin 12.3.8; Plutarch, *Alexander* 45.2; Ephippus in Athenaeus 537E.

[30] Arrian, *Anabasis* 3.25.3; cf. Xenophon, *Anabasis* 2.5.23.

F. Schachermeyr.[31] In its original 19th century form the *Einquellen-theorie* asserted that Diodorus slavishly epitomised a succession of earlier historians with little modification of their language or perspectives in compiling his *Bibliotheke*. In so doing, he confined himself to a single source over long sections of his work, often extending to an entire book or more. In the 20th century, Schwartz advocated relaxation of the strict *Einquellenprinzip* to the effect that Diodorus generally based his narrative upon a single main source, but sometimes intermingled material from another source and occasionally offered personal contributions.[32]

It is beyond the scope of this article to argue the point in detail, but it is pertinent to outline the main strands of the case that Cleitarchus was the major source for Diodorus 17:

- Because he had already been a source for Diodorus in Book 2.

- Because of the high proportion of the fragments of Cleitarchus which are closely echoed in Diodorus 17.

- Because Jacoby's testimonies reveal that Cleitarchus' history was extremely popular in Italy in the late Republican period: many episodes in Diodorus have detailed parallels in Curtius, who therefore seems independently to have elected to use the same source as Diodorus for much of his account of Alexander and Cleitarchus would have been the obvious choice for both of them.

These facts make it almost unavoidable that Cleitarchus was the principal source for both Diodorus 17 and Curtius. Hammond's conjecture that Diyllus was a significant secondary source for Diodorus 17 proves untenable, because it requires (on his own admission) that Curtius independently chose Diyllus as a secondary source for exactly the same set of episodes as Diodorus, which is a statistical impossibility. Similarly Luisa Prandi's advocacy of Duris as a secondary source for Diodorus is unconvincing, because her reasons for rejecting Cleitarchus do not stand up to scrutiny (e.g. of Bosworth) and because she cannot escape the same *impasse* as encountered by Hammond. In fact Diodorus 17 appears to be dominated by Cleitarchus, but it is epitomised down to only ~10%-20% of the length of the original.[33]

---

[31] F. Schachermeyr, *Alexander der Grosse: Das Problem seiner Persönlichkeit und seines Wirkens*, (Vienna 1973) Anhang nr. 2: Der Weg zu Kleitarch 658-662.

[32] For a good discussion of the use of sources by Diodorus see Hornblower (above, n.11) 18-32.

[33] Diodorus 17 is an exceptionally long book for a Greek work, so it is unlikely that Cleitarchus' 13 books averaged more than 75% of its length – conversely, Cleitarchus' work seems to have been substantial, so it seems improbable that his books averaged less that 40% of the length of Diodorus 17.

An Update On The Organisation And Structure Of Cleitarchus

The main chronological scheme utilised by Diodorus is Athenian Archon-years, which have seemingly been applied retrospectively (and rather clumsily) by Diodorus himself and are not derived from his sources. There are many errors and Diodorus often instigates an Archon-year among events that happened at a very different time of year than the beginning of the Archon-year in midsummer.

However, there is another type of sub-division that seemingly occurs even more erratically within Diodorus' text in the form of a variety of curiously bland boundary phrases that contain no historical details, but simply indicate the end of one account and the beginning of another. Are they mere rhetorical flourishes or do they have some ulterior significance?

In general we can see that this type of formula is used by Diodorus to indicate major changes in the focus of his account, not only in Book 17, but also in parts of his history based on different sources than Cleitarchus. For example he gives "This was the state of affairs concerning Philip," at Diodorus 16.89.3 before moving on to deal with Timoleon's activities in Sicily. Diodorus himself provides strong clues as to his inspiration for these curious phrases. For example, Diodorus 16.76.4 closes his account of the siege of Perinthus with Καὶ τὰ μὲν περὶ Περινθίους καὶ Βυζαντίους ἐν τούτοις ἦν ("Such was the situation at Perinthus and Byzantium"). But most interestingly he immediately goes on to comment that this was the point at which his source, Ephorus of Kyme, had closed his history. The obvious inference is that such phrases may often mark book boundaries or other significant termini in Diodorus' source texts, most of which are now lost.

This hypothesis is particularly rewarding for the question of the book termini relating to Cleitarchus in Diodorus 17. Starting from the hypothesis that Cleitarchus had one book for each year of Alexander's reign, it transpires that some of these boundary phrases in Diodorus 17 can be associated with Cleitarchan book termini as follows:

1) Diodorus 17.47.6 gives Ἡμεῖς δ' ἐπεὶ τὰ περὶ τὸν Ἀλέξανδρον διήλθομεν, μεταληψόμεθα τὴν διήγησιν ("Now we have described things concerning Alexander, we shall turn our narrative in another direction") and this appears to be in about the right place for the end of the narrative of Alexander's activities in Cleitarchus' Book 4 at the appointment of "Balonymus" as King of Tyre. It is followed by a digression on events in Europe and then the material of the next book began with Diodorus' Archon-year boundary and mention of the siege of Gaza.

2) Diodorus 17.63.5 has Ἡμεῖς δὲ διεληλυθότες τὰ πραχθέντα κατὰ τὴν Εὐρώπην ἐν μέρει τὰ κατὰ τὴν Ἀσίαν συντελεσθέντα διέξιμεν ("Now that we have run through the events in Europe, we may in turn pass on to what occurred in Asia"). This ends the

digression on the rebellion of Agis in Greece, which seems to have closed Cleitarchus' Book 5.

3) Diodorus 17.83.3 gives Καὶ τὰ μὲν περὶ Ἀλέξανδρον ἐν τούτοις ἦν ("These were the concerns of Alexander"). This is a plausible juncture for the end of Cleitarchus' Book 7 with Alexander's crossing of the Paropamisus range. The narrative focus then shifts from Alexander himself to the activities of his generals in Aria.

4) Diodorus 17.108.3 also has Καὶ τὰ μὲν περὶ Ἀλέξανδρον ἐν τούτοις ἦν ("These were the concerns of Alexander"). This is a plausible location for the end of Cleitarchus' Book 12. Again it marks a shift in the narrative focus from Alexander himself to the activities of Harpalus.

5) Diodorus 17.73.4 concludes with Καὶ τὰ μὲν κατὰ τὴν Ἀσίαν ἐν τούτοις ἦν ("That was the situation in Asia"). This is very likely to have been the end of the narrative of Alexander's activities in Cleitarchus' Book 6 with the death of Darius. Again it is followed by a short digression on events in Europe.

Virtually all of the boundary phrases of this type in Diodorus 17 (such that the narrative focus shifts from Alexander's activities to a digression on events elsewhere or back again) can be closely associated with a Cleitarchan book terminus.[34] It looks as though Diodorus is faithfully echoing these scene shifts from Cleitarchus' work. The phrases themselves may have been read from Cleitarchus' text, especially since 1, 3 & 4 incorporate the title of Cleitarchus' work - Περὶ Ἀλεξάνδρου. Cleitarchus himself seems to have followed the tidy policy of placing digressions on events remote from Alexander's operations at either the end or occasionally the beginning of his books. This is why these scene shifting boundary phrases are evidently giving good indications of the Cleitarchan book termini. It is a corollary that significant digressions in Diodorus may mark Cleitarchan book termini, even where there is no boundary phrase, especially if the same digression occurs at the same point in Curtius. An excellent example would be the digression on events in Bactria at Diodorus 17.99.5-6 and Curtius 9.7.1-11, which appears to mark the end of Cleitarchus' Book 11.

Two other types of boundary phrase occur in Diodorus 17, but appear to be less significant:

---

[34] With the sole exception of the phrases at Diodorus 17.5.1 and 17.7.10, which bound a passage giving historical background on the Persian Empire: this appears to have been embedded in Book 1 of Cleitarchus, since it is also echoed in Book 10 of Justin; Cleitarchus' father, Deinon, had written a history of the Persian Empire.

An Update On The Organisation And Structure Of Cleitarchus

a) Diodorus 17.61.3 has "This was the outcome of the battle near Arbela" at the end of the narrative of Alexander's activities in Cleitarchus' Book 5. However, there is a similar phrase at Diodorus 17.36.6: "This was the result of the battle at Issus in Cilicia". This latter cannot easily have been a book boundary in Cleitarchus, because Fragment 2 shows that the fourth book dealing with the fourth year of the reign had already opened and had another ten or eleven months to run.

b) There are four instances of "This is what happened in this year" at Diodorus 17.28.5 (autumn 334BC), 17.39.4 (January 332BC), 17.86.7 (April 326BC) and 17.112.6 (April 323BC), which all immediately precede Diodorus' own Archon-year boundaries. It is possible that the first of these is at the terminus of Book 2 of Cleitarchus, since it occurs just after the Siege of Halicarnassus, which probably ended just before the second anniversary of the reign. But the others are widely displaced from the expected Cleitarchan book boundaries.

The dates of the termini of Books 1, 2, 4 and 5 can all now be recognised to occur in late September to October of their respective years, so they appear specifically to be marking the anniversaries of Alexander's accession. From Book 6 onwards, the termini seem to shift into the summer months. On this point it may be relevant that the manuscripts of Diodorus declared an end to the first part of his 17th book at the same point as Cleitarchus' Book 5 closed. It is possible that this reflected a division of Cleitarchus' work at this point. If so then it could help to explain the change in practice regarding the end points of the books, although Cleitarchus nevertheless held to the pattern of one book per year. Obviously, the termini needed to shift into the summer at some stage, since the reign ended in June. It is also possible that Cleitarchus was unable precisely to locate the anniversaries of the accession accurately among the events once Alexander had moved into the wilds of the eastern satrapies.

The ends of Cleitarchus' Books 8 & 9 are lost in the Great Lacuna in Diodorus 17 and there are no boundary phrases to be found for the expected termini of Books 1, 3, 10, 11 and 13. However, five of the book termini of Cleitarchus seem to be marked by the boundary phrases associated with digressions. The hypothesis that Diodorus 17 is essentially an epitome of Cleitarchus is greatly strengthened by the presence of these vestiges of his book structure.

The Date of Accession of Alexander the Great

On the best evidence the assassination of Philip took place in October of 336BC. The key arguments may be summarised as follows. Alexander's death is fixed to 10th June 323BC (Julian Calendar) according to Plutarch citing the *Ephemerides* (composed by Eumenes of Cardia)[35] or 11th June according to

---

[35] Plutarch, *Alexander* 76.4; A. E. Samuel, *Ptolemaic Chronology* (Munich 1962) 46-47.

Aristobulus and the Babylonian Astronomical Diaries.[36] Arrian attributes a reign of 12 years and 8 months to Alexander, whilst Diodorus approximately concurs with 12 years and 7 months.[37] Hammond has further argued that the festival at which the assassination took place should be identified with the Dia held in honour of Zeus, which took place in the eponymously named Macedonian month of Dios.[38] E. Grzybek pointed out in 1990 that Josephus (*Antiquities of the Jews* 19.1.13) might indicate that the day number within the month was 24.[39] Unfortunately, we cannot be sure of the Julian equivalent date for 24th Dios in 336BC, but it fell roughly in October. There is a further supporting argument from Arrian, *Indica* 21.1, where it is stated that Nearchus set sail from India on 20th Boedromion in the Attic Calendar in 325BC and that this was within the eleventh year of Alexander's reign. Hence the anniversary of the accession was after 20th Boedromion, which occurred on about 18th September (Julian calendar) in 325BC (assuming that Nearchus was having to resort to direct lunisolar observations to derive calendar dates in Southern India).[40] However, this has been the limit of our knowledge of the date of the assassination of Philip and its exact day in the Julian calendar has never been precisely established (which is the same as stating that it has only been located to within tens of days on the standard axis of Universal Time).[41]

I have already argued that there are strong reasons to suppose that Cleitarchus ended his fifth book with the Battle of Arbela (Gaugamela). Justin 11.14.6 comments on this battle, "It was with this engagement that [Alexander] seized control of Asia, in the fifth year after his accession to the throne." This implies that Cleitarchus (Justin's probable ultimate source) had made a special point of noting that the day of the battle fell within the fifth year of the reign. Furthermore, Cleitarchus' book boundaries appear to coincide with the

---

[36] Plutarch, *Alexander* 75.4; L. Depuydt, "The Time of Death of Alexander the Great: 11 June 323 BC, ca. 4:00-5:00 PM," *Die Welt des Orients* 28 (1997) 117–135.

[37] Arrian, *Anabasis* 7.28.1; Diodorus 17.117.5; other ancient accounts rounded the reign to either 12 years (in two instances) or 13 years (also two instances.)

[38] Hammond (above, n.17 on *Regnal Years*) 358.

[39] E. Grzybek, *Du calendrier Macédonien au calendrier Ptolémaïque* (Basel 1990) 21-28; Josephus states that Philip died on the same day as Caligula, who was assassinated on 24th January AD41.

[40] The Attic Calendar was lunar, so its months drifted backwards and forwards slightly from year to year relative to the fixed dates in a solar calendar, such as the Julian scheme, which we use for dates in Antiquity; but Boedromion was always in the vicinity of late August to mid-October.

[41] In fact there are even voices (K.J. Beloch, W.W. Tarn, J.R. Hamilton, R. Lane Fox…) that have argued vociferously for a date of accession in the summer of 336BC, despite the consequential complete inconsistency with the reign durations given independently by Arrian and Diodorus, which should be accurate to within a month or so, and the fact that Nearchus specifically placed 20th Boedromion 325BC within Alexander's 11th regnal year. It seems that these authors base their case on the several references that make Alexander twenty at his accession (Arrian *Anabasis* 1.1.1; Plutarch, *Alexander* 11.1; Justin 11.1.9), but he was still twenty in the autumn and none of the ancient souces suggests that he was *exactly* twenty when Philip died.

anniversaries of the accession at least up to this point in the first half of his history. It is therefore highly significant that the next definite event recorded by Cleitarchus after the battle, which is Alexander's arrival in the town of Arbela, he evidently placed at the beginning of the sixth book of his history. Diodorus recounts this at 17.64.3 *after* the boundary phrases signifying the end of the fifth book of Cleitarchus. Arrian 3.15.5 states that Alexander reached Arbela on the day after the battle, which is perfectly consistent with a hot pursuit on horseback.[42] Curtius actually takes up the story with Darius' flight from *midnight* on the day of the battle at the very beginning of his fifth book, implying that he too was reflecting a major division in his source between the day of the battle and the following day with midnight as the specific point of division. *It may reasonably be inferred that Cleitarchus believed the day after the Battle of Arbela to be the fifth anniversary of Alexander's accession.*

This is highly significant, because we have incontrovertible dates for the Battle of Arbela in both the Julian and Attic calendars. The Julian date comes from the lunar eclipse that was observed by Alexander's forces at around 21:00 local time on the evening of 20th September 331BC. It is easy to calculate from analysis of the various sources that the battle itself took place eleven days later on 1st October.[43] Furthermore, Plutarch, *Camillus* 19.3 states that the battle took place on the Attic date of 26th Boedromion. It is important to notice that these dates are entirely independent in their derivation, since the Julian derives from modern astronomical calculations. Yet they agree with one another in a highly specific way. The date of the eclipse is of course also the date of the Full Moon in that month. The synodic lunar month (the month as defined by repetition of the phases) has a duration of 29.53 days. The New Moon had therefore occurred 14.765 days before 21:00 on 20th September in 331BC, i.e. on 6th September.[44] In principle, for Greek lunar calendars (as in the case of most lunar calendars) the New Moon (more strictly the first evening observation of the crescent after the New Moon) defines the first day of the month. We can see that the 6th September was indeed the 1st Boedromion from Plutarch's date for the battle, so Plutarch's date gives exactly the correct lunar phase as predicted from the eclipse. But actually this is rather surprising, because the standard Attic calendar used by the Archon for setting the date of festivals and also used for most other practical purposes was demonstrably normally out of

---

[42] The distance was in range 500 to 600 stades according to Arrian, *Anabasis* 6.11.5; modern estimates are in the range 80 to 95km although the precise site of the battle remains controversial; see Bosworth (above, n.19) 293-294.

[43] See of Brunt (above, n.29) Section 5 of Appendix VIII for the details.

[44] In fact the orbit of the Moon is slightly elliptical, which results in the Moon having a slightly higher angular velocity around the Earth in the half of its orbit where it is slightly closer to the Earth. Hence the New Moon does not in general occur precisely halfway between two successive Full Moons, but the discrepancy will only be of the order of a few hours. It is doubtful whether the ancients could establish the precise time of the New Moon any more accurately than this.

synchrony with the lunar phases (mostly due to tampering by the Archons): there was also an Attic Lunar Regulatory Calendar, which *was* strictly based on the lunar phases, but it was hardly ever used for practical purposes.[45] Nevertheless, it would appear that Plutarch did indeed use the Attic Lunar Regulatory scheme for his date, because Arrian, *Anabasis* 3.15.7 states that Gaugamela took place in the next Attic month of Pyanepsion and he is presumably referencing the standard Attic Archon/Festival Calendar, which was as usual out-of-step with the lunar phases. In fact it was quite normal for the various *civil* lunar calendars in the Greek world at the time to be out of precise synchrony with the lunar phases: that is why the possible Macedonian date for the assassination of Philip of 24th Dios cannot readily be translated to a Julian date.

Why might Plutarch have used such a specialised and pedantic dating scheme? There is a straightforward answer. He was probably getting his dates directly or indirectly from a famously pedantic Greek chronologist and historian of the late 4th and early 3rd centuries BC: Timaeus of Tauromenium. Though originally from Sicily, Timaeus was educated in Athens and spent most of his life there. Diodorus and Polybius record his special attention to matters of accurate chronology.[46] There is strong evidence from elsewhere that both Cleitarchus and Plutarch were virtual disciples of the work of Timaeus. Hammond has shown that Plutarch's date of 6th Hecatombaeon for Alexander's birth comes from Timaeus, because Cicero gives many of the same details in his mentions of the stories about Alexander's birth and he names Timaeus as his source in one instance.[47] Cleitarchus himself definitely used Timaeus, since Fragment 7 of Cleitarchus couples him with Timaeus as its co-source and it mentions the Heracleidae, Alexander's putative ancestors.[48] Then Fragment 36 from Suidas seems to make Cleitarchus a follower of Timaeus and Anaximenes.[49] This makes it quite likely that Plutarch got 6th Hecatombaeon from Cleitarchus (although Plutarch did also use Timaeus directly, for example, in his Life of Timoleon.) There is also a strong possibility that Plutarch's date for Gaugamela came from Cleitarchus – for instance, when he gives its date in his Life of Camillus he calls it the Battle of Arbela, which is the Cleitarchan name. Certainly, Plutarch had read Cleitarchus and it may be inferred that Cleitarchus

---

[45] Alan E. Samuel, *Greek & Roman Chronology* (Munich 1972) 57-58.

[46] Diodorus 5.1.3 & Polybius 12.11.1.

[47] N. G. L. Hammond, *Sources for Alexander the Great* (Cambridge 1993) 19-20; Jacoby (above, n.2) 566 F150a of Timaeus (Cicero, *N.D.* 2.69); Cicero, *Div.* 1.47; Hammond also believed that Timaeus was born in the same year as Alexander; it is an obvious corollary that Alexander was born on the sixth day after a New Moon in July of 356BC and a New Moon occurred on 15th July (Julian), so Alexander was born on 20th July 356BC in the Julian Calendar.

[48] Jacoby (above, n.2) 137 F7 (Clement of Alexandria, *Strom.* 1.139.4).

[49] Jacoby (above, n.2) 137 F36 (Suidas s.v. ἔχετον).

gave a date for the battle, since otherwise it would have been difficult for him to demonstrate his point that it fell within the fifth year of the reign.

It being established that Cleitarchus considered 2nd October 331BC (=27th Boedromion in the Attic Lunar Regulatory Calendar) to be the fifth anniversary of Alexander's accession, how can we calculate the Julian date of the accession itself in 336BC? The obvious date of 2nd October 336BC is probably incorrect, because Cleitarchus is not likely to have had a source for the key dates in a solar calendar. Rather we need to identify the Julian date for 27th Boedromion in 336BC. If the Attic date had been given in the standard Archon/Festival Calendar, then the situation would be difficult, because the Athenians regularly and arbitrarily added and subtracted days from that scheme to suit various social and political purposes. However, as I have argued, there are strong reasons to suppose that Cleitarchus was using Timaeus' accurate dating system and that this involved citing dates aligned with lunar phases according to the Attic Lunar Regulatory Calendar. Therefore, we need only establish the dates of the New Moons in the autumn of 336BC to calculate the possible Julian equivalents for the 27th Boedromion in that year. This is easily done: for example, NASA has calculated that a partial lunar eclipse occurred at around 04:30 (local time at Athens) on the morning of 14th December 336BC (Julian Calendar).[50] Hence there would have been a New Moon on 1st September; so 27th Boedromion should be 27th September (Julian) in 336BC. There is a slight possibility that the true date was exactly one synodic month earlier or later than this date, but these alternatives would appear to be too early or too late to fit in well with other aspects of the historical record and they would represent rather extreme excursions for the month of Boedromion. The earlier date would give Alexander a reign of well over 12 years and 9 months, which is too long according to both Arrian and Diodorus. The later date would not readily have allowed Alexander enough time to make his reported expedition into Southern Greece as described by Arrian, *Anabasis* 1.1.1-3 and Diodorus 17.4 before winter set in. Conversely, the date of 27th September gives Alexander a reign of 12 years 8 months and 14 days and fits perfectly with all the other historical information. If the rule suggested by Plato, *Laws* 767C was applied in the Attic Lunar Regulatory Calendar, then the Attic New Year in 336BC would have fallen on the first New Moon after the Summer Solstice,[51] which was about 3rd July in that year. In that case 27th Boedromion was indeed 27th September in 336BC.[52] Finally, I note that 27th September 336BC in the Julian calendar is 22nd

---

[50] NASA Five Millennium Catalog of Lunar Eclipses.

[51] The solstice fell on ~26th June in the Julian Calendar in that era, due to slippage relative to the Gregorian Calendar of about 3 days in every 4 centuries: the two coincide in the early 4th century AD.

[52] Plutarch's date for Gaugamela does obey Plato's rule, but I am aware that there is ongoing controversy on Athenian practice regarding the date of the New Year: see W. Kendrick Pritchett, "Postscript: The Athenian Calendars," *ZPE* 128 (1999) 79-93.

September 336BC in the retro-projected Gregorian calendar. This means that the festival of the gods at which Philip was assassinated was being held on the Autumnal Equinox. I believe this significantly corroborates Cleitarchus' date for the event, since the Equinoxes have always been popular days for pagan holy festivals. Indeed, the Autumnal Equinox was specially significant in Macedon, because the Macedonian calendar began its year on the first New Moon after the Autumnal Equinox.[53]

Book Boundaries and Fragment Locations in Cleitarchus

The location of the boundaries between Cleitarchus' books is a topic that is intertwined with the fragment locations. It is clear that the starting point for seeking book boundaries for the first five books should normally be the anniversary of Alexander's accession at around the start of October. This is most clearly signalled by the division between the Battle of Arbela itself at the end of Book 5 and the subsequent advance to the town of Arbela, which falls into Book 6. However, from the death of Darius onwards, it appears that Cleitarchus allowed the book boundaries to creep backwards into summer. Although he successfully retained the scheme of one book per year, many of the later book boundaries significantly antedate the anniversary of the accession. It seems that Cleitarchus may have been especially vague on chronology in India, where even the Winter-Summer cycle of the weather was largely missing as a guide. Throughout the texts of Diodorus and Curtius a helpful additional indication of the Cleitarchan book boundaries is the occurrence of digressions, since Cleitarchus seems to have pursued the neat practice of placing them preferentially at the beginnings or ends of his books. Due to the secondary authors in some cases having moved the digressions, their Cleitarchan locations can only be reliably identified wherever Diodorus and Curtius relate a particular digression at the same juncture. However, the boundary phrases marking digressions in the text of Diodorus 17 do appear to be reliable indications of Cleitarchan boundaries even in isolation. Indeed, the occurrences of digression boundary phrases in Diodorus 17 can safely take precedence as the primary guide wherever they are available. The normal book and chapter divisions in Curtius and Justin and the chapter ends or Attic year boundaries in Diodorus 17 do not, in general, follow Cleitarchus' scheme. Yet in some instances, particularly where a boundary is found at the same point in all the extant followers of Cleitarchus, there may nevertheless be evidence of a Cleitarchan boundary: e.g. Curtius' fifth book opens where Cleitarchus began his sixth. The broad conclusions on the book structure of Cleitarchus and the locations of his Fragments are detailed below and summarised in Table 8.1.

---

[53] Samuel (above, n.45) 142; Hammond (above, n.17 on *Regnal Years*) 355 & 358.

An Update On The Organisation And Structure Of Cleitarchus

Book 1: It is likely that Cleitarchus began with an outline of Alexander's birth and ancestry resembling Plutarch, *Alexander* 2.1 & 3.3-5. As already noted Hammond has shown that Plutarch's date of 6th Hecatombaeon for Alexander's birth comes from Timaeus, a rough contemporary of Cleitarchus, because Cicero gives many of the same details and names Timaeus as his source. However, there is good evidence that Cleitarchus himself used Timaeus, who was the leading authority on chronological issues in the early 3rd century BC. Fragment 7 of Cleitarchus couples him with Timaeus as its co-source and it mentions the Heracleidae, Alexander's putative ancestors.[54] Then Fragment 36 from Suidas seems to make Cleitarchus a follower of Timaeus and Anaximenes.[55] In this context Plutarch also gives Hegesias as the source of a quip about the conflagration of the Temple at Ephesus on the day of Alexander's birth.[56] Hegesias is another near contemporary of Cleitarchus, but immediately precedes him in a list of ancient writers given by Philodemus, who usually arranged his lists in date order.[57] A famous fragment of Hegesias describes the killing of Betis at the siege of Gaza, but very similar details of this event are given by Curtius, who usually followed Cleitarchus for such histrionic anecdotes.[58] Furthermore, Curtius' version of Gaza emphasises Alexander's emulation of Achilles, which is a familiar Cleitarchan theme. The end of Plutarch's passage on Alexander's birth cites a prophecy that Alexander would be *aniketos* (= Latin *invictus* = invincible), an epithet for the king, which is strongly associated with the Cleitarchan tradition.[59] Finally, Hegesias was renowned for being perhaps the earliest author to employ a curious metrical device known as Asianic rhythms and there are some hints among the fragments of Cleitarchus that he too occasionally practised this type of prose poetry.[60] In summary, there are indications that both Timaeus and Hegesias were sources for Cleitarchus, so when material is found from both, which is also linked to familiar Cleitarchan themes such as *aniketos*, descent from Heracles and Achilles and a fascination for chronology and the calendar, all these things being found together in a short passage, then there are cumulatively strong grounds to suspect that Cleitarchus is Plutarch's immediate source of inspiration. Book 1 evidently extended as far as the end of the campaigning

---

[54] Jacoby (above, n.2) 137 F7 (Clement of Alexandria, *Strom.* 1.139.4).

[55] Jacoby (above, n.2) 137 F36 (Suidas s.v. ἔχετον).

[56] Jacoby (above, n.2) 142 F3 of Hegesias.

[57] Jacoby (above, n.2) 137 T12 (Philodemus, *Rhet.* 4.1 col. 21).

[58] Jacoby (above, n.2) 142 F5 of Hegesias; Curtius 4.6.12-16.

[59] Plutarch, *Alexander* 3.5 & 14.4-5; Diodorus 17.93.4 & 17.51.3-4; Curtius 4.7.27; Livy 9.18; Justin 11.11.10; Cleitarchus' use of this epithet may reflect contemporary practice, since Hypereides I, col.32, 5 referred to a proposal to erect a statue of Alexander as θεὸς ἀνίκητος according to the interpretation of H. Berve, "Review of W I" *Gnomon* 5 (1929) 376 n.2.

[60] Pearson (above, n.8) 213, n.9 & 227, n.59.

season in 335BC and the sack of Thebes, since Fragment 1, dealing with the aftermath of its fall, is from Book 1. The last known event of the season in the Vulgate tradition was Alexander's visit to Delphi whilst heading back towards Macedon.[61] Thebes fell at the beginning of October and the anniversary of Alexander's accession (27th Boedromion) fell on 16th October in 335BC leaving ample time for the visit to Delphi in Book 1.

Book 2: The second book may have opened with Alexander's return to Macedon and various stories telling of Alexander's theatrical preparations for the campaign against the Persian Empire during the winter of 335-334BC. Surviving versions of the stories are found in Justin and Frontinus (transmitted via Trogus) and in Plutarch (probably directly from Cleitarchus).[62] Fragment 7, noting that Alexander's invasion came 820 years after that by the Heracleidae, must be derived from the opening of this book.[63] I infer that Cleitarchus mentioned an otherwise unreported visit of Alexander to the tomb of Themistocles at Magnesia, because Fragments 33 and 34 are from a digression on the career of Themistocles.[64] We should expect this book to have closed in early October 334BC after the conclusion of the siege of Halicarnassus. It is likely that Alexander's encounter with the Marmares on the frontier of Lycia, which is uniquely recounted by Diodorus 17.28, was virtually the last event described by Cleitarchus in his second book. The accession anniversary was 6th October in 334BC, which would be a credible date. The boundary phrase at the end of 17.28 ("This is what happened in this year") possibly marks the end of Cleitarchus' second book. This is underscored by the opening of the next Attic Archon-year in the ensuing section – several months late!

Book 3: Opened with winter campaigning in Pamphylia. Cleitarchus seems to have inserted a group of digressions on the activities and death of Memnon (see Diodorus 17.29, Plutarch, *Alexander* 18.3 and Curtius 3.2.1) and the preparations of Darius at Babylon (Diodorus 17.30.1-31.2 and Curtius 3.2.2-19). The surviving part of the account of Curtius opens with the episode of the Gordian

---

[61] Plutarch, *Alexander* 14.4-5; Diodorus 17.93.4; W. Dittenberger (ed.), *Sylloge Inscriptionum Graecarum, editio tertia* vol 1 (Leipzig 1915) 251H, col. II, lines 9-10 436-7 is an inscription from Delphi recording a gift to the shrine at this time of 150 gold coins minted by Philip II, but Alexander is the only likely donor of Macedonian coinage on this scale at this juncture.

[62] Justin 11.5.1-9; Plutarch, *Alexander* 15.2-3; Frontinus, *Strat.* 2.11.3 & 1.11.14.

[63] Jacoby (above, n.2) 137 F7 (Clement of Alexandria, *Strom.* 1.139.4).

[64] Jacoby (above, n.2) 137 F33 & F34 (Plutarch, *Themistocles* 27.1-2 & Cicero, *Brut.* 42-43); the surrender of Magnesia (Arrian, *Anabasis* 1.18.1) is the most likely occasion for Cleitarchus' digression on Themistocles, since his tomb lay there. Cleitarchus' father Deinon had evidently told the story of Themistocles, since Plutarch cites Deinon for the same story in Fragment 33. It is possible that Cleitarchus drew a comparison between Themistocles' submission to Xerxes and Charidemus' allegiance to Darius, since they were both exiled Athenians serving Persian kings. Arrian, *Anabasis* 1.18.2 may implicitly be contradicting Cleitarchus when he makes a point of stating that Alexander stayed at Ephesus when Magnesia surrendered.

knot. Alexander probably arrived at Gordion in April of 333BC, but lingered during midsummer, departing perhaps as late as the end of July.[65] Diodorus omitted Gordion along with most of the other events from this book in his epitome: the only part of Alexander's activities that he included from Cleitarchus' third book seems to be the passage at Diodorus 17.31.3-6, mainly dealing with Alexander's illness. Alexander arrived at Tarsus in Cilicia early in September of 333BC and immediately fell seriously ill. His recovery may have been the last major event of this book, because Fragment 2, relating to Alexander's campaign in western Cilicia immediately after his recovery, was in the fourth book. The accession anniversary was 25th September in 333BC.

Book 4: Fragment 2 shows that Alexander's Cilician campaign towards Soli and Anchiale, west of Tarsus, was related at the beginning of this book. This is from Curtius 3.7 and Diodorus 32.2. Its major events must have been firstly the Battle of Issus (Fragment 8)[66] on around 5th November 333BC and subsequently the siege of Tyre (Fragment 9).[67] It ended with the story of the appointment of "Balonymus" as King of Tyre. This has been believed by some to be an error by Cleitarchus for the appointment of Abdalonymus as King of Sidon. Curtius gives what seems a correct version of the story with Abdalonymus appointed King of Sidon before the siege of Tyre on the recommendation of Hephaistion, whereas the manuscripts of Diodorus do not mention Sidon. Prandi, Bosworth and others have highlighted and discussed the case of Abdalonymus,[68] because it appears to present an intractable local difficulty for the reconstruction of the Cleitarchan version. However, Curtius 4.1.26 mentions that an area surrounding Sidon was added to Abdalonymus' dominions by Alexander. Perhaps Cleitarchus therefore mentioned that he was given control of Tyre after its fall and that was what prompted Diodorus to tell the story of his original appointment as a king in the context of the fall of Tyre. Perhaps Diodorus in his original manuscript correctly referred the story of Abdalonymus' appointment back to Sidon in Section 17.47, having noted his appointment as King of Tyre in Section 17.46.6. If so, given the curious order in which Diodorus presents the matter, an ancient editor of Diodorus would obviously have assumed that the mentions of Sidon were errors for Tyre and incorrectly corrected them in some later manuscript that became the prototype for our surviving versions of Diodorus. This seems to constitute a logical and viable way of explaining the confusion through an understandable rather than a crass error, which also allows that Diodorus, Curtius and Trogus (Justin) were all still following Cleitarchus. Although it might be objected that Philotas was

---

[65] D. W. Engels (above, n.25) 37.

[66] Jacoby (above, n.2) 137 F8 (Cicero, *Ad f.* 2.10.3).

[67] Jacoby (above, n.2) 137 F9 (Schol. Plato *Resp.* 337A cf. Photius: Σαρδόνιος γέλως).

[68] Luisa Prandi, "Fortuna è Realtà dell'Opera di Clitarco" *Historia Einzelschriften* 104 (Stuttgart 1996) 102; Bosworth (above, n.8).

made garrison commander in Tyre according to Curtius 4.5.9, I cannot see that this excludes Abdalonymus as its king. The end of the narrative on Alexander in Book 4 in the aftermath of Tyre is clearly marked by a boundary phrase "Now we have described things concerning Alexander, we shall turn our narrative in another direction" at Diodorus 17.47.6. It probably had a digression on events elsewhere (e.g. Agis' activities in Crete in Diodorus 17.48.1-2) as indicated by this boundary phrase and by analogy with the end of Book 5 as described next.[69]

Book 5: Opened from the accession anniversary on 14th October 332BC with the siege of Gaza, the advance into Egypt, the visit to Siwa and **afterwards** the foundation of Alexandria. Cleitarchus probably described Alexander's return up the Levantine coast after Egypt, because this would explain why Fragment 3, which seems to relate to a visit of Alexander to Byblos on the Lebanese coast, is located in Book 5 by Stobaeus. The narrative of Alexander's activities within Book 5 seems to have ended on schedule on 1st October 331BC with the Battle of Arbela (Gaugamela). This account terminated with the boundary phrase "This was the outcome of the battle near Arbela". Book 5 then concluded with the digression on events in Europe and specifically the rebellion of Agis, since Fragment 4 attributes mention of the 50 Spartan hostages received by Antipater to Book 5. Conjecturally, other events in Europe were related by Cleitarchus at this point, such as the death of Alexander of Epirus, given in Justin 12.2.1-15. For example, Curtius 8.1.37 mentions a complaint by Alexander of Epirus (whilst he died of a wound according to Livy) that he had encountered men in Italy, whilst his nephew was up against women in Persia.[70] The relevant section of Livy has some Cleitarchan elements, such as referring to the "Invincible Alexander".[71] The final close of Book 5 is indicated by the boundary phrase "Now that we have run through the events in Europe, we may in turn pass on to what occurred in Asia" at Diodorus 17.63.5.

Book 6: Opened with the immediate aftermath of the Battle of Arbela, including the flight of Darius and Alexander's arrival at Darius' base in Arbela the day after the battle. This book incorporated Fragment 10 (description of Babylon) and Fragment 11 (the razing of Persepolis).[72] The narrative on Alexander's activities seems to have ended in July 330BC with the death of Darius, which was also the end of Curtius' fifth book and the 11th book of Justin/Trogus. Diodorus 17.73.4 concludes with the boundary phrase, "And

---

[69] Diodorus 17.48.1-2; Curtius 4.1.39-40; note that there are additional digressions in Curtius 4.5.11-22 immediately following Curtius' account of Tyre and including the tale of Aristonicus the Pirate.

[70] Aulus Gellius, *NA* 17.21.33; Livy 9.19.10-11.

[71] See N. G. L. Hammond, *Three Historians of Alexander the Great* (Cambridge 1983) 112 on Cleitarchus as Livy's probable source.

[72] Jacoby (above, n.2) 137 F10 & F11 (Diodorus 2.7.3-4 cf. Tzetzes, *Chil.* 9.569; Athenaeus 576D-E).

that was the situation in Asia", before catching up with the matter of the Spartan hostages, which Cleitarchus had treated at the end of his fifth book. It looks as though Diodorus related the matter here, because Cleitarchus recorded the departure of the Spartan envoys to Alexander on the subject of the Spartan hostages at this point (Diodorus 17.73.6 & Curtius 6.1.20). Perhaps the actual arrival of the Spartan envoys in Alexander's camp is indicated by Curtius 7.4.32, when Alexander receives news from Greece of the Spartan rebellion.

Book 7: The first events must have been persuasion of the troops to continue the war and the advance to Hecatompylus, but Fragments 12-14,[73] Diodorus 17.75 and Curtius 6.4.1-22 show that Cleitarchus provided significant digressions on the geography of the Caspian region and the natural history of Hyrcania at the beginning of this book. Fragments 15 and 16 relate the visit of Thalestris, Queen of the Amazons, and Fragment 32 on the castration of a transgressing male also best fits the context of a digression on Amazon practices.[74] Following Alexander's first crossing of the Hindu Kush in the summer of 329BC Diodorus 17.83.3 has the boundary phrase, Καὶ τὰ μὲν περὶ Ἀλέξανδρον ἐν τούτοις ἦν ("These were the concerns of Alexander"), which probably indicates the end of Book 7 of Cleitarchus.

Book 8: Began with a digression on events in the camp of Bessus echoed in both Curtius 7.4.1-19 and Diodorus 17.83.7, followed by news reaching Alexander from Greece and elsewhere (Curtius 7.4.32-40 and Diodorus 17.83.4-6), then the march to the River Oxus (Diodorus, List of Contents for Book 17; Curtius 7.5.9-12; Frontinus, *Strat.* 1.7.7). The end of Book 8 falls in the great lacuna in Diodorus 17, but the *Metz Epitome* has opened and continues to provide corroboration of Cleitarchan material in Curtius down to Alexander's arrival in the Indus Delta. The closing event of this book seems to have been Alexander's capture of the Rock of Ariamazes (i.e. the Sogdian Rock), which Cleitarchus treated as the climax of the campaigning year of 328BC (*Metz Epitome* 15-18; Curtius 7.11.1-25; Polyaenus 4.3.29; Diodorus 17 – Contents; Strabo 11.11.4.). This also ended the seventh book of Curtius.

Book 9: Probably opened with Scythian peace overtures including the offer of the Scythian king's daughter to Alexander in marriage (Curtius 8.1.1-10). It continued with the first campaign against the Massagetae and the Dahae: Alexander's 3-column campaign through Sogdiana. This book seems to have climaxed in a similar way to Book 8 with the capture of the Rock of Chorienes. It therefore closed in the late Spring of 327BC with the marriage of Alexander to Roxane, who had fallen into his hands with the surrender of this strong point (*Metz Epitome* 28-31; Curtius 8.4.20-30; Diodorus - Contents).

---

[73] Jacoby (above, n.2) 137 F12 (Pliny, *N.H.* 6.36-38), F13 (Strabo 11.1.5), F14 (Demetrius, *De eloc.* 304 cf. Tzetzes, *Chil.* 7.49, 11.832).

[74] T. S. Brown, "Clitarchus," *American Journal of Philology* 71 (1950) 149; Jacoby (above, n.2) 137 F15 (Plutarch, *Alexander* 46), F16 (Strabo 11.5.4), F32 (*Pap. Oxyrh.* 2.218 col. 2).

Book 10: Commenced with Alexander's preparations for the invasion of India and also mentioned his orders for the training of native youths in Macedonian arms to augment the *Epigoni*. Several Fragments (20-22) seem to be from an introductory description of Indian royal processions by virtue of parallels in Curtius.[75] A little later Alexander's visit to Nysa and the discovery of the ivy of Dionysus were related by Cleitarchus (Fragment 17).[76] This was the first book of the Indian campaigns. Its climax was the battle against Porus (the Hydaspes) and it closed with the re-instatement of Porus as king in the same place as the close of Curtius' eighth book and the 89th chapter of Diodorus (Curtius 8.14.5; Diodorus 17.89.6; Justin 12.8.7; *Metz Epitome* 61). This was in June of 326BC. Jacoby Fragment 5 of Cleitarchus, which is stated to be derived from Book 10, was likely part of a digression on the revolt of Baryaxes that ended this book.[77]

Book 11: Opened with a discussion of Alexander's plans to reach the ends of India and to visit the Ocean (*Metz Epitome* 63; Curtius 9.1.1-6; Diodorus 17.89.3-90.6). There is copious evidence from the Fragments and other Vulgate sources for digressions on the geography and natural history of India near the beginning of this book: specifically, sixteen cubit serpents in Fragment 18[78] (Diodorus 17.90.1 and Curtius 9.1.4) and troops of monkeys and their ensnarement in Fragment 19[79] (Diodorus 17.90.2-3). A visit to salt mines in Fragment 28 probably relates to the start of the voyage down the Hydaspes, when the expedition would have passed the famous and ancient salt mines at Khewra.[80] There is also a fragment of Onesicritus at Strabo 15.1.30, which mentions a mountain of salt in the kingdom of Sopeithes. According to Arrian 6.2.2 Hephaistion was ordered to hurry to the capital of King Sopeithes at the start of the river voyage. Fragment 24 suggesting that Ptolemy was present when Alexander was wounded at the Mallian town was part of the climax of this book.[81] The best indications are that Cleitarchus' 11th book closed soon after the successful treatment of Alexander's Mallian chest wound by Critobulus in the Spring of 325BC. The main evidence for this is the insertion of a digression on a revolt of the Greeks settled in Bactria by both Diodorus and Curtius at this point (Diodorus 17.99.5-6; Curtius 9.7.1-11). Conversely, the Vulgate narrative is relatively seamless through Alexander's visit to the Ocean and subsequent

---

[75] Curtius 8.9.23-26; Jacoby (above, n.2) 137 F20 (Strabo 15.1.69l), F21 (Aelian, *N.A.* 17.23), F22 (Aelian, *N.A.* 17.22).

[76] Jacoby (above, n.2) 137 F17 (Scholia on Apollonius Rhodius 2.904).

[77] It is also feasible that it was in a digression at the beginning of Book 10.

[78] Jacoby (above, n.2) 137 F18 (Aelian, *N.A.* 17.2).

[79] Jacoby (above, n.2) 137 F19 (Aelian, *N.A.* 17.25).

[80] Jacoby (above, n.2) 137 F28 (Strabo 5.2.6).

[81] Jacoby (above, n.2) 137 F24 (Curtius 9.5.21).

march into Gedrosia, despite this seeming perhaps to modern sensibilities to be a more logical point to close the second book of the Indian campaign.

Book 12: Began with the surrender of the Mallians and Oxydracae and a celebratory banquet after which the contest between Coragus and Dioxippus took place.[82] F25 relates the killing of 80,000 Indians in the Kingdom of Sambus.[83] F23 telling of Mandi women bearing children at age 7 and being old at 40 is difficult to place exactly, but most probably comes from a digression during the progress down the Indus.[84] It is co-attributed to Megasthenes. Fragment 26 clearly refers to the tidal bore in the Indus Delta described also by Curtius.[85] The location of F27 among the Oreitae and the Ichthyophagi in Gedrosia is self-explanatory.[86] F29 cites stories told to Alexander about the Indian Ocean voyage and may securely be placed at the return of Nearchus and Onesicritus, since there are matching tales related by these men at Curtius 10.1.11.[87] F6 shows that Book 12 extended at least as far as the suicide of Calanus. Its end is clearly indicated following the arrival of the Persian *Epigoni* in summer 324BC (Diodorus 17.108.3) with a recurrence of the terminal sentence, Καὶ τὰ μὲν περὶ Ἀλέξανδρον ἐν τούτοις ἦν, incorporating Cleitarchus' title.

Book 13: Opened with a digression on the extravagance of Harpalus towards his mistresses (Fragment 30) and an account of his flight to Athens.[88] Subsequently, Cleitarchus evidently claimed that a Roman delegation met Alexander at Babylon in April-May of 323BC (Fragment 31).[89] There is significant evidence that Cleitarchus' account extended beyond Alexander's death in June 323BC in an epilogue focussed on the fate of his corpse. A similar version of the suicide of Sisygambis is found in Diodorus 17 and Curtius. Pausanias 1.6.3 speaks of Alexander's body being laid to rest with Macedonian rites at Memphis in about 321BC and he does so shortly after giving a Cleitarchan version of the story that Ptolemy had saved Alexander's life in India. Similarly, Curtius 7.9.21 speaks of the bones of dead Macedonians being laid to rest in accordance with the rites of their fatherland in a passage likely to be derived from Cleitarchus. Furthermore, Curtius' account closes with a mention of Alexander's entombment at Memphis. This raises the possibility that

---

[82] Exclusively a Cleitarchan story: Diodorus 17.100.1-101.6; Curtius 9.7.12-26.

[83] Jacoby (above, n.2) 137 F25 (Curtius 9.8.15), which had 800,000 (DCCC milia) in the manuscripts, which is usually amended to 80,000 (LXXX milia) on the basis of Diodorus 17.102.5-7, which speaks of "more than eight myriad of the barbarians".

[84] Jacoby (above, n.2) 137 F23 (Pliny, *N.H.* 7.28-29).

[85] Jacoby (above, n.2) 137 F26 (Strabo 7.2.1-2); Curtius 9.9.9-21.

[86] Jacoby (above, n.2) 137 F27 (Pliny, *N.H.* 7.30).

[87] Jacoby (above, n.2) 137 F29 (Pliny, *N.H.* 6.198).

[88] Jacoby (above, n.2) 137 F30 (Athenaeus 586C-D); Diodorus 17.108.4-8; Curtius 10.2.1-3.

[89] Jacoby (above, n.2) 137 F31 (Pliny, *N.H.* 3.57); cf. Arrian, Anabasis 7.15.5-6.

both Pausanias and Curtius are following a description of how Alexander's body reached Memphis given by Cleitarchus (Curtius 9.8.22 also shares the statement in Pausanias 1.6.2 that Ptolemy was not sired by Lagus, presumably both following Cleitarchus again.) Another significant indicator for Cleitarchus' account having extended beyond Alexander's death is provided by closely matching comments on the suppression of poisoning rumours under Antipater and Cassander in Diodorus 17.118.2 and Curtius 10.10.18-19 with further echoes in Pausanias 9.7.2. There are also 3-way matches between the accounts of these authors encompassing Cassander's actions: murder of Olympias; restoration of Thebes; slaughter of all Alexander's relatives. Schachermeyr has also argued that Curtius was still drawing on Cleitarchus for his account of events after Alexander's death.[90] It is additionally pertinent that Jane Hornblower has concluded in the context of a detailed study of Book 18 of Diodorus[91] that the historian continued to follow his source for Book 17 (i.e. Cleitarchus) in several chapters near the beginning of Book 18 culminating in the review of Alexander's Last Plans (*hypomnemata*). She saw the geographical review of Asia in Diodorus 18.5 as the start of the material from Hieronymus. I tend to share the view that the Last Plans are from Cleitarchus, but for different reasons: specifically, I find many echoes of the Last Plans in other Cleitarchan material (notably: Hephaistion's memorial in Plutarch, *Alexander* 72.3; campaign against the Carthaginians, march to Pillars of Heracles and return via Spain and Italy in Curtius 10.1.17-19; 10,000 talents on temples in Greece in Plutarch, *Moralia* 343D; temple of Athena at Troy in Strabo 13.1.26). Hornblower also suspected that Cleitarchus might be the source for Diodorus' version of Alexander's entombment in Alexandria at 18.28.3-6, but I consider that Diodorus was drawing on his personal experience of having visited the tomb in Alexandria for this, since Cleitarchus could not have implied that Ptolemy Soter created the Alexandrian tomb as early as 321BC. Nevertheless, Curtius also mentions the transfer from Memphis to Alexandria in his last sentence. It is likely that Cleitarchus' account extended at least as far as the entombment at Memphis in 321BC and a possibility exists that he finished with the transfer of the body to Alexandria in ~280BC.[92] Indeed it is that event that may have prompted him as a resident of Alexandria to compose his history.

Other Fragments: As regards F35 and F36 and also the aphorisms attributed to Cleitarchus by several Christian writers in the doubtful Fragments 37-52, none can be placed with certainty.[93] However F36 from the Suda is helpful in that it extends the evidence for Cleitarchus having used Timaeus as a source.

---

[90] F. Schachermeyr, *Alexander in Babylon und die Reichsordnung nach seiner Tode* (Vienna 1970) 92.

[91] Hornblower (above, n.11) 92-97.

[92] A.M. Chugg, "The Sarcophagus of Aleander the Great?" *Greece & Rome* 49.1 (April 2002) 14-15.

[93] There are echoes of the philosophy of the Cynics and mentions of the diadem in F37-52, which is enough to make it seem credible that they were indeed extracted from Cleitarchus' work: F48

An Update On The Organisation And Structure Of Cleitarchus

Conclusions

A revised analysis of the book-numbered fragments of Cleitarchus has shown that he organised his history *Concerning Alexander* into thirteen books, one for each year of Alexander's reign. Echoes of the *termini* of five of Cleitarchus' books have been discerned in Diodorus' seventeenth book in the form of boundary phrases marking digressions on events elsewhere that Cleitarchus placed at the ends of his books. Cleitarchus' work may have been divided into two parts in the same place as Diodorus 17 is divided (between its 63rd and 64th chapters). The five books in the first part of Cleitarchus had *termini* located quite precisely on the anniversaries of the accession corresponding to mid-September to mid-October in the Julian calendar. However, Books 6 to 13 comprising the second part of the work generally ended in the summer months.

This improved understanding of the structure of Cleitarchus' work has yielded startling new information on key details of Alexander's reign. It has emerged that Alexander's route probably hugged the Mediterranean coast for as long as possible for the march between Tyre and Thapsacus in 331BC. This means that most modern reconstructions of his path are in error in making him march inland from Tyre. It has become clear that Cleitarchus paid detailed attention to events beyond the narrow focus of Alexander's expedition in a more comprehensive sense than has previously been realised and he was scrupulous about chronology. For example, he appears to have given a detailed account of the revolt of Baryaxes in Persia in its correct context, whilst Alexander was in India. It has also been demonstrated that Cleitarchus believed the Battle of Arbela (or Gaugamela) to have taken place on the day before the fifth anniversary of Alexander's accession. Since this battle can be dated accurately in the Julian Calendar using an antecedent lunar eclipse and Plutarch has provided an Attic date for the event, which is synchronised with the lunar phases, it has been possible for the first time to calculate a Julian date for the festival of the gods at which Philip was assassinated of 27th September 336BC, which was the autumnal equinox (it was 22nd September in the Gregorian Calendar).

The first book of Cleitarchus opened with some details of Alexander's birth and ancestry. The last book probably extended to note Alexander's entombment at Memphis and seems briefly to have alluded to attempts by Antipater and Cassander to suppress rumours that they had poisoned Alexander. Possibly it closed with the transfer of Alexander's corpse to Alexandria. It appears certain that Diodorus' seventeenth book is essentially solely an epitome of Cleitarchus' work, despite some modern speculation that he incorporated a significant admixture of a second early author.

---

might be associated with Curtius 8.12.17-18; F39 with Diodorus 17.100.1-101.6 & Curtius 9.7.12-26; F41 with Diodorus 17.114.2; F52 with Diodorus 17.116.3; F49 with Arrian, *Anabasis* 4.9.6.

Alexander the Great in Afghanistan by Andrew Chugg

Table 8.1: The Books and Fragments of Cleitarchus

bk	START	END	FRAGMENTS
1	**Spring 336BC** Alexander's birth & ancestry; Philip sends a vanguard under Parmenion & Attalus into Asia	**15th October 335BC** Razing of Thebes Alexander's visit to Delphi(?)	F1* - the wealth of Thebes was just 440 talents
2	**16th October 335BC** Alexander's preparations for the invasion of Asia	**5th October 334BC** Capture of Halicarnassus The Marmares(?) "This is what happened in this year" Diodorus 17.28.5	F7 – 820 years between invasion of the Heracleidae and Alexander's invasion F33 & F34 – Themistocles at the court of Xerxes (the context is Alexander's visit to the tomb of Themistocles at Magnesia)
3	**6th October 334BC** Pamphylian campaigns	**24th September 333BC** Alexander's recovery from illness at Tarsus	
4	**25th September 333BC** Campaign in western Cilicia and visit to Anchiale Battle of Issus	**13th October 332BC** Balonymus appointed king of Tyre "Now we have described things concerning Alexander..." Diodorus 17.47.6, digression on events elsewhere: Agis conquers Crete...	F2* - Death of Sardanapalus (the context is Alexander's visit to his tomb at Anchiale near Tarsus) F8 – Battle of Issus (November 333BC) F9 – Tyrian sacrifice of a boy
5	**14th October 332BC** Siege of Gaza	**1st October 331BC** Battle of Arbela (Gaugamela) "This was the outcome of the battle near Arbela" D 17.61.3 Digression on Agis' rebellion in Greece: "Now that we have run through the events in Europe, we may in turn pass on to what occurred in Asia" D 17.63.5	F3* - Story of Theias Byblios F4* - 50 Spartan hostages given to Antipater
6	**2nd October 331BC** Capture of Darius' base at Arbela	**Late July 330BC** Pursuit & death of Darius "That was the situation in Asia" Diodorus 17.73.4, digression?	F10 - Description of Babylon F11 – Razing of Persepolis
7	**August 330BC** Advance to Hecatompylus	**June 329BC** First crossing of the "Caucasus" (actually Paropamisus – modern Hindu Kush) "These were the concerns of Alexander" Diodorus 17.83.3	F12 – Caspian Sea equal to the Euxine F13 – Flooding of isthmus between Euxine and Caspian F14 – a wasp in Hyrcania F15 & F16 - Visit of Thalestria, Queen of the Amazons F32 – Castration of man (spouse of an Amazon?) for adultery

An Update On The Organisation And Structure Of Cleitarchus

8	**July 329BC** Digression on quarrel of Bessus & Bagodaras at a banquet	**Autumn 328BC** Capture of the Rock of Ariamazes	
9	**Autumn 328BC** Scythian king offers Alexander his daughter in marriage	**May 327BC** Marriage to Roxane	
10	**June 327BC** Preparations for the invasion of India. Alexander orders the formation of the Epigoni	**June 326BC** Re-instatement of Porus as king following his defeat at the Hydaspes Report of the revolt of Baryaxes in Media	F20-22 – Indian processions with trees drawn on carriages and tame birds in their branches F17 – Ivy of Dionysus at Nysa F5* - Only the Persian king may wear the tiara upright (revolt of Baryaxes)
11	**July 326BC** Foundation of Bucephala Digression on wonders of India and Alexander's geographical objectives	**Late Spring 325BC** Treatment of the Mallian wound by Critobulus Digression on the revolt of the Greeks in Bactria	F18 –16 cubit serpents F19 – Troops of monkeys and an entrapment technique F28- A salt mine F24 – Ptolemy saves wounded Alexander at the Mallian town
12	**Late Spring 325BC** Surrender of Mallians & Oxydracae Contest between Coragus & Dioxippus	**June 324BC** The arrival of 30,000 Epigoni at Susa "These were the concerns of Alexander" Diodorus 17.108.3	F25 – 80,000 Indians slain in the Kingdom of Sambus F23 – Mandi women bear children at 7 and are old at 40 F26 – Tidal bore in Indus Delta F27- Oreitae & Ichthyophagi F29 – Nearchus & Onesicritus arrive with stories of the Ocean F6* - Gymnosophists scorn death
13	**July 324BC** The extravagance of Harpalus & his flight to Athens The exiles decree & the mutiny	**June 323BC (Epilogue 280BC?)** Death of Alexander First Division of the Satrapies Entombment in Alexandria?	F30 – The courtesans of Harpalus F31 – Roman Embassy at Babylon

* Fragment with the book number in Cleitarchus

9. Bibliography

1) Atkinson, JE, "A Commentary on Quintus Curtius Rufus' Historiae Alexandri Magni, Books 3 & 4", Amsterdam 1980.

2) Atkinson, JE, "A Commentary on Quintus Curtius Rufus' Historiae Alexandri Magni, Books 5 to 7.2", Amsterdam 1994.

3) Atkinson, JE, "Quintus Curtius Rufus' *Historiae Alexandri Magni*", ANRW II (H. temporini ed., Aufsteig und Niedergang der römischen Welt, Berlin), 34.4: 3447-83, 1998.

4) Atkinson, John E, "Curzio Rufo: Storie di Alessandro Magno. Volume I (Libri III-V) & Volume II (Libri VI-X)", tr. Virginio Antelami and Maurizio Giangiulio, Milan: Fondazione Lorenzo Valla/Arnoldo Mondadori Editore, 1998 & 2000.

5) Atkinson, JE, "Originality and its Limits in the Alexander Sources of the Early Empire" in *Alexander the Great in Fact and Fiction* (editors: AB Bosworth & EJ Baynham), Oxford 2000, pp. 307-25.

6) Atkinson, JE, & Yardley, JC, "Curtius Rufus: Histories of Alexander the Great, Books 10", Oxford 2009.

7) Badian, E, "The Date of Clitarchus" Proceedings African Classical Associations 8 (1965): 5-11.

8) Bardon, H., "Quinte-Curce: Histoires", Paris, Tome I (1947) & Tome II (1948).

9) Baynham, Elizabeth, "Alexander the Great: The Unique History of Quintus Curtius", Ann Arbor 1998.

10) Baynham, Elizabeth, "An Introduction to the *Metz Epitome*: its traditions and value", Antichthon 29 (1995) 60-77.

11) Berve, H, "Review of W I", Gnomon 5, 1929.

12) Billows, Richard, "Polybius and Alexander Historiography" in *Alexander the Great in Fact and Fiction*, ed. A.B. Bosworth and E.J. Baynham, Oxford 2000.

13) Borza, EN, 1968, "Cleitarchus & Diodorus' Account of Alexander" Proceedings African Classical Associations 11:25-45.

14) Bosworth, AB, "A Missing Year in the History of Alexander the Great", Journal of Hellenic Studies, Vol. 101, pp. 17-39, 1981.

15) Bosworth, AB, "From Arrian to Alexander", Oxford, 1988.

Bibliography

16) Bosworth, AB, "Conquest & Empire: The Reign of Alexander the Great", Cambridge, 1988.

17) Bosworth, AB, "Commentary on Arrian's History of Alexander II" Oxford 1995.

18) Bosworth, AB, "The Historical Setting of Megasthenes' Indica," Classical Philology 91, 1996.

19) Bosworth, AB, "In Search of Cleitarchus: Review-Discussion of Luisa Prandi: Fortuna è Realtà dell'Opera di Clitarco" in Histos (University of Durham, electronic journal of historiography), Vol. 1, Aug. 1997.

20) Bradford Welles, C, "Diodorus Siculus: Library of History," Vol. 8, Loeb, Harvard, 1963.

21) Brown, TS, 1949, "Onesicritus", Berkeley.

22) Brown, TS, 1950, "Clitarchus" American Journal Philology 71: 134-55.

23) Brown, TS, "The Merits and Weaknesses of Megasthenes," Phoenix 11, 1957.

24) Brunt, PA, "Arrian: History of Alexander and Indica", Loeb, Harvard, 1976 & 1983.

25) Chugg, AM, "The Journal of Alexander the Great", Ancient History Bulletin 19.3-4 (2005) 155-175.

26) Chugg, AM, "The Sarcophagus of Aleander the Great?" Greece & Rome, Vol. 49.1, April 2002.

27) Chugg, AM, "The Quest for the Tomb of Alexander the Great", AMC Publications, 2007

28) Chugg, AM, "Alexander the Great in India: A Reconstruction of Cleitarchus", AMC Publications, 2009.

29) Chugg, AM, "The Death of Alexander the Great: A Reconstruction of Cleitarchus", AMC Publications, 2009.

30) Depuydt, L., "The Time of Death of Alexander the Great: 11 June 323 BC, ca. 4:00-5:00 PM," Die Welt des Orients 28 (1997) 117–135.

31) Engels, Donald W, "Alexander the Great and the Logistics of the Macedonian Army", University of California, 1978.

32) Errington, RM, "Bias in Ptolemy's History of Alexander", *Classical Quarterly* 19, 1969, 233-242.

33) Errington, RM, "From Babylon to Triparadeisos, 323-320BC," *JHS* 90 (1970) 72-75.

34) Fontana, M, "Il problema delle fonti per il XVII Libro di Diodoro Siculo," *Kokalos* I (1955), 155-190.

35) Goralski, Walter J., "Arrian's Events After Alexander," *Ancient World* 19, 1989.

36) Goukowsky, P, 1969, "Clitarque seul? Remarques sur les sources du livre xvii de Diodore de Sicile" Revue des Etudes Anciennes 71: 320-6.

37) Grzybek, E., "Du calendrier Macédonien au calendrier Ptolémaïque", Basel, 1990.

38) Gunderson, Lloyd L, "Quintus Curtius Rufus: On His Historical Methods in the *Historiae Alexandri*" in Philip II, Alexander the Great and the Macedonian Heritage, eds. WL Adams & E N Borza, Lanham, 1982, pp.177-196.

39) Hamilton, JR, 1961, "Cleitarchus & Aristobulus" *Historia* 10: 448-59.

40) Hamilton, JR, "Plutarch, Alexander: A Commentary", Oxford 1969.

41) Hamilton, JR, 1977, "Cleitarchus and Diodorus 17" in Greece & the Ancient Mediterranean in History and Prehistory, ed KH Kinzl, Berlin, 126-46.

42) Hammond, NGL, "Three Historians of Alexander the Great", Cambridge 1983.

43) Hammond, NGL, "The Miracle that was Macedonia", London 1991.

44) Hammond, NGL, "The Regnal Years of Philip and Alexander," Greek, Roman and Byzantine Studies, Vol. 33, 1992, 355-373.

45) Hammond, NGL, "Sources for Alexander the Great", Cambridge 1993.

46) Heckel, W, "The Last Days & Testament of Alexander the Great", Historia Einzelschriften, Heft 56, Stuttgart 1988.

47) Heckel, W, "The Marshals of Alexander's Empire", Routledge, 1992.

48) Heckel, W, "The Earliest Evidence for the Plot to Poison Alexander" in *Alexander's Empire: Formulation to Decay*, California 2007.

49) Heckel, W, "Who's Who in the Age of Alexander the Great", Blackwell 2006.

50) Holt, Frank, "Alexander the Great and Bactria", supplement to Mnemosyne 104, 1989.

51) Holt, Frank, "Alexander the Great and the Mystery of the Elephant Medallions", California, 2003.

52) Hornblower, Jane, "Hieronymus of Cardia", OUP, 1981.

53) Howard, CL, Review of the Teubner Edition of the *Metz Epitome*, Classical Philology 58, pp. 129-131.

54) Hunt, JM, "An Emendation in the *Epitoma Metensis*", Classical Philology 67, pp. 287-288.

Bibliography

55) Hunt, JM, "More Emendations in the *Epitoma Metensis*", Classical Philology 80, pp. 335-337.

56) Jacoby, F, FGrH 137, "Kleitarchos".

57) Karageorghis, V, "Cyprus", London, 1969.

58) Koldewey, R, "The Excavations at Babylon", London, 1914.

59) Markle, Minor, "A Shield Monument from Veria and the Chronology of Macedonian Shield Types", *Hesperia* 68.2, 1999.

60) Merkelbach, Reinhold, "Die Quellen des Griechischen Alexanderromans," *Zetema Monographien zur Klassischen Altertumswissenschaft*, Heft 9, Munich 1954.

61) Müller, Konrad & Schönfeld, Herbert, "Q. Curtius Rufus: Geschichte Alexanders des Grossen", Tusculum, Munich, 1954.

62) Oldach, David W. & Richard, Robert E., "A Mysterious Death", *The New England Journal of Medicine*, June 11, 1998, Volume 338, Number 24.

63) Palagia, Olga, *Hephaestion's Pyre and the Royal Hunt of Alexander*, pp. 167-206 in "Alexander the Great in Fact and Fiction", edited by A. B. Bosworth & E. J. Baynham, Oxford, 2000.

64) Pearson, Lionel, 1960, "Cleitarchus" in The Lost Histories of Alexander the Great, American Philological Association, London and New York.

65) Pédech, P., "Deux campagnes d'Antiochus III chez Polybe," Revue des Études Anciennes, 60 (1958), 67-81.

66) Prandi, Luisa, "Callistene. Uno storico tra Aristotele e i re macedoni", Milan, 1985.

67) Prandi, Luisa, "Fortuna è Realtà dell'Opera di Clitarco" in Historia Einzelschriften 104, Steiner, Stuttgart 1996.

68) Pritchett, W. Kendrick, "Postscript: The Athenian Calendars," ZPE 128 (1999) 79-93.

69) Rolfe, John C, "Quintus Curtius: History of Alexander, Loeb, Harvard, 1946.

70) Samuel, Alan E., Ptolemaic Chronology, Munich, 1962.

71) Samuel, Alan E., Greek & Roman Chronology, Munich, 1972.

72) Schachermeyr, F, "Alexander der Grosse: Das Problem seiner Persönlichkeit und seines Wirkens", Vienna, 1973.

73) Schachermeyr, F, "Alexander in Babylon und die Reichsordnung nach seiner Tod", Vienna, 1970.

74) Schwartz, E, Paulys Real-Encyclopädie, Vol. 4, 1901, s.v. Q. Curtius Rufus, cols. 1871-1891, & Vol 5, 1905, s.v. Diodoros, cols. 682-684.

75) Steele, R. B., "Quintus Curtius Rufus", *AJP* 36, 1915.

76) Tarn, WW, "Alexander the Great, Vol II, Sources and Studies", Part One, The So-Called 'Vulgate' and its Sources, pp. 1-133, Cambridge 1948.

77) Thomas, PH, Editor, "Incerti Auctoris Epitoma Rerum Gestarum Alexandri Magni cum Libro de Morte Testamentoque Alexandri" (The *Metz Epitome*), Teubner, Leipzig 1966.

78) Wood, Michael, "Footsteps of Alexander", BBC, 1997.

79) Yardley, JC & Heckel, W, "Quintus Curtius Rufus: The History of Alexander", Penguin Classics, 1984.

80) Yardley, JC & Heckel, W, "Justin: Epitome of the Philippic History of Pompeius Trogus, Vol I, Books 11-12, Alexander the Great", Oxford 1997.

81) Zeller, Eduard, "Die Philosophie der Griechen", 4th ed., Part II, Leipzig, 1889.

Selected Ancient Sources

Aelian, Varia Historia, N.G. Wilson, Loeb, Harvard, 1997

Aelian, On The Characteristics of Animals, trans. A.F. Scholfield in 3 volumes, Loeb, Harvard, 1958

Agatharchides, Agatharchides of Cnidus on the Erythraean Sea, Stanley M. Burstein, Translator and Editor, Hakluyt Society, London, 1989

Arrian, Anabasis Alexandri and Indica, P.A. Brunt, Loeb, Harvard, 1976 and 1983

Arrian, Epitome of the History of Events After Alexander, *Photius* 92, Photius, Bibliothèque, vol. II, René Henry, Paris, 1960

Athenaeus, Deipnosophistae, Charles Burton Gulick, Loeb, Harvard, 1927-41

Curtius, The History of Alexander, John C. Rolfe, Loeb, Harvard, 1946; The History of Alexander, trans. John Yardley, Penguin Classics, 1984; Historiae Alexandri Magni, ed. E. Hedicke, Teubner, 1908; De Rebus Gestis Alexandri Magni, Freinshem et al., Petrus vander Aa, Lugduni Batavorum, 1696; Konrad Müller & Herbert Schönfeld, Geschichte Alexanders des Grossen, Tusculum, Munich, 1954; H. Bardon, Quinte-Curce: Histoires, Paris, Tome I, 1947 & Tome II, 1948

Dexippus, *Photius* 82, Photius, Bibliothèque, vol. I, René Henry, Paris, 1959

Bibliography

Diodorus Siculus, Library of History, vol. VII, Charles L. Sherman, Loeb, Harvard, 1952; vol. VIII, C. Bradford Welles, Loeb, Harvard, 1963; vol. IX, Russel M. Geer, Loeb, Harvard, 1947

Diogenes Laertius, Lives of Eminent Philosophers

Dio Cassius, Roman History, Loeb, translated by Earnest Cary, based on translation by H.B. Foster - reprints of the editions published from 1914-1927

Ephemerides, FrGrHist 2.117

Hegesias, FrGrHist 2.142

Homer, Iliad, trans. A.T. Murray, revised William F. Wyatt, Loeb, Harvard, 1999

Justin, Epitome of the Philippic History of Pompeius Trogus, Books 11-12, J.C. Yardley and W. Heckel, Oxford, 1997; Justin, Cornelius Nepos and Eutropius, Rev. John Selby Watson, London, 1853

Livy, History of Rome, Loeb Classical Library in 14 Volumes

Lucian, Dialogues of the Dead, XIII, vol. 7, M.D. MacLeod, Loeb, Harvard, 1961

Lucian, Essay on How to Write History, vol. 6, K. Kilburn, Loeb, 1959

Lucian, Calumniae non temere credendum, Lucian: Vol. I, A. M. Harmon, Loeb, 1913

Macrobius, Saturnalia, Macrobius: Opera: Band I Saturnalia, Saur Verlag, 1994

Martial, Liber de Spectaculis, De Spectaculis Liber, Shackleton Bailey, Loeb, 1994

Metz Epitome & Liber de Morte, P.H. Thomas, Ed., Incerti Auctoris Epitoma Rerum Gestarum Alexandri Magni cum Libro de Morte Testamentoque Alexandri, Teubner, Leipzig 1966

Nepos, Eumenes in Justin; Cornelius Nepos and Eutropius, Rev. John Selby Watson, London, 1853

Pausanias, Description of Greece, vol. 1, W.H.S. Jones, Loeb, Harvard, 1918

Pliny the Elder, Natural History, H. Rackham, W.H.S. Jones, D.E. Eichholz, Loeb, Harvard, 1938-62

Plutarch, Agesilaus, Lives vol. 5, B. Perrin, Loeb, Harvard, 1917

Plutarch, Alexander & Caesar and Cicero & Demosthenes, Lives vol. 7, B. Perrin, Loeb, Harvard, 1919; Plutarch: The Age of Alexander, trans. Ian Scott-Kilvert, Penguin 1973

Plutarch, Eumenes, Lives vol. 8, B. Perrin, Loeb, Harvard, 1919

Plutarch, Demetrius, Antony & Pyrrhus, Lives vol. 9, B. Perrin, Loeb, Harvard, 1920

Plutarch, Moralia, vols. 3 and 4, Frank Cole Babbitt, Loeb, Harvard, 1931 and 1936

Polyaenus, Stratagems of War, trans. Peter Krentz & Everett L. Wheeler, Ares, Chicago, 1994

Polybius, The Histories, W.R. Paton, Loeb, Harvard, 1922-7

Pseudo-Callisthenes, Alexander Romance, e.g. Guilelmus Kroll, Historia Alexandri Magni, vol, 1, Weidmann, 1926

Claudius Ptolemy, Geographia, ed. C.F.A Nobbe, Leipzig, 1843-1845

Stephanus Byzantinus, Augustus Meineke, Stephani Byzantii, Ethnicorum, Berlin, 1849

Strabo, Geography, H.L. Jones, Loeb, Harvard, 1917-32

Suidae Lexicon (a.k.a. The Suda), Ada Adler (ed.), Leipzig, 1928-35

10. Acknowledgements

I would like to express my particular gratitude to the following for their assistance in the research reported in this book:-

The staff of Bristol University Arts and Social Sciences Library

Matthew Wofinden and Centonex for website support

Visitors to the Cleitarchus Reconstruction pages at www.alexanderstomb.com

C. Bradford Welles for recognizing the usefulness of a reconstruction

A. B. Bosworth for endorsing the feasibility of reconstruction

Index

A

Abdalonymus 119, 177
Abii 99
Abradatas 7, 40
Achaeans 42
Achilles 141, 161, 175
Adler, Ada 23, 95, 192
Adonis 162
Aelian 23, 24, 73, 95, 96, 153, 157, 180, 190
Afghanistan ....i, iv, 1, 5, 6, 12, 16, 55, 57, 91, 114, 144, 146, 148, 150
Africa 186
Agatharchides 190
Agesilaus 191
Agis the Argive 130, 132
Agis, King..48, 90, 130, 160, 164, 165, 168, 178, 184
Ai Khanum 112, 147
Aldus 33, 141, 156
Aleppo 163
Alexander IV 31
Alexander Lyncestes 21, 73, 75, 76, 135, 136, 151
Alexander Mosaic 8
Alexander of Epirus ..25, 121, 178
Alexander Romance 192
Alexandria....1, 16, 56, 58, 84, 86, 100, 145, 146, 152, 153, 157, 161, 172, 175, 176, 178, 182, 183, 185
Amazon 46, 50, 52
Amazons .iv, 1, 14, 34, 36, 39, 46, 50, 51, 52, 150, 179, 184
Amedines 84
Ammon 25, 27, 66, 70, 71
Amu-Darya 92, 146
Amuq Plain 163

Amyntas.... 20, 21, 44, 59, 66, 67, 69, 75, 76, 78, 79, 125, 162
Anabasis .. 6, 7, 14, 16, 17, 25, 31, 32, 35, 44, 48, 50, 55, 56, 66, 73, 83, 86, 92, 94, 98, 100, 103, 107, 123, 124, 138, 144, 145, 146, 147, 159, 162, 163, 165, 170, 171, 172, 173, 176, 181, 190
Anaximenes 172, 175
Anchiale 162, 177, 184
Andromache . 24, 25, 27, 120, 123
Andromeda 25
Andronicus 84
aniketos 175
anthredon 47, 149
Anticleides 14
Anticles 133
Antigenes 14
Antigone 18
Antioch 163
Antiochus............ 10, 45, 144, 189
Antipater.. 14, 42, 57, 75, 90, 112, 149, 164, 178, 182, 183, 184
Antipater the son of Asclepiodorus 133
Antiphanes 76, 77
Antiquities of the Jews 170
Antonius 34, 124
Anzob Pass 147
Aphobetus 59
Apollo 22, 23
Arabs 80
Arachosia 12, 84
Arachosii 80, 84
Aral Sea 149
Araxes River 85
Arbela 169, 170, 171, 172, 174, 178, 183, 184
Archepolis 59

Index

Ares 192
Aria... 16, 56, 58, 83, 84, 145, 168
Ariamazes ...... iv, 1, 87, 113, 115, 116, 117, 147, 154, 179, 185
Arian Satrapy 55, 56
Arians 56, 90
Arimaspians 83, 145
Aristander . 27, 101, 102, 103, 154
Aristobulus 14, 17, 26, 31, 103, 123, 138, 149, 153, 154, 162, 170, 188
Aristonous 27
Aristotle 30, 124
Armenia 11, 43, 85, 86
Arrhidaeus 32
Arrian. 6, 7, 14, 16, 17, 18, 19, 23, 25, 26, 32, 33, 35, 44, 48, 50, 55, 56, 66, 73, 83, 86, 92, 94, 98, 100, 103, 107, 123, 124, 138, 144, 145, 146, 147, 151, 155, 156, 159, 162, 163, 165, 170, 171, 172, 173, 176, 180, 181, 186, 187, 188, 190
Arsaces 83, 130
Artabazus.. iv, 1, 5, 39, 48, 50, 84, 91, 113, 116, 118, 119, 150
Artacana 56, 57, 145
Artacoana 56, 145
Artaxerxes (Bessus) 55
Artaxerxes III 7
Artemus of Colophon 27
Asander 112
Asclepiodorus 112, 133
Asia 11, 41, 49, 53, 54, 73, 74, 85, 101, 102, 105, 106, 109, 114, 120, 121, 137, 143, 150, 167, 168, 170, 178, 179, 182, 184
Asianic rhythms 175
Asiatic officials 53
Assembly ... 19, 20, 21, 28, 30, 71, 118, 138
astrology 158
astronomy 158
Atarrhias 63, 75, 121

Athena 127, 182
Athenaeus...25, 31, 105, 150, 159, 161, 162, 165, 178, 181, 190
Athenian Archon-years 167
Athenians 120, 173, 176
Athens .7, 162, 172, 173, 181, 185
Atkinson, JE 186
Atropates 130, 165
Attalus..32, 66, 74, 121, 123, 135, 137, 184
Attic Calendar 170
Attic Lunar Regulatory Calendar 172, 173
Attica 162
Attinas 117
Audata the Illyrian 32
Augustus 192
Aulus Gellius 25, 121, 178
Azov, Sea of.... 11, 12, 34, 46, 149

B

Babylon 25, 160, 161, 176, 178, 181, 182, 184, 185, 187, 189
Babylonia 130
Babylonian Astronomical Diaries 170
Bacchae 25
Bactra 16, 43, 56, 90, 92, 101, 109, 110, 112, 146, 150, 155
Bactria....5, 12, 22, 24, 39, 56, 73, 84, 86, 90, 99, 106, 112, 125, 126, 145, 146, 147, 148, 152, 154, 155, 160, 168, 180, 185, 188
Bactrians 88, 89, 99, 101, 102, 103, 106
Bactrus River 90
Badian, E 186
Bagoas 5, 10, 43, 45, 50, 109, 150, 154
Bagodaras 36, 88, 89, 152, 185
Balkh 16, 92, 146
Balonymus 167, 177, 184

195

Barbarians .. 23, 27, 29, 32, 33, 43, 49, 50, 52, 57, 67, 84, 89, 90, 91, 98, 104, 108, 113, 114, 115, 117, 118, 126, 127, 132, 136, 140, 141, 181
Bardon, H 186, 190
Barsine 31, 32
Baryaxes 165, 180, 183, 185
Barzaentes 39, 57, 150
Basista .... iv, 1, 117, 118, 119, 155
Baynham, E 150, 186
Begram 145
bematists 16, 58, 144
Benefactors 83, 152
Berlin 186, 188, 192
Berve, H 186
Bessus .... iv, 1, 22, 26, 36, 39, 43, 44, 45, 55, 57, 84, 86, 87, 88, 89, 90, 91, 94, 95, 96, 97, 99, 110, 146, 149, 152, 153, 154, 165, 179, 185
Bibliotheke 165
Billows, R 186
Black Sea ... 10, 11, 12, 14, 34, 46, 50, 84, 90, 99, 149
boar 28, 133
Bodyguard 8, 20, 26, 27, 59, 62, 71, 97, 102, 124, 138
Boedromion 162, 170, 171, 173
Boeotia 42
Bolon 70
Borysthenes 41
Borza, EN 186, 188
Bosphorus, Cimmerian 11, 14, 41, 99, 118
Bosworth, AB 112, 146, 147, 157, 159, 162, 166, 171, 177, 186, 187, 189, 193
Branchidae .... iv, 1, 22, 23, 24, 87, 95, 96, 153
British Museum 8, 9
Brown, TS 187
Brunt, PA 144, 145, 146, 147, 156, 165, 171, 187, 190

Bucephalus .... iv, 1, 39, 49, 150
Burstein, SM 190
Byblios 162, 184
Byblos 162, 178
Byzantium 167

C

Caesar 191
Calanus 159, 165, 181
Caligula 28, 170
Calis 74
Callisthenes. iv, 10, 25, 28, 29, 30, 31, 124, 131, 132, 134, 135, 138, 147, 155, 156, 162
Camillus 162, 171, 172
Cappadocia 43, 86
Caranus 84, 90, 159, 160
Cardia 160, 161, 169, 188
Caria 43
Cariatae 135, 147
Carthage 182
Carthaginians 182
Carthasis 101, 154
Caspian ... iv, 1, 10, 11, 12, 14, 34, 36, 39, 44, 46, 50, 85, 90, 149, 179, 184
Caspian Gates 50
Cassander 161, 182, 183
Castaigne, A 97, 122, 142
Castor & Pollux 131
Catanes 94, 97, 99, 153, 155
Caucasus 11, 36, 50, 85, 86, 89, 145, 149, 150, 152, 184
cavalry . 26, 44, 53, 56, 57, 62, 66, 67, 72, 76, 78, 79, 84, 98, 99, 103, 104, 107, 108, 109, 112, 117, 127, 150, 153, 154
Cebalinus ... 19, 59, 60, 61, 62, 65, 68, 69, 70, 151
Cercatae 46
Chaeronaea 119
Chaldean priests 25
Chalybes 46

Index

Chares 14, 30, 31, 138
Charikar 145
Chesmeh-i-Ali 45, 144
Choerilus 130
Choras................................ 118
Chorienes. 33, 140, 141, 148, 156, 179
Chortacana..................... 56, 145
Christianity 8, 53
Chugg, AM .... i, ii, 182, 187
Cicero 105, 172, 175, 176, 177, 191
Cilicia 18, 43, 85, 87, 113, 169, 177, 184
Cleander....................... 22, 80, 82
Cleitarchus.... i, iv, 1, 2, 3, 5, 7, 8, 10, 11, 12, 13, 14, 17, 31, 33, 34, 35, 36, 37, 39, 41, 46, 47, 50, 52, 53, 55, 58, 87, 91, 92, 99, 105, 112, 113, 114, 117, 118, 124, 141, 144, 146, 147, 149, 150, 151, 152, 153, 154, 155, 156, 157, 158, 159, 160, 161, 162, 163, 164, 165, 166, 167, 168, 169, 170, 172, 173, 174, 175, 176, 177, 178, 179, 180, 181, 182, 183, 184, 185, 186, 187, 188, 189, 193
Cleitus..... iv, 1, 24, 25, 26, 36, 77, 117, 119, 120, 121, 122, 123, 124, 125, 135, 137, 138, 143, 147, 155
Cleomantis the Lacedaemonian 27
Cleon of Sicily 130, 131, 132
Cleopatra 32
Coenus 19, 62, 67, 71, 117
Cohortandus..................... 33, 141
Companion Cavalry.................... 5
Companions............................ 124
conspiracy.... iv, 1, 17, 18, 28, 29, 58, 117, 147
Cophes 113, 115
Corianus............................... 33
Corinth................................ 49

Cothelas.............................. 32
Crassus 163
Craterus 18, 19, 44, 47, 56, 57, 61, 62, 71, 72, 99, 100, 102, 109, 117, 146
Critobulus...................... 180, 185
Ctesias 162
Curtius....2, 3, 5, 7, 10, 11, 12, 14, 17, 19, 20, 21, 22, 24, 25, 26, 29, 30, 33, 34, 35, 37, 44, 46, 51, 55, 56, 58, 60, 61, 64, 69, 71, 75, 77, 81, 83, 84, 86, 88, 91, 93, 94, 95, 96, 98, 99, 100, 104, 105, 107, 109, 111, 112, 113, 114, 116, 118, 123, 130, 138, 141, 145, 147, 149, 150, 151, 152, 153, 154, 155, 156, 157, 159, 160, 161, 163, 164, 165, 166, 168, 171, 174, 175, 176, 177, 178, 179, 180, 181, 183, 186, 188, 189, 190
Cynics 8, 53, 182
Cynna 32
Cyprus 189
Cyropaidia 6, 7, 8, 40
Cyropolis.................. 99, 100, 146
Cyrus ..... iv, 6, 7, 8, 10, 40, 43, 83, 99, 100, 101, 152
Cyrus the Younger 7, 163

D

Dahae .43, 88, 103, 117, 127, 130, 155, 179
Damascus 18, 163
Damghan 144
Darius.1, 3, 5, 7, 8, 10, 18, 20, 21, 23, 24, 26, 31, 32, 39, 40, 41, 43, 44, 45, 47, 48, 50, 53, 54, 55, 73, 84, 87, 91, 93, 94, 95, 96, 97, 101, 110, 121, 141, 144, 150, 160, 164, 168, 171, 174, 176, 178, 184
Dataphernes.......94, 130, 153, 155

de Vaugelas.........................51, 81
Deinon....150, 152, 160, 162, 168, 176
Deipnosophistae......................190
Delphi.............................176, 184
Demaratus of Corinth..............49
Demetrius.34, 47, 59, 65, 74, 149, 179, 191
Democrates of Athens..............48
Derdas........................32, 99, 118
Dexippus..............................190
Dia.......................................170
diadem......8, 53, 86, 150, 165, 182
Dialogues of the Dead.............191
Dicaearchus.....................32, 150
Didyma..............................22, 23
Didymeon.........................22, 95
Dimnus...5, 16, 17, 18, 21, 58, 59, 60, 61, 63, 65, 68, 69, 73, 151
Dio Cassius 191
Diodorus.....2, 3, 5, 10, 11, 17, 23, 33, 34, 35, 36, 37, 41, 46, 47, 56, 58, 61, 71, 75, 86, 88, 95, 109, 112, 114, 118, 130, 145, 149, 150, 151, 152, 153, 154, 155, 156, 157, 158, 159, 160, 161, 162, 164, 165, 166, 167, 168, 169, 170, 171, 172, 173, 174, 175, 176, 177, 178, 179, 180, 181, 183, 184, 185, 186, 187, 188, 191
Diogenes 191
Diogenes Laertius 6, 159, 160, 165
Dionysus ..35, 108, 124, 131, 154, 155, 180, 185
Dios 170, 172
Dioscuri.................................27
Dioxenus................................59
Disorderly Division..................83
Ditamenes.............................130
Diyllus.....149, 151, 152, 161, 166
Don, River......11, 41, 88, 99, 101, 132, 146, 153
Drangiana 16, 57, 145
Drangians.......... 16, 17, 57, 58, 83
Duris of Samos 14, 151, 166

E

Ecbatana 41, 80, 110, 154
Egypt 17, 25, 48, 105, 161, 178
Einquellenprinzip 37, 165
Elaphthonius........................... 133
Engels, D . 56, 144, 145, 146, 163, 177, 187
English................................... 21
Ephemerides 169, 191
Ephorus........................... 161, 167
Epigoni 55, 180, 181, 185
Epimenes 133, 134
Epirus................................... 178
equinox 2, 158, 174, 183
Eratosthenes.............. 12, 149, 165
Erigyius 44, 47, 62, 84, 90, 91, 102, 103, 127, 152
Errington, RM........................ 187
Erythraean Sea....................... 190
Ethymantus, River 12, 91
Euergetae ... iv, 1, 39, 83, 145, 152
Eumenes 31, 161, 169, 191
Euphrates River 163
Euripides. 24, 25, 27, 96, 120, 123
Europa 32
Europe 11, 14, 41, 53, 99, 101, 102, 105, 106, 143, 167, 168, 178, 184
Eurylochus............................. 134
Euxine 11, 12, 34, 36, 46, 90, 149, 184

F

Farah........... 5, 16, 17, 57, 80, 145
Favoured Villages.................... 47
figs.. 47
First Division of the Satrapies 161, 185
flogging 29

Index

Florilegium 159, 162
Fontana, M. 187
Fortune..... 8, 53, 57, 76, 106, 107, 113, 127, 128, 141
Fraxkar-Peroz 17
Freinshem 190
Friends.... 5, 6, 19, 24, 33, 41, 58, 59, 61, 62, 63, 65, 71, 74, 77, 79, 83, 92, 99, 101, 118, 119, 121, 131, 140, 141, 143, 159
Frontinus... 93, 153, 156, 176, 179

G

Garfield, James 28
Gaugamela..... 164, 170, 172, 173, 178, 183, 184
Gaza............... 167, 175, 178, 184
Gazaba 138, 140, 147
Ghazni 145
Google 92, 146
Goralski, WJ 188
Gordian knot 75, 177
Gorgatas 78
Gorgias 78
Goukowsky, P 188
Granicus, Battle of the 24, 26, 119
Great King 7
Great Lacuna 169
Great Mysteries 162
Greece.. 22, 23, 24, 32, 40, 57, 90, 95, 120, 152, 158, 164, 168, 173, 179, 182, 184, 187, 188, 191
Greek Mercenaries........... iv, 1, 39
Greeks 3, 5, 12, 23, 27, 41, 48, 80, 84, 106, 109, 112, 114, 120, 130, 131, 138, 180, 185, 188
Gregorian Calendar 158, 173, 174
Grzybek, E 170, 188
Guiteau, Charles 28
Gunderson, LJ 188

H

Halicarnassus .. 121, 169, 176, 184
Hamah 163
Hamilton, J 37, 150, 151, 170, 188
Hammond, NGL 73, 149, 150, 151, 152, 153, 154, 155, 156, 161, 166, 170, 172, 175, 178, 188
harem 150
Harpalus 168, 181, 185
Harpocration 160, 164
Heaven 131
Hecataeus 14, 78
Hecataeus of Eretria 14
Hecatombaeon 172, 175
Hecatompylus .... iv, 1, 36, 39, 41, 45, 144, 149, 179, 184
Heckel, W 152, 156, 157, 159, 188, 190, 191
Hector 67
Hedicke, E 190
Hegelochus 20, 21, 72, 73
Hegesias 175, 191
Hellanice 119
Hellas 27
Hellespont 42, 44
Helmand, River ... 12, 91, 145, 150
Hephaistion 29, 40, 62, 71, 102, 109, 117, 118, 119, 125, 131, 177, 180, 182
Heracleidae 172, 175, 176, 184
Heracles..... 31, 32, 44, 67, 69, 77, 78, 102, 103, 131, 136, 161, 175
Herat 16, 56, 58, 145
Hermolaus 6, 28, 29, 30, 133, 134, 135, 136, 137
Hieronymus 160, 161, 182, 188
Himalayas 11
Hindu Kush 11, 36, 145, 152, 179, 184
Hippostratus 32

199

Hissar Range 147
Holt, F 188
Homer 191
Homs 163
Hornblower, J.. 160, 166, 182, 188
House of the Faun 8
Howard, CL.............................. 188
Hunt, JM 188, 189
Hydaspes 180, 185
hypaspists 56, 107, 108, 155
hypomnemata 182
Hypsides.................................. 104
Hyrcania.... iv, 1, 5, 14, 36, 39, 41, 43, 44, 46, 47, 48, 49, 50, 130, 144, 145, 149, 150, 179, 184
Hystaspes 7, 40

I

Ichthyophagi 181, 185
Iliad 191
Illyria.. 57
Illyrians 32, 42, 73, 120
India . 1, 2, 5, 6, 12, 30, 42, 47, 55, 57, 77, 84, 86, 89, 91, 106, 114, 126, 145, 146, 148, 150, 155, 159, 160, 165, 170, 174, 180, 181, 183, 185, 187
Indians......... 43, 88, 137, 181, 185
Indica 144, 165, 170, 187, 190
Indus, River. 12, 84, 179, 181, 185
invictus 175
Iolaus.. 59
Ionians...................................... 43
Iran 5
Iron Gate Pass 147
Isidorus of Charax..................... 16
Islam.................................... 8, 53
Issus 169, 177, 184
Istanbul..................................... 11
Ister 14, 94
Ister River............................... 101
isthmus 11, 34, 36, 46, 149, 184
Italy 25, 121, 166, 178

ivy 108, 180

J

Jacoby, F.... 16, 34, 37, 38, 46, 47, 52, 124, 149, 150, 157, 159, 160, 161, 162, 165, 166, 172, 175, 176, 177, 178, 179, 180, 181, 189
Jaxartes, River . 10, 11, 14, 41, 88, 101, 146
Julian (Emperor)..................... 163
Julian Calendar 158, 161, 162, 164, 169, 170, 171, 172, 173, 183
Justin.. 2, 3, 21, 25, 34, 37, 41, 52, 55, 66, 73, 75, 100, 123, 130, 138, 146, 149, 150, 151, 152, 153, 154, 155, 156, 157, 159, 160, 164, 165, 168, 170, 174, 175, 176, 177, 178, 180, 190, 191

K

Kabul 145
Kafirnigan River..................... 147
Kalat-i-Nadiri 56, 145
Kandahar 16, 84, 145
Karageorghis, V...................... 189
Kashka-Darya 126, 147
Kazakhstan 5
Kedrosia................................. 181
Kedrosians 84
Kennedy, John 28
Kerch, Strait of 11, 41, 99
Khawak Pass.......................... 146
Khewra 180
Khodjend 146
Khujand 100, 146
Kochka River.................. 112, 147
Koldewey, R 189
Kroll, G 192
Kunduz 112, 147
Kushka 56, 145

Index

Kyme 167
Kyrgyzstan 5

L

Lagus 17, 26, 31, 182
Larissa 12, 32
Last Plans 182
Latin. 2, 12, 17, 20, 21, 30, 44, 55, 58, 69, 71, 84, 98, 107, 109, 116, 175
Laws 173
Leonidas 83
Leonnatus 62, 121, 134
Leucosyri 46
Levantine littoral 163, 178
Liber de Morte 191
Liber de Spectaculis 191
Library 191, 193
lice 30, 138
Lincoln, Abraham 28
Livy 25, 121, 175, 178, 191
Loeb 187, 189, 190, 191, 192
London 191
Lucian 191
lunar eclipse 164, 171, 173, 183
Lycia 176
Lydia 43, 57, 105
Lysimachus .. 8, 14, 118, 121, 127, 138

M

Macedon 54, 66, 69, 73, 106, 151, 157, 176
Macedonians 5, 17, 18, 26, 27, 28, 29, 33, 41, 44, 54, 60, 63, 67, 69, 71, 74, 82, 84, 85, 89, 90, 96, 97, 98, 101, 102, 107, 108, 109, 110, 113, 114, 118, 124, 125, 126, 128, 130, 131, 132, 135, 136, 137, 141, 163, 181, 187, 188
Machatas 32
Macrobius 191
Maenidas 112
Maeotic Marsh 11, 34, 46
Magnesia 34, 52, 176, 184
Mallians 180, 181, 185
Manapis 48
Mandi 181, 185
Maracanda .... iv, 1, 5, 14, 87, 98, 100, 109, 118, 119, 125, 146, 147, 153, 154, 155
Mardians 49, 50, 130
Margania 112, 147, 154
Margiana 112, 147, 154
Mark Antony 191
Markle, M 189
Marmares 176, 184
marriage . 1, 14, 31, 32, 33, 36, 54, 118, 141, 142, 148, 155, 179, 185
Martial 191
Massagetae 43, 117, 155, 179
Mazaeus 130
Meda 32
Medeia 25
Medes 43, 83, 88, 105, 165
Media ... 41, 63, 65, 66, 71, 80, 86, 130, 145, 165, 185
Median dress 8
Mediterranean 183, 188
Megasthenes 181, 187
Meleager 100
Melissa 34, 124
Memaceni 99, 100
Memnon 176
Memphis 109, 181, 183
Menedemus 100, 103, 104, 109, 154
Menon 84
mercenaries 150
Merkelbach, R 189
Merv 112, 147, 154
Meshed 144
Metron 60, 65
Metz Epitome 3, 33, 35, 57, 84, 98, 100, 104, 112, 113, 116, 125,

145, 150, 152, 153, 154, 155, 156, 157, 165, 179, 180, 186, 188, 190, 191
Milesians 23, 24, 95, 96
Miletus 22, 34, 52, 95, 96, 124
Molossians 32
Moon.........46, 162, 171, 172, 173
Moralia ..8, 10, 22, 24, 95, 96, 98, 153, 162, 182, 192
Mossyni......................................46
Müller, K.................157, 189, 190
Myrra..162

N

Nabarzanes....iv, 1, 39, 43, 45, 50, 109, 150
NASA.......................................173
Natural History 10, 16, 34, 46, 144, 191
Nature. 52, 56, 102, 113, 114, 123, 131, 139
Nautaca 126, 147, 148
Nearchus 170, 181, 185
Nepos 191
Nero..28
Nicanor.....................55, 59, 65, 67
Nicesipolis of Pherae 32
Nicomachus..... 58, 59, 60, 61, 62, 65, 68, 74
Nicostratus 133
Nysa 180, 185

O

obeisance............................27, 29
Ocean 10, 47, 77, 84, 180, 181, 185
Ochus 7, 40, 48, 112, 154
Ochus River 112, 147
Oldach & Richards..................189
Olympias...... 21, 25, 32, 73, 121, 151, 182
Olynthian..........................30, 138

Onesicritus...... 6, 14, 46, 50, 149, 150, 155, 180, 181, 185, 187
Oracle of Ammon 25, 66, 121
Oreitae 181, 185
Orexartes, River....................... 11
Orient................................. 42, 73
Oxartes.......................... 126, 127
Oxathres...... 5, 40, 41, 53, 97, 153
Oxus River.... iv, 1, 87, 89, 92, 93, 94, 112, 146, 147, 153, 154, 179
Oxyartes.............. 32, 33, 141, 156
Oxydates 41, 130
Oxydracae..................... 181, 185

P

Pages. iv, 1, 6, 19, 28, 29, 60, 117, 133, 147
Palagia, Olga.......................... 189
Pamphylia.......................... 43, 176
Pantheia 7, 40
Paphlagonia 43
Paphlagonians........................... 71
papyrus 34, 52
Paris 8, 9, 162, 186, 190
Parmenion... iv, 1, 3, 6, 17, 18, 19, 20, 21, 22, 25, 27, 39, 41, 55, 58, 59, 62, 63, 65, 67, 70, 72, 73, 74, 77, 79, 80, 81, 82, 84, 120, 121, 123, 135, 136, 152, 184
Paropamisadae.................. 84, 152
Paropamisus.. iv, 1, 11, 36, 39, 85, 90, 92, 114, 168, 184
Parsagada................................... 6
Parthia............... 5, 41, 43, 44, 53
Parthians 41
Patrocles 10, 11, 34, 149
Pausanias 21, 25, 73, 75, 109, 181, 191
Pearson, L 150, 152, 153, 154, 157, 159, 160, 162, 175, 189
Pédech, P 45, 144, 189

Index

Peloponnese 42
Peloponnesians 90
Penguin 190
Perdiccas 62, 66, 69, 73, 100, 121, 123
Perinthus 167
Peroz 17
Persepolis 178, 184
Persia 7, 40, 43, 106, 165, 178, 183
Persian dress 1, 7, 8, 9, 150
Persian Empire 7, 168, 176
Persian rod-bearers 10
Persianising .... iv, 5, 6, 7, 10, 40
Persians.... 5, 8, 23, 25, 26, 27, 29, 39, 44, 46, 53, 83, 96, 97, 105, 112, 131, 132, 135, 136, 137, 140, 141, 165
Persica 162
Peucolaus 59, 65, 110
phalanx .. 23, 45, 46, 95, 104, 107, 108, 109, 127
Phasis River 50
Phila 32
Philadelphus 31
Philinna of Larissa 32
Philip 2, 14, 25, 26, 27, 31, 48, 54, 57, 66, 72, 73, 74, 75, 82, 118, 119, 120, 123, 136, 157, 158, 161, 167, 169, 170, 172, 174, 176, 183, 184, 188
Philip II 2, 66, 157, 158, 176
Philip of Theangela 14
Philip the Chalcidian 14
Philip the Physician 70
Philip, brother of Lysimachus 127
Philippic History 190, 191
Philippus 155
Philo the Theban 14
Philodemus 175
Philotas . iv, 1, 3, 5, 16, 17, 18, 19, 20, 21, 22, 26, 39, 55, 58, 59, 60, 61, 62, 63, 64, 65, 66, 67, 69, 70, 71, 72, 73, 74, 75, 77, 79, 80, 82, 134, 135, 136, 138, 145, 151, 155, 177
Philotas the Page 133
Phoenicia 43
Photius 190
Phrada 16, 58
Phradates 47, 50, 130, 150
Phrataphernes 47, 118, 130, 150
Phrygia 43
Phrygians 71
Pierio 27
Pillars of Heracles 182
Pinelli 125
Pisidians 43
Plato 7, 173, 177
Pliny .10, 16, 34, 46, 57, 118, 144, 149, 157, 179, 181, 191
Plutarch ..2, 3, 6, 8, 10, 11, 12, 14, 18, 22, 24, 25, 26, 29, 30, 32, 34, 46, 52, 53, 55, 66, 91, 93, 95, 96, 98, 112, 120, 123, 138, 149, 150, 151, 153, 155, 157, 159, 160, 161, 162, 163, 165, 169, 170, 171, 172, 173, 175, 176, 179, 182, 183, 188, 191, 192
Polemon 20, 21, 75, 78, 79
Policy of Fusion 29
Polyaenus ... 12, 55, 113, 150, 152, 154, 157, 179, 192
Polybius 172, 186, 192
Polycleitus of Larissa .. 12, 14, 149
Polydamas 22, 79, 80, 82, 152
Polyperchon 132
Polytimetus River 110, 146
Pompeii 8, 15
Pontic Sea 10, 11, 12, 46, 90
Pope John Paul II 28
Porus 180, 185
Poseidium of the Milesians 22
Prandi, L..159, 166, 177, 187, 189
Pranichus 27
Pritchett, W Kendrick 173, 189
Prometheus 86, 152

203

Prophthasia .. iv, 5, 16, 57, 80, 144, 145
proskynesis 1, 10, 29, 147, 155
Pseudo-Callisthenes 192
Ptolemaeus 112
Ptolemy .. 3, 14, 16, 17, 26, 31, 56, 57, 109, 121, 123, 134, 138, 165, 180, 181, 185, 187
Ptolemy, Claudius 11, 16, 145, 192
Pydna 18
Pyrrhus 191

R

Reagan, Ronald 28
Renaissance 33
Republic 7
Rhidagnus 45
Rhosaces 119
Rolfe, J 189, 190
Roman 188
Rome 187
Roxane ...... iv, 1, 6, 31, 32, 33, 36, 117, 141, 142, 148, 156, 179, 185
Royal Eunuchs 8
Royal Youths 29
Russian Steppes 14

S

Sacae 43, 88, 109, 140, 154
Sahr-i Qumis 144
Samarkand 5, 98, 118, 146, 147
Sambus 181, 185
Samothrace 120
Samuel, AE 169, 172, 189
Sardanapalus 162, 184
Sari 50, 144
Sarmatians 101
Sassanian Empire 17
Satibarzanes .. iv, 1, 12, 39, 55, 56, 57, 84, 90, 91, 144, 145, 150, 152

Satyrus 32
scepter 15, 53
Schachermeyr, F 166, 182, 189
Scholia on Apollonius Rhodius 159, 180
Scholia on Aristophanes 164
Schönfeld, H 189, 190
Schwartz, E .. 5, 37, 149, 150, 151, 152, 153, 154, 155, 165, 166, 190
Scythia 85, 125, 147, 154, 155
Scythian king 14, 36, 179, 185
Scythians ... 12, 14, 41, 55, 88, 90, 99, 101, 102, 105, 106, 107, 108, 109, 118, 152, 154
Seistan 16, 58, 145
Sejanus 17, 58
Seleucia 163
Semiramis 100
Shakhrisyabz 126, 147
Shirabad River 147
Sicily 167, 172
Sidon 177
Simmias 20, 75
Sinope 48
Sisimithres .... iv, 1, 116, 117, 126, 140, 147, 155, 156
Sisygambis 181
Siwa 73, 178
skins 92, 93, 94, 104, 107, 153
Socrates 6
Sogdian Rock 32, 33, 36, 154, 179
Sogdiana 5, 22, 87, 91, 94, 106, 110, 112, 121, 146, 154, 155, 179
Sogdians 43, 89, 99, 110, 117, 154
Soli 177
Solstice 173
Sopeithes 180
Sopolis 135
Sostratus 29, 133
Sousia 55, 144
Spain 182
Sparta 42, 48, 152

Index

Spartan hostages 160, 164, 178, 179, 184
Spartans 42, 48, 90, 91
Spitamenes.... iv, 1, 87, 94, 96, 99, 100, 103, 104, 109, 117, 127, 128, 129, 130, 147, 153, 154, 155, 159
Stasanor 83, 84, 130
Stathmoi............................ 16, 144
Steele, RB 190
Stephanus Byzantinus. 16, 58, 192
Stiboeites River 45, 144
Stobaeus.................. 159, 162, 178
Strabo.... 6, 10, 11, 12, 16, 22, 24, 34, 46, 47, 52, 56, 57, 80, 84, 86, 95, 96, 101, 135, 144, 145, 147, 149, 150, 152, 153, 154, 155, 162, 179, 180, 181, 182, 192
Suda ... 23, 95, 153, 162, 164, 172, 175, 182, 192
Surkhab River................. 112, 147
Surkhan River........................ 147
Susa 33, 165, 185
Susianê.................................... 159
Syr-Darya 11, 14, 41, 88, 90, 101, 108, 146, 153
Syria.. 43, 105, 106, 112, 118, 163

T

Tajikistan 5, 147
Tanais River . iv, 1, 10, 11, 12, 14, 41, 55, 87, 88, 90, 96, 98, 99, 100, 101, 102, 106, 108, 109, 146, 153, 154
Tapurians 47, 48, 130
Tarn, WW 5, 11, 16, 23, 24, 58, 149, 170, 190
Tarsus 162, 177, 184
Taurus Mountains..................... 86
Tempesta, Antonio 119
Teubner.................. 188, 190, 191

Thalestris.... 14, 15, 34, 36, 50, 51, 52, 150, 179, 184
Thapsacus...................... 163, 183
Thebes 42, 55, 120, 161, 162, 176, 182, 184
Theis....................................... 162
Themiscyra...............................50
Themistocles 176, 184
Thermodon, River 14, 50, 150
Thessalians........................ 32, 57
Thomas, PH.................... 190, 191
Thrace 32, 41, 42, 101, 106
Thracians................................. 32
Thucydides............................ 160
tiara 164, 165, 185
Timaeus of Tauromenium 34, 149, 172, 173, 175, 182
Timagenes 3, 164
Timoleon 167, 172
Tiridates 84, 134
torture ... 19, 20, 21, 30, 67, 68, 70, 71, 72, 74, 79, 151, 153
Trajan 163
Triballians 42
Trogus ..3, 93, 159, 164, 176, 177, 178, 190, 191
Troy..182
Turkey 11
Turkmenistan 5
Tus 55, 56, 144, 145
Tyre. 163, 167, 177, 178, 183, 184

U

Underworld 96
Universal Time....................... 170
Uzbekistan.......................... 5, 146

V

Vakhsh River 147
Varia Historia 190
Vulgate 3, 157, 164, 165, 176, 180, 190

W

Welles, C Bradford 5, 160, 187, 191, 193
Wood, Michael 190

X

Xenippa 125, 147
Xenodochus of Cardia 27
Xenophon 6, 7, 8, 40, 160, 165
Xerxes 22, 23, 24, 95, 96, 176, 184

Y

Yardley, J 152, 186, 190, 191

Z

Zadracarta 50, 144
Zarangians 16, 58
Zariaspa 146
Zeller, E 190
Zeravshan River 146, 147
Zeus 69, 71, 72, 73, 130, 136, 137, 170
Zoilus 57
Zopyrus 34, 52

www.ingramcontent.com/pod-product-compliance
Ingram Content Group UK Ltd.
Pitfield, Milton Keynes, MK11 3LW, UK
UKHW041438180426
11947UKWH00007B/512